QUANTUM
LEAN

Taking Lean
Systems
to the
Next Level

Sean Fields, P.E., LSSBB, MSIE
and **Michael Sanders**, Ph.D., LSSBB

J.ROSS
PUBLISHING

ISBN-13: 978-1-60427-175-1

Printed and bound in the U.S.A. Printed on acid-free paper.

Credit for the illustrations in this book belongs to Meredith Fields.

10 9 8 7 6 5 4 3 2 1

Library of Congress Cataloging-in-Publication Data
Names: Fields, Sean, 1965- author. | Sanders, Michael S., author.
Title: Quantum lean : taking lean systems to the next level / Sean Fields,
    Michael Sanders.
Description: Plantation, FL : J. Ross Publishing, [2020] | Includes
    bibliographical references and index.
Identifiers: LCCN 2020033182 (print) | LCCN 2020033183 (ebook) | ISBN
    9781604271751 (paperback ; alk. paper) | ISBN 9781604278262 (epub)
Subjects: LCSH: Lean manufacturing. | Production control. | Organizational
    effectiveness.
Classification: LCC TS155 .F53 2020 (print) | LCC TS155 (ebook) | DDC
    658.5--dc23
LC record available at https://lccn.loc.gov/2020033182
LC ebook record available at https://lccn.loc.gov/2020033183

Direct all inquiries to J. Ross Publishing, Inc., 151 N. Nob Hill Rd., Suite 476, Plantation, FL 33324.

Phone: (954) 727-9333
Fax: (561) 892-0700
Web: www.jrosspub.com

CONTENTS

FOREWORD

One of the privileges of working in a university environment is being surrounded by and working with some of the most gifted academics in the world. An additional benefit of being a dean, particularly in a school of business, is being surrounded by and working with some of the most gifted practitioners in the world. I have often observed that academics and practitioners do not always appropriately value each other's contributions to education, research, and the practice of business. However, it is vital that serious scholars continually push the knowledge discovery envelope and that dedicated practitioners put that knowledge to the test in the real world. It is rare to find individuals who bring together the thought process that is typically associated with academics and the vast experiences of long-term practitioners. Sean Fields is one of those rare individuals.

While reading *Quantum Lean*, I was not surprised to find that the author would take a process with which he is very familiar, analyze it thoroughly, look for improvements, add his observations and experiences from years of consulting work, and ultimately turn that process on its head. I was not surprised because the author, Sean Fields, has been a lifelong improver of processes. I know this because Sean is my younger brother. From a very early age, his brilliance and inquisitiveness were evident. He was always thinking, reading, and learning. In high school, when most young people just wanted to take their classes and hang out with their friends, Sean actually took summer school classes so he could free up time for math and science courses during the regular school year. When he had taken all of the math classes that were available in our district, his math teacher (herself an engineer) created advanced math independent studies for Sean to take for no credit during summer vacation. In his undergraduate and master's programs, he was a curve-busting engineering student. Across my 30 years in the academy, I have known many astonishingly smart people. I have yet to meet anyone who has greater native intelligence or natural curiosity than Sean.

Some academically gifted individuals who become experts in a chosen field have *challenging* personalities. Not only is Sean an academically accomplished individual with an impressive practical background, he is also an amazingly down-to-earth man. As you read *Quantum Lean*, you will see this attitude reflected through his tone and concern for all parties in the company—from people who work on the shop floor to high-level decision makers. Make no mistake, he does hold strong opinions and convictions. But these convictions are shared in the way that an accomplished teacher shares information—by being thorough, organized, and evidence-driven.

Sean displays an appreciation and understanding of traditional lean theoretical foundations. However, the focus of *Quantum Lean* is on the product rather than on waste minimization, like is so often seen in business. As mentioned in Chapter 1, some practitioners might be tempted to say that this difference of focus is a "difference without a distinction." Nothing could be further from the truth. Sean provides logical arguments associated with his expertise in traditional lean to show that by following Quantum Lean principles and being product-focused, firms may also ultimately achieve traditional lean objectives including waste reduction. Additionally, he uses his 30+ years of industrial engineering consulting experience with companies in a variety of industries to describe and assess the effectiveness of numerous lean tools. He lays out the pros and cons of popular tools such as 5S, drum-buffer-rope, kanban, and huddle boards. His assessments take into account the potential impact for tool usage as informed by both the manufacturing particulars and the human elements facing decision makers in the real world. In short, *Quantum Lean* provides an uncomplicated, straightforward decision-making framework for potentially realizing all of the promised results that have previously eluded the many believers in and practitioners of typical lean.

L. Paige Fields
Dean, H.D. Price Professor
University of Kansas School of Business

PREFACE

WHY THIS BOOK?

With all of the books about lean manufacturing, you might wonder what possible benefit one more could bring. If I were in your place, I would be asking the same question. However, since we are wondering about the same thing and great minds think alike, wouldn't it stand to reason that you would want to read this book? Further reinforcing our common ground is the fact that I, and in all probability you, have experienced the following:

- When someone says to think outside of the box, *in-the-box* thinking is about to follow
- The moment someone tells you that things will be different, you can be sure that things will be the same
- When someone tells you that things will be the same, you can bet that things will be different
- When you hear businesses say that people are their most valuable resource, you will find that these precious assets are the first to be unloaded when times get hard
- When your work area was changed, you were asked for input, but you will find that your advice was completely ignored

As you can see, we have a lot in common! And the fact that the aforementioned situations are so common is a key motivation for this book. Although no explanation has been found, societal discourse is replete with mixed signals. Whether it's politics, religion, or business, hypocrisy rules the day. This aspect of everyday living is so time-honored that it is the basis for the fairy tale *The Emperor's New Clothes*. On the rare occasion when someone tells it like it is, most people feel an immediate sense of relief and validation. In our minds, we think, "Maybe I'm not so crazy after all!"

With lean as a case in point where one thing is said but something else is done, the goal is to tell it like it is and communicate an interpretation of lean systems that cuts to the chase. If you have studied this subject, this book will be different from what you're used to. And regardless of your background, I am confident that you will be pleased with what you read.

THE BACKSTORY

"This doesn't work!" This was the thought several years ago when implementing lean at a job shop for custom products. As one example of how the standard approaches weren't fleshing out, the lean team had developed a *value stream map* that revealed nothing. It was all there with the correct symbols, but there was no indication of where any waste existed. All it showed was a sequence of operations, minimal work-in-process (WIP) inventory, and little else. While it was otherwise obvious that the operations were inefficient, one would never know it from the diagram.

To make a long story short, the team relied on common sense in lieu of lean doctrine. While some excellent ideas resulted, it caused a serious reassessment. With job shops constituting a significant portion of the manufacturing sector and my client base, I realized a new angle was essential. And knowing that I couldn't rely on every future group to come up with their own answers, this new approach would need to work in a wide variety of situations.

With logic, inspiration, and real-world application, a new system was developed to implement lean systems. For these situations, it is easy to apply, accurately identifies opportunities, and indicates corresponding solutions. Every. Single. Time. Even better, it can be used in practically any business environment—whether it's mass production, job shops, or services. In order to help others adopt this approach, this book was written to provide explanations, examples, and key details to facilitate the implementation of this system.

INTENDED AUDIENCE

This book is intended for people who work in all economic sectors including service, manufacturing, and government. Some of the types of people who will be interested in this book include:

- Executive level personnel—CEO, COO, president, vice president
- Business owners
- Operations managers
- Plant managers
- Production managers

- Consultants
- Engineers—industrial, manufacturing, production, quality
- Supervisors, lead men, superintendents, foremen
- Rank and file employees

BOOK STRUCTURE

Like any broad-based framework, this fresh approach called Quantum Lean (QL) is an integrated system with the following key pillars:

- *Framework*—to lay a sound foundation, a reexamination of lean principles is presented along with the benefits it brings. To demonstrate QL's power, several pictorial examples are reviewed in order to highlight the waste elimination made possible by the new framework. Where conventional methods might identify two or three forms of waste, the new approach will typically find at least six. By internalizing the QL paradigm, a practitioner will have the grounding to successfully apply QL.
- *Product path diagramming*—with a new view of lean, the next step is *learning to see* using product path diagramming (PPD). For those exposed to value stream mapping (VSM), PPD might seem similar, except that PPD has several edges. Among other things, PPD works. Compared to VSM with its many symbols, PPD is simpler and only has three. In addition, easy-to-follow rules allow rapid prioritization and selection of improvement techniques.
- *Lean tools*—with a new view of lean and knowledge of PPD under the belt, frequently used lean tools are reexamined in light of the new framework. By doing this, one gains an enhanced understanding of the rationale behind lean tools, how they reinforce each other, and when to apply them. Best of all, an understanding of when to avoid lean building blocks is acquired. The tools that will be revisited include:
  - *Product-based layout*—where many businesses lay out shops departmentally (lathes with lathes, mills with mills, etc.) to maximize resource utilization, product-based layout is arranging resources so that product flow is facilitated.
  - *One-Piece Flow (aka Make One-Move One)*—to reduce lead time, this practice immediately moves a product to the next stage of production once an operation is finished.
  - *Kanban*—as a way to regulate inventory levels and flow, kanban signals what to buy/build, when to do it, and in what amount.

- *Drum-buffer-rope*—this approach for scheduling to the pace of an operation's bottleneck improves shop floor control and minimizes lead time.
- *5S*—organizing and cleaning up the workplace.
- *Andon*—a method for signaling the state of the product or process so that responses to breakdowns, parts outages, or slowdowns can be addressed in a timely manner.
- *Quick changeover*—many companies require significant time to switch production from one product to another. Quick changeover seeks setup times so low that they have no influence on a production schedule.
- *Cells*—product-based layout on steroids.
- *QLM (Quantum Lean maintenance)*—harmonizes a lean tool called total productive maintenance (TPM) to the QL framework so that maintenance is subordinated to QL objectives.
- *Work balancing*—distributing work among resources so that efforts are equalized.
- *Standardized work*—improving work methods so that variation in time and quality are minimized and speed is optimized.
- *Quality@Source*—optimizing processes to eliminate product variation and improve quality.

While the first chapters cover the pillars, theory needs know-how. To address this, the chapters that follow include deeper dives into lean tools and other topics that will have tremendous influence on your implementation:

- *QL versus other approaches*—although QL gets a great reception, there will be holdouts who can't see the difference between QL and typical approaches. To help address this, important differences among the systems are elaborated in further detail.
- *Inventory*—a lack of necessary material is a literal showstopper. Techniques to assure a reliable supply of inventory are covered.
- *Shop-floor control/logistics/scheduling*—improper shop-floor control aggravates virtually every efficiency problem an operation will encounter. For a functioning system, groundwork in scheduling, procurement, sales, production, shop-floor control, and inventory control is needed.
- *5S (workplace organization)*—although 5S is spelled out in the S's, reading between the lines is key. Limiting yourself to the 5S script can leave you with equally limited results. To avoid this, guidance is given to get the most from this vital tool.

- *Kanban*—the deep dive on this topic is using this building block in support of inventory control.
- *Quick changeover*—in QL, the criticality of proper scheduling can't be overstated. Without it, efforts at improving efficiency amount to nibbling around edges. At companies with lengthy changeovers, the same can be said about setup reduction. Quick changeover in QL is similar to a technique called *single minute exchange of dies* (SMED). The QL approach is covered in detail.
- *QLM*—by diffracting TPM through a QL lens, the benefits of a maintenance program can be elevated while minimizing the liabilities. The elements of this system are explained along with implementation tips.
- *Standard work*—as QL implementations progress, there comes a point where standardizing work shows up on the radar. In addition to reducing labor costs, substantial benefits can accrue from variation reduction. This chapter covers variation reduction techniques to improve consistency and using the product path diagram to increase speed.
- *Work balancing*—one good way to elevate efficiency is by adopting an assembly line or cellular production. However, like anything worthwhile, legwork is necessary. To cut things down to size, this chapter details a structured approach for efficient and effective work balancing.
- *Cellular production*—of all the concepts that get missed about lean production, cellular flow stands apart. In this deep dive, the power of cellular production is highlighted along with two critical principles to assure that this building block achieves full potential.
- *Quality@Source*—as this lean tool often requires statistical knowledge, coverage is provided on the necessary body of knowledge to maximize this lean tool.
- *Lean implementations*—ask a practitioner about the success rate of lean initiatives (other than theirs) and you might be surprised at how low it can go. Depending on the source, failure rates as high as 95% have been claimed. However, it shouldn't be too surprising since implementations have obstacles that can stymie the most seasoned professionals. Although there are no guarantees, this deep dive offers food for thought on ways to improve the odds.
- Potemkin lean—in a lot of workplaces, all kinds of tools are deployed with the nominal goal of improvement. However, many of these *aids* are just a distraction from productive efforts. At the same time, they are sometimes used to paint a pretty picture that is at odds with a gritty reality. As a way out, an approach that gets great results and maintains appearances is outlined.

ABOUT THE AUTHORS

SEAN FIELDS

Sean Fields, P.E., LSSBB, MSIE, has over 30 years of experience in a wide variety of industries, including oil field equipment manufacturing, food processing, and job shops. As a seasoned industry professional, he has worked in all phases of business, including the shop floor, quality, safety, and engineering. Over the years, he found himself in a great deal of situations where he was expected to implement lean approaches in environments where conventional lean methods were impractical. However, by returning to the fundamentals pioneered by Henry Ford, Fields found that lean could be sustain-  ably applied in practically any setting. With successful implementations in the most challenging environments, he now wants to share his experiences, ideas, and approaches for businesses to reach the next level of success.

In addition to being an active lean practitioner, Sean is a network member of the non-profit organization BeehiveFund, that assists companies with production scheduling, inventory control, and developing quality management systems (ISO 9000, AS9100, and API Q1). He is also a columnist for the Lubbock Avalanche Journal, a licensed professional engineer in the state of Texas, a certified Six Sigma Master Black Belt, and a certified QMS auditor. He resides in Lubbock, TX, with his wife and has two adult daughters. For further information, please refer to his LinkedIn profile: https://www.linkedin.com/in/sean-fields-21290b45/.

Acknowledgments

I have been blessed by so many outstanding people in my life that I can't give proper acknowledgment to any one person without short selling someone else. With that being said, I couldn't imagine a better family (including in-laws!) than the one I have. They are better than any mortal deserves. On top of this, I have so many colleagues, mentors, coworkers, and friends who have influenced my thinking and helped me through thick and thin that I can't extend enough gratitude. You know who you are, it's all remembered, and will always be appreciated.

MICHAEL SANDERS

Michael Sanders, PhD, LSSBB, MBA, is the cofounder of BeehiveFund, a non-profit organization dedicated to assisting industry. Michael has worked in every phase of the supply chain at a wide variety of companies, including serving as CEO and president of food, energy, distribution, and high-tech firms. Along this journey, he and Sean have collaborated extensively to refine the Quantum Lean framework and successfully deliver their lean methods to numerous companies.

In addition to his work as a seasoned executive and practitioner, Dr. Sanders is sought after for his expertise in negotiation, organizational psychology, Six Sigma, quality systems, and regulatory compliance. He has delivered speeches worldwide on topics that include global supply chain optimization, lean and beyond lean production systems, quality and regulatory systems, optimal and effective leadership, product-centered sustainable growth, organizational culture transition, and emerging technologies. Michael has a PhD in Industrial Engineering and an MBA from Texas Tech University. In addition, he holds a certification as a Six Sigma Master Black Belt. He resides in Houston, TX, with his wife, two sons, and one daughter. For further information, please refer to his LinkedIn profile: https://www.linkedin.com/in/dr-michael-sanders-8049a290/.

Acknowledgments

This book would not have been possible without the guidance and support of my family, friends, and clients who are still the greatest teachers of my living days. My most heartfelt appreciation goes to Sanju, my wife and the most intelligent member of my family, and her unbridled love and care through many years of joint learning and global experience. Thanks for challenging me on every important thought and guiding me to produce the best outcomes at every turn.

My deep gratitude also goes to my coauthor, Sean, whose persistence and strong belief made this book a reality. I have learned invaluable lessons from Sean over the years that have validated many of my organizational improvement approaches and methods that have resulted in unprecedented successes. Finally, my thanks to all of my family members and friends who have supported me unconditionally over the years, making it possible to field-test and confirm my theories on organizational improvement.

 Web Added Value™

At J. Ross Publishing we are committed to providing today's professional with practical, hands-on tools that enhance the learning experience and give readers an opportunity to apply what they have learned. That is why we offer free ancillary materials available for download on this book and all participating Web Added Value™ publications. These online resources may include interactive versions of the material that appears in the book or supplemental templates, worksheets, models, plans, case studies, proposals, spreadsheets and assessment tools, among other things. Whenever you see the WAV™ symbol in any of our publications, it means bonus materials accompany the book and are available from the Web Added Value Download Resource Center at www.jrosspub.com.

Downloads for *Quantum Lean: Taking Lean Systems to the Next Level* include a/an:

- Overall Equipment Effectiveness Data Collection Form—A form to facilitate data collection for overall equipment effectiveness.
- Time Study Data Collection Sheet—A form to facilitate data collection for time studies.
- Lean Assessment Sheet—A customizable spreadsheet to benchmark an operation against Quantum Lean standards
- Job Information Sheet—A form to document the inputs necessary for developing standard work methods. It also serves as a memory jogger to assure due diligence in developing consistent methods.
- Standard Work Priority Method—An instruction sheet to assess jobs and determine priority for developing standard work methods.
- Reorder Point Spreadsheet (Data Poor Cases)—To aid in estimating reorder points, this spreadsheet generates random usage data based on triangular distribution. Using this data, maximum usages can be estimated for various lead times.

CHAPTER 1

DEFINING QUANTUM LEAN: PART 1

"Lean is a way of thinking, not a list of things to do."

Shigeo Shingo

Before implementing lean, you need to know it; and in order to really know it, a consistent understanding is critical. When lean is mentioned, everyone imagines a different picture. Think about the inkblot tests psychologists give. The image is only a random splash. What's seen says everything about the patient and nothing about the inkblot. Similarly, interpretations of lean vary according to individual motivations. This inconsistency poses a barrier to effective execution. To address this, Quantum Lean (QL) operates from one ironclad viewpoint. However, before embarking on a QL journey, consider the following example to help establish your baseline mindset regarding lean.

Imagine a business where customers contact the company for information by phone. In one situation, an employee picks up the phone and handles the caller's inquiry (see Figure 1.1).

Hi, how can I help you?

Figure 1.1 Human versus automated: human

In the second case, an automated answering system greets the customer, and the caller navigates a menu until they address their problem or reach someone who can (see Figure 1.2).

Figure 1.2   Human versus automated: automated

Which system is lean? While QL provides an answer, baselining perceptions is the object for now. Make a note of which scenario you consider lean and why. As you make your way through this book, you might change your mind! With your interpretation established, it's time to introduce the QL understanding of lean and contrast it with more conventional approaches.

In a nutshell, QL's mission is to minimize the time required to give the product what it needs. As an illustration of this idea, consider the movie *Castaway*. In this film, Tom Hanks plays a FedEx employee who gets stranded on a desert island. While the entire movie is worth watching, the part that speaks to my inner lean practitioner is a scene where Tom enters a FedEx facility. Upon his arrival, a kid hands him a package, which is then opened. And what is in this package? A clock that shows 72 hours. In other words, Tom mailed himself a clock to determine how long a package spends in the FedEx system. With a 24-hour turnaround being the goal, the fact that this shipment had taken three times as long was a pretty bad sign.

Think of your company in the same way. If you dropped material to your shop floor and placed a timer on it, what would it say when the order is ready to ship? In this book, I will argue there is no better measure of the health of your business than *time*. If it takes a long time to finish a product, you are inefficient. If the product moves quickly, you probably run a tight ship. Ultimately, the goal should be for the product's clock to show the lowest possible number. In a perfect world, it would register zero.

Expanding on this point, lean has been described as: *eliminating waste through flowing the product.* Too often, typical approaches stop with the first two words—eliminating waste—and ignore the rest. By contrast, QL focuses on minimizing a product's time in the system by flowing the product (see Figure 1.3).

	Typical Lean	**Quantum Lean**
Definition/ Objective	Eliminate waste to minimize cost	Eliminate a product's time in the system to eliminate waste and minimize cost

Figure 1.3   Typical versus QL

Although the QL wrinkle might seem like a distinction without a difference, it's a subtle twist that allows for a radical improvement in simplicity and effectiveness.

While confronting waste head-on might seem like the best way to eliminate it, QL leverages the fact that wastes share time as a common denominator. The idea is similar to a strategy that contributed to winning World War II. Rather than munitions, weapons, transportation, and other military assets, the Allies prioritized ball-bearing facilities as a target. By eliminating the one thing upon which everything else depended, the Axis war machine was ground to a halt (see Figure 1.4).

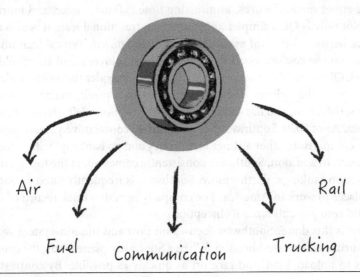

Figure 1.4   Bearings and products

In other words, victory became simpler. Similarly, by attacking a product's time-in-system, addressing waste is simpler as well. Time-in-system is the fuel that feeds waste. You can attack waste in its multitude of forms, or you can focus on one thing (see Figure 1.5).

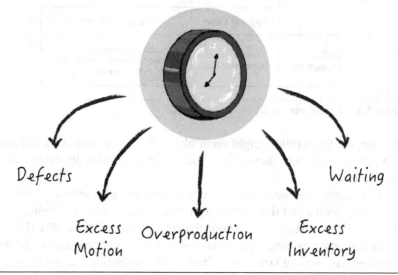

Defects

Waiting

Excess
Motion

Overproduction

Excess
Inventory

Figure 1.5 Time and wastes

While either method works, minimizing time is faster, easier, and more effective. Not only is QL a simpler approach than traditional lean, it is also the difference between *lean and mean* and *skinny and pissed*. Typical lean initiatives can become so cost-obsessed that customers, employees, and shareholders get shafted. QL avoids this trap. As a case in point, consider the airline industry.

Out of all the airlines, one consistently earns a profit, maintains high customer satisfaction, and has excellent employee relations. Which one? Southwest Airlines. As of 2020, Southwest has achieved 47 consecutive years of profitability. By comparison, other airlines lose money and go bankrupt with astonishing frequency. In addition, Southwest consistently comes out at the top of customer satisfaction rankings. Furthermore, Southwest is frequently rated as one of the best places to work in America. The company heralds a track record of zero lay offs and zero pay cuts since its inception.

How is this done? Southwest focuses on flow and time-in-system while the other airlines are waste-obsessed. When a Southwest plane lands, the overriding goal is to unload, load, and take off as quickly as possible. By contrast, other airlines squeeze in more customers and employees while remaining indifferent to gate times.

During a lengthy layover with one of Southwest's competitors, a plane arrived at my gate three hours before my departure. When a fellow passenger asked if I thought that was our flight, I replied that it wasn't possible. No airline would allow that much idle time. As it turned out, it was our flight!

If you are wondering why this matters, one major benefit from quick turn-arounds is that freed-up time allows more flights to be scheduled. Since airlines make their money at every departure, Southwest maximizes the number of times they can earn. In addition to increased cash flow, this unique approach optimizes the company's cost structure.

Like many breakthroughs, Southwest stumbled onto this. In the beginning, they owned two planes and borrowed one to serve three cities. Eventually, the loaner's owner wanted their plane back. With a smaller fleet, Southwest faced a dilemma. Lacking capital, they couldn't acquire a plane. On top of this, they couldn't afford to cut their service. Instead, they investigated how to handle their routes with the remaining planes. In the end, they found that minimizing gate time enabled just that. In this happy ending, Southwest served all their customers with two rather than three planes. In other words, they achieved the same sales with two thirds of the overhead. Doing so converted a moderately profitable business into an industry leader.

In addition to increasing profitability directly, minimizing time-in-system accomplishes indirect benefits as well. When flow is achieved, the following benefits occur:

- *Customer satisfaction increases*—facilitating the product is another way of prioritizing the customer. Even if the two never meet, an employee indirectly serves the customer by serving the product.
- *Employee morale increases*—if the product is truly prioritized, barriers to employee effectiveness are minimized. The job gets easier and innate satisfaction comes with a job well done.
- *Shareholder morale increases*—with more money from increased cash and reduced cost, how could it not?

Real-world examples, like Southwest, demonstrate how QL enables employees, shareholders, and customers to share in the benefits for a win/win/win situation. When following the central organizing principle that time is money, much can be accomplished. In addition to being conceptually sound, the fact that practically everyone agrees on this point makes for a unifying principle. Ironically, even though most agree with the phrase: *time is money,* few can explain why this is true—and this should be expected. Since most of us have been exposed to this notion from infancy, it's not human nature to question long-held beliefs. However, to implement QL effectively, it's essential to grasp this point on an intellectual, not just visceral, level. With illustrations of the power behind this adage, you will gain this understanding along with a renewed gut-level appreciation for this phrase.

SIDEBAR—WHY DO WE RESIST CHANGE?

Investigating a new idea is ultimately entertaining the possibility of change. At the same time, for all that we explore, isn't it amazing how few of us take the next step? Taken further, it could be argued that people resist change at every turn. Why? All kinds of reasons are offered:

- *Comfort zone*—people are in a groove and want to continue in it
- *Discipline*—the effort to sustain a change is too great
- *Fear*—change is unknown and people fear this
- *Company politics*—turf battles block change
- *Apathy*—people don't want to be bothered

While all of these explanations are valid, what's annoying is that they are offered to the exclusion of the elephant in the room: change is bad. By an overwhelming margin, changes typically offer no benefit or they create massive burdens. Sometimes, they offer both. Consider:

- Do bills generally increase or decrease?
- How often is the new plan better?
- When an employer changes a business, how often does it bring better customer relations, an improved workplace, or increased employee morale?
- How often do beloved products and services get discontinued?
- After an election and regardless of who wins, do the people not lose?

There is more, but the most likely reason that people resist change is due to its bad track record. If you doubt this, consider a winning $100,000,000 lottery ticket. Upheaval is in store for anyone who accepts it. Hasn't everyone heard about lottery winners who consider it the worst thing that ever happened to them? Despite the barriers to *buy-in*, what's the chance that someone would decide to go ahead and buy a winning ticket? Conservatively, 100%! Even though this option plows uncharted territory for most and will shake a person out of their comfort zone, who wouldn't jump on this with both hands and feet? Obviously, the reason is that this particular change is perceived as beneficial. To this point, if a plan offers a credible prospect for low risk, high reward, and minimal cost, buy-in is not nearly as difficult. The frequently mentioned reasons to resist change remain, but the biggest reason for pushback will disappear.

And the good news is that lean systems offer overwhelmingly positive change when done correctly. The key lies in an approach called QL that casts aside the tired approaches that come with typical programs. This book presents an explanation of this system, what makes it tick, and the benefits that it offers.

CHAPTER 2

DEFINING QUANTUM LEAN: PART 2

"The longer an article is in the process of manufacture, the greater is its ultimate cost."

Henry Ford

"Time isn't the main thing. It's the only thing."

Miles Davis

While it's one thing for a stranger to say that time is money, none other than Henry Ford made this idea the basis for his success. The key insight that drove Ford's approach is that the longer a product stays in production, the more it will cost. Although the idea may seem obvious, few can explain why this is true. Ironically, as little as people ponder this, there is a lot of science to back it up. Consider an equation called Little's Law (see Figure 2.1):

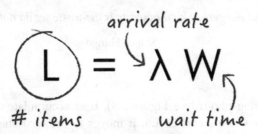

Figure 2.1 Little's Law

We can think of this formula in terms of a town's population:

Population of a town =
(arrival rate of new citizens) × (average time that citizens live in town)

For example, if 1,000 people arrive per year and each person lives there 10 years, this means that the average number of people living in the city is 10,000:

Population of town = (1,000 people/year) × (10 years) = 10,000 people

For a business, the amount of money tied up in production can be thought of as is depicted in Figure 2.2:

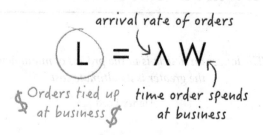

Figure 2.2   Little's Law explained

Orders that stay at a company longer mean that more orders will be tied up at any one time. Since orders are denominated in dollars, that also means more money is tied up, resulting in greater costs. Since you may be wondering how this translates into cold hard cash, a few tangible illustrations will drive the point home.

TIME IS MONEY

> *"The most dangerous kind of waste is the waste we do not recognize."*
>
> Shigeo Shingo

Tires

In the correlating photo (see Figure 2.3), tires accumulate on carts at a tire retread facility. Once a cart is full, it moves to the next stage of fulfillment. Thinking of the buildup on the cart as a batch where tires wait to be moved to the next step, it's clear that the first tire will be there awhile. In other words, this accumulation represents time. Why does it cost money? Here are two common answers that people will give:

- *Carrying cost*—a frequent answer is that the excess work-in-process (WIP) inventory represents tied-up money. Although accurate, how much does this matter when interest rates are low?

Figure 2.3 The tires

- *Sales lag*—people might also respond that delaying the semi-finished product means a slower turnaround on sales. While true, this affects cash flow and opportunity cost, but not operating expense.

Once these answers are given, most people will be at a loss to come up with more. Let's dig deeper:

- *Handling*—when WIP inventory accumulates, handling follows. Picking up, putting down, stacking, unstacking, and counting are a few possibilities.
- *Aggravated defects*—if the operation underway was done improperly, that means the entire cart will be bad. By contrast, if a completed sub-assembly could be sent to the next station right away, how much bad product might be prevented? In addition, other risk-related costs from this WIP include:
  - *Disposition*—obviously, evaluating bad product requires time, paperwork, and effort
  - *Scrap/rework*—lost material in the case of scrap and squandered man-hours are experienced in the case of rework
  - *Storage*—storage in the form of cabinets for the scrap, disposition, and rework records and extra office space for the cabinets must be provided

- *Cart*—the carts that carry the tires didn't miraculously appear; someone had to buy the materials and build them. Other costs include:
  - *Maintenance*—anyone who has used a shopping cart has probably been annoyed by casters with wobbly wheels. The carts in the picture have casters that need periodic replacement.
  - *Miscellaneous*—the casters on these carts are too small. Combined with the joints that concrete floors have, these carts get stuck.
  - *Safety*—with such a narrow base, the cart might occasionally fall over when it gets stuck.
  - *Space*—the excess WIP occupies excess space.

Stampings

Looking at the basket brimming with fabricated pieces (see Figure 2.4), the pieces that are at the bottom are going to be there quite a while. How does this represent money? Consider some of the added expenses that are related to this:

- *Baskets*—baskets aren't cheap.
- *Cosmetics*—as the parts rub together while they sit in the basket, cosmetics are compromised. Some additional costs from this include:
  - *Rework*
  - *Scrap*
  - *Lengthy Debates*—when cosmetics enter the picture, debates soon follow. Since appearance standards are typically vague, dispositioning questionable parts has a way of degenerating into a back-and-forth between production and quality. To make a long story short: some good product gets scrapped, some bad product gets sent, and employees waste a lot of time in discussions in order to arrive at this ideal outcome.
- *Material handling equipment*—since the baskets are too large for an employee to pick up or drag around, a material handling device like a forklift is necessary. On the one hand, there are many costs associated with forklifts, including capital expenditure, safety risks, training, fuel, and maintenance. On the other hand, some businesses might try to avoid using forklifts by equipping the containers with casters or using a less expensive device like a pallet jack. These options are not free. For the basket with casters, the wheels need to be periodically replaced. For the other option, the business has to buy the pallet jack.

Figure 2.4 The baskets

- *Safety*
  - To get parts at the bottom of the basket, people must stoop. This means awkward body mechanics that increase the odds of injury.
    - To address this, some companies might invest in a lifting and/or tilting device. Again, the devices cost money.
  - When stooping, people will lean against the baskets and increase the chances that the baskets collapse.
  - Since material handling equipment is necessary, forklifts entail elevated safety risks due to power and mass.
  - If a pallet truck is used, pallet trucks are trip hazards.
  - If a pallet truck or wheeled basket is used, manually driven transportation requires exertion which always adds risk.
- *Space*—empty or full, additional room must be made for:
  - *Baskets*
  - *Pallet trucks*—if they are used.
- *Handling*—besides the full baskets, empty baskets must be dealt with. If space is limited, someone must collapse the baskets so they can be stacked higher and free up space.

The Gathering

In many plants, the sight of a room cluttered with baskets, trays, and carts (see Figure 2.5) is extremely common. As WIP is built up, it has to be sent somewhere to wait. In addition to all of the costs that were enumerated in the previous two scenarios, there could be further costs:

- *Misplaced material*—anyone who has worked in even the smallest facilities knows that misplaced orders are a fact of life. Adding insult to injury, scattered WIP compounds this problem with the following side effects:
  - *Late delivery*—while most jobs will eventually be found, the time spent retrieving necessary parts increases the prospect for a late delivery
  - *Effort*—personnel must be assigned to and paid for finding the lost orders
  - *Write-offs*—occasionally, jobs aren't found and the materials must be written off
- *Pilferage*—just as no one is likely to notice when a small quantity of material or a small item is stolen, it's much easier to steal from a crowded space than it is from a clear one. And no matter how trustworthy a workforce may be, the chance of pilferage remains because a company has no control over the integrity of outsiders.
  - *Added security*—if the merchandise is valuable enough, businesses will invest in personnel and/or equipment to secure and to insure their valuables

Figure 2.5   The gathering

- *Handling*—beyond the normal handling, baskets must be moved out of the way to get to the load an operator needs; and then must be returned to their original positions.
- *Damage*—the longer that product sits in storage, the greater the chances of deterioration, damage, or obsolescence. To address this, some companies might apply coatings or wraps for protection which entails:
  - *Labor*—the time required to coat, wrap, or otherwise protect the parts
  - *Protectant*—the applied protectants cost money
- *Materials management*—there is a significant amount of manpower necessary to track orders, maintain traceability, and account for quantity and location

The Tote

In the corresponding figure (see Figure 2.6), a company handles subassemblies by the tote bin. While it may seem harmless enough, there are costs.

- *Tote bins*—the cost of the tote bins must be considered
- *Safety*—having so many parts in one tote bin results in a heavy container, which increases the chance of injury when it's lifted
- *Product*—being so heavy and girthy, there is a chance that a bin will be dropped every now and then resulting in possible:
  - *Product damage*

Figure 2.6   The tote

       ▫ *Injury*—when parts fall from an elevated height, the chances of foot injury significantly increase

           ○ To address these types of risks, a business might require steel-toed shoes, which entails expense

The Partial

In the photo depicting a stockpile of partial orders (see Figure 2.7), a company wanted to improve delivery by producing components ahead of time, storing them until an order came in, and then assembling them into finished product. As the thinking went, the lead time would be reduced and on-time delivery improved. But, at what cost?

- *Transportation*—to put the components in hibernation, they have to be moved into storage.
- *Obsolete product*—what if you build it and no one comes?
- *Skid*—in this case, a skid is necessary for efficient movement. And no matter how you slice it, skids cost money. In particular, free skids are expensive as they are often in poor shape and break, thereby damaging product, property, and people.

Figure 2.7   The partial

- *Mishaps*—is it possible that these skids have been spilled?
  - *Time*—someone has to put the pieces back together
  - *Safety*—falling product puts bystanders at risk
  - *Product damage*
- *Stretch wrap/straps*—to prevent spillage, some companies might want to use strapping or stretch wrap. Strapping requires straps, an application tool, and the labor to install. In addition, straps are often over-tensioned and fly away when cut. This causes safety issues. If stretch wrap is the choice, consider some of the costs:
  - The stretch wrap itself
  - Manual stretch wrap applicator
  - Excess stretch wrap when applied manually
  - Time to apply stretch wrap
  - Time to remove stretch wrap
  - Box cutters to remove stretch wrap
  - First aid when people cut themselves using box cutters
  - Gloves to avoid cuts from box cutters
  - Disposal cost of stretch wrap
  - Automatic stretch wrap machines are often purchased after employees tire of manually applying stretch wrap and management grows weary of excessive stretch wrap usage (although these machines are very efficient, they are costly and must be maintained)
- *Rework*—these skids are stored outside. When the metal pieces rust, the rust will have to be removed before assembly can take place.
- *Protectant*—to prevent rust, protectant may need to be applied.

The Staging

In the Buddhist faith, it has been said that monks painstakingly carve intricate figures out of butter and let them melt in order to reinforce the idea that all things are temporary. Whether or not this is true, I choose to believe it because I want to make a point. Like the carving, the skids in the staging photo (see Figure 2.8) represent a significant time investment. And, like the butter, this work will melt away when it's time to load trailers. However, unlike the Buddhist handiwork, insult is added to injury as an equal amount of time and effort will be required to undo all of the staging. Based on the previous examples, are you starting to see the cost implications of handling, floor space, product damage, investment, and workplace safety?

Figure 2.8   The staging

TIME AND WASTE

In the previous section's examples, costs weren't enumerated repeatedly. Instead, new costs were identified in every case. Like the proverbial onion, the interplay between costs and time often results in a staggering number of layers underneath the surface. Although it's not critical to be able to recite all of the expenses that accrue from time, an appreciation of this relationship is crucial. The beauty of Quantum Lean (QL) is that while focusing on minimizing time, its application imparts an ability to reflexively identify waste.

While time is money, what makes matters worse is that once time is allowed a toehold, the resulting wastes feed off of each other and require even more time, creating a vicious cycle. Fortunately, when time is drained, this vicious cycle reverses itself and becomes a virtuous cycle. A visualization of how these elements feed off each other is shown in Figure 2.9:

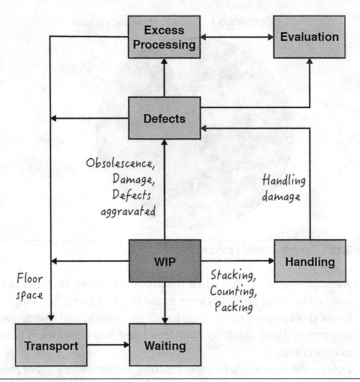

Figure 2.9 WIP and waste

The common factor behind these wastes that feed off each other is time. As was stated before, *attack time and the wastes go away!*

QL FOUNDATION

With a gut-level understanding that time is money, it follows that QL's mission is minimizing the time required to give the product what it needs. Ultimately, the goal should be for a product's clock to show the lowest possible number. In a perfect world, it would be zero.

When minimizing time, categorizing it will help prioritize your efforts (see Figure 2.10). In QL, a product's time in fulfillment is classified in one of three ways:

- *Conversion*—this is when the product is being transformed by a resource into a configuration that is closer to finished form. Although typical lean approaches use the term *value added*, QL uses the term *conversion* for reasons that will be explained later.

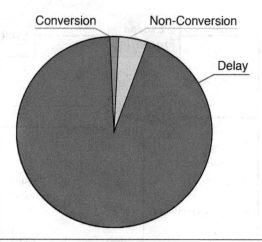

Figure 2.10   Time-in-system pie chart

- *Non-conversion*—this is when the product is being attended to by a resource but is not brought closer to the finished form. For simplicity, QL limits this category to moving, handling, rework, and inspection. If the resource is doing anything outside of these four activities, it is classified as conversion.
- *Delay*—the time when no man, machine, or any other kind of resource is expending effort on the product is delay. Put another way, delay is when the product is collecting dust.

When you consider time, remember that this is all strictly from the standpoint of the product. That is, you should only concern yourself with the resource's time when it is serving the product. From the pie chart in Figure 2.10, you can see that most of the time a product spends at an average business is in a delay mode. This means that the product is sitting with nothing being done to it. However, the good news is that this common situation allows a lot of opportunity for improvement. While time should be minimized regardless of its form, it pays to focus on where most of the time is spent. As the saying goes, hunt where the ducks are. If most of the time lies in conversion, prioritize reduction in conversions. If most of the time is tied up in non-conversion, try to eliminate that instead. However, in most cases, delays should be attacked first since they typically consume most of the product's time. Here are some additional reasons why delays are a great initial target:

- Where there is a delay, it often creates the need for a non-conversion activity. If you can eliminate the delay, you generally get rid of non-conversion at the same time. It's like killing two birds with one stone.

- Delays impair the efficiency of conversion operations. When delays are eliminated, conversion steps tend to get quicker. At the same time, as delays cause the lion's share of your workforce's frustrations, employees will appreciate life being made easier.
- Too many businesses initially look at conversion to make efficiency improvements. In a sense, this amounts to blaming the workforce for a business's shortcomings. By attacking delay first, the focus is on a system that is probably victimizing its employees. In addition to being the most effective initial step, focusing on delay rather than on conversion shows a vote of confidence in your people.

I cannot emphasize enough that the objective of the QL process must be minimizing the time required for a product to get what it needs. While typical explanations of lean revolve around the idea of *eliminating waste* until only *value-added* processes remain, nothing should be considered off limits. After all, if you could drain a *value-added* process of all its time and still get the same quality product, why wouldn't you? Again, as long as the product gets what it needs, the whole mission should be to eliminate time, regardless of its form. The only question is where the richest opportunities lie. In the absence of hard data, the order of attack should be:

- Delays
- Non-conversion
- Conversion

Although the idea is simple enough, QL is a comprehensive framework that provides a foundation that supports the objective of giving the product what it needs as quickly as possible.

SIDEBAR—CAUTIONARY TALE

When attacking time-in-system, avoid the trap that Schlitz Beer fell into back in the 1970s. Many years ago, Schlitz consistently occupied one of the top two spots in the United States market. However, along the way, Schlitz started tampering with their processes to reduce brewing time. Early on, a lot more beer was produced from the same plants and the margins reflected this. The downside was that all the production changes added up to plummeting quality. Over time, Schlitz fell from its lofty perch and, by the 1980s, had to close their flagship Milwaukee plant. Shortly after, they were acquired by another company and have remained insignificant ever since. Schlitz never recovered from shortchanging the product. Don't make the same mistake!

CHAPTER 3

DEFINING QUANTUM LEAN: PART 3

To realize Quantum Lean's (QL's) full potential, we must first establish its foundation. This solid foundation, in turn, allows the implementation of QL to undergird other initiatives that can be used to bolster an organization. In order to understand how QL fits in a comprehensive management system, it is critical to describe each foundation stone and the sequence in which each one is laid—known as the QL Hierarchy—in order to usher in the best possible outcomes (see Figure 3.1).

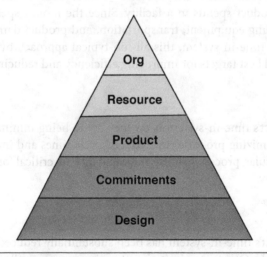

Figure 3.1 QL Hierarchy

CLARIFICATION OF EACH FOUNDATION STONE

Design

Product design has a significant impact on every other aspect of an organization's ability to serve customers. Improper specification, inadequate design criteria, and indifference to downstream processes enshrine inefficiency and alienate buyers. A design that ensures maximum function while using minimal resources lays a perfect foundation for effective sales and operations.

Commitments

A company is only as good as its ability to fulfill commitments. If deliveries are late, quality is suspect, or service is inadequate, the first order of business should be getting these shortcomings addressed. However inefficient it may be, a company should institute immediate action to reestablish its solid footing. With the customer base secured, time can be bought to achieve sustainable improvement.

Product

Ideally, with commitments kept and design under control, QL is introduced by prioritizing, analyzing, and optimizing a product's time-in-system. As a contrast, typical organizations often obsess over labor hours at the expense of the time that a product spends in a facility. Since the money spent on facilities, material handling equipment, transportation, and product damage is dictated by a product's time-in-system, this all-too-typical approach bypasses some of the biggest and best targets for improving efficiency and reducing costs.

Process

Once a product's time-in-system is on the way to being minimized, QL's next priority is optimizing processes for reduced cycle times and improved consistency. In particular, process stability and capability are critical for uninterrupted flow and quality.

Resource

Once a product's time-in-system has been substantially reduced and processes are largely stable, QL's next priority is increasing resource utilization and minimizing operating costs. These efforts may include automation, software applications, and other resources to optimize the results achieved in the previous QL stages.

Organization

Since prior foundation stones have largely been laid at this point, additional improvement is made possible by harmonizing the remaining portions of the organization that have not been aligned to the QL system.

While it's entirely possible to pursue every foundation stone simultaneously, the QL hierarchy represents an ideal order of attack for enhancing an organization. Although it is unlikely that any company can follow this hierarchy precisely, the main point of describing this scheme is to suggest an orderly, staged approach to thinking about improvement. Again, perfection is not expected, but having a proper framework from which to work will provide guideposts on the path to excellence. Ultimately, the good news is that maintaining product centricity offers great prospects for success regardless of the sequence in which improvements are carried out.

Organization

Since prior foundation studies have largely been laid at this point, additional improvement is made possible by harmonizing the remaining portions of the organization that have not been aligned to the QL system.

While it may be possible to pursue every foundation some simultaneously, the QL improvement presents an ideal order of attack for enhancing an organization. Although it is unlikely that any company can follow this precisely, clearly the main point of describing this ideal is not to suggest a concrete, staged approach to thinking about improvement. Again, perfection is not expected, but having a proper framework from which to work will provide guideposts on the path to excellence. Ultimately, the good news is that each improvement produces great prospects for success regardless of the sequence in which improvements are carried out.

CHAPTER **4**

PRODUCT PATH DIAGRAM

"Simplicity is the ultimate sophistication."

Leonardo da Vinci

To help minimize the time required to serve a product, Quantum Lean (QL) frequently relies on twelve specific tools[4-1] (see Figure 4.1).

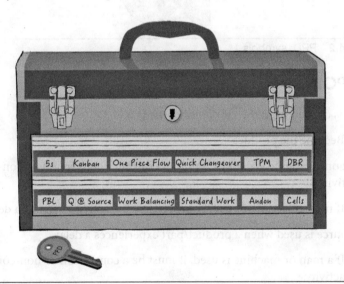

Figure 4.1   Lean tools

Despite the fact that every tool is useful, no situation requires them all. To pick the ones that offer genuine impact for a particular problem, product path diagrams (PPDs) are the key to identifying improvement opportunities, unlocking the lean toolbox, and accessing the relevant tools. To minimize cost by minimizing a product's time-in-system, PPD starts with the idea that a product's time falls under the categories of conversion, non-conversion, and delay—and puts each of these types in symbol form (see Figure 4.2).

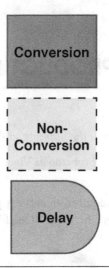

Figure 4.2   PPD: symbols

KEY POINTS

A PPD is created from the viewpoint of the product.

- Become the product!

At least one resource is used by a product during a conversion or non-conversion activity.

- If neither a man nor a machine is used, the activity must be a delay.

No resource is used when a product/part experiences a delay.

- If a man or machine is used, it must be a conversion or non-conversion activity.

To illustrate these principles, a few examples follow.

EXAMPLE—FABRICATION

Consider the steps in the following fabrication operation (see Figure 4.3):

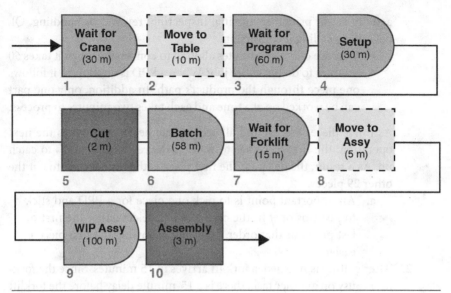

Figure 4.3 PPD: fabrication

1. An operator waits 30 minutes to get access to a crane. When it is time to start an order, the operator has to wait on a crane to become available so that sheet metal can be moved to a cutting table. Since the operator is waiting, the sheet metal is waiting too. Because no man or machine is doing anything to the sheet metal during this time, this is a delay.
2. Using the crane, it takes 10 minutes for the sheet metal to be removed from a shelf and moved to a computer-controlled cutting table. Why is this non-conversion? First, a man and a machine (the crane) are attending to the sheet metal. Second, the activity is primarily handling and transportation. And if it is moving, handling, rework, or inspection, it is a non-conversion activity.
3. Due to a lack of coordination, the program needed to run the table will not be available for an hour. Consequently, the sheet metal has to wait for a program. Although the table is tied up, no resource is actually attending to the product. Therefore, it is a delay.
4. Once a program is available to run the cutting table, setup operations require 30 minutes. With the program ready, the operator has to load the file and make adjustments. Again, since the product is unattended, it is experiencing a delay.
5. After setup, the sheet metal is cut into 30 pieces at a rate of two minutes per piece. Why is this conversion? Since a man and a machine are processing the material, it must be conversion or non-conversion. Since the

activity is not primarily moving, inspecting, rework, or handling, QL defaults to calling it conversion.

- Why are only two minutes allotted to conversion when it takes 60 minutes to do the entire job? When a PPD is developed, it follows one piece through the product's path. In addition, only one part can be worked on at a time and each takes two minutes to process.

1. As thirty pieces are cut and all accumulate before moving to the next operation, the first piece has to wait on the remaining pieces to catch up. As a result, the delay for the first piece is the time it took to cut the other 29 pieces.

   a. An important point is to pick one piece for a PPD and stick to just this one. In the case of a job, select either the first or last piece for that order. Typically, following the first piece is easier.

2. After cutting is finished, a forklift arrives in 15 minutes. Since the forklift is busy on another task, there is a 15-minute delay before the forklift is available.

3. Once the forklift picks up the parts, a five-minute movement takes place. Since a man and machine are involved, this activity is non-conversion.

4. Typically, since the cutting table is much quicker than subsequent operations, there is work-in-process (WIP). Since assembly is working on another order, the parts are placed in queue. Since no resource is attending to the 30 cut pieces, this portion of time is a delay.

5. Assembly takes three minutes. Since the task isn't any of the four non-conversion types, it's treated as conversion.

To gain a little more familiarity, see if your answers to these questions match the answers provided:

Question: For the cutting table, what is the setup time?

- Answer: 30 minutes

Question: What are the delays and non-conversion activities?

- Answer: Delay—wait for crane
- Answer: Delay—wait for program
- Answer: Delay—setup
- Answer: Delay—batching after cutting table
- Answer: Delay—wait for forklift
- Answer: Delay—WIP before assembly
- Answer: Non-conversion (transportation/handling)—before and after cutting table

Question: Based on the information in Figure 4.3, how long is material in the system before it gets to the *next station*?

- Answer: Adding up the times in the first nine icons results in 310 minutes. While there are many ways to visualize a system, a PPD not only helps you analyze events in sequence, but also helps you recognize which category of time monopolizes the system. Here, delay makes up about 94% of a product's time-in-system (see Figure 4.4).

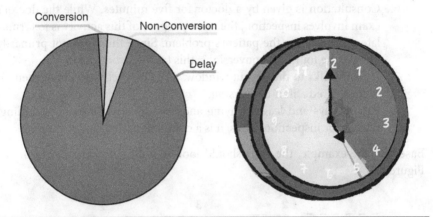

Figure 4.4   Pie chart: fabrication

EXAMPLE—CLINIC

Leaving the manufacturing sector, let's enter a doctor's office and formulate a PPD. Since patients are being processed by a medical office, they will be considered the product. With this in mind, the following steps would be involved in a typical medical practice:

1. Patient is signed in at the desk and takes 10 minutes to fill out paperwork. Since the patient is being attended to, it's either a non-conversion or conversion. Since the task isn't primarily moving, handling, rework, or inspection, this assigned a conversion symbol.
2. Patient waits in the lobby for two hours. By definition, this is a delay.
3. Patient is escorted to the examination room. Since the patient is attended to and this task is primarily moving, it is assigned the non-conversion symbol.
4. Vital signs are taken and that requires about two minutes. Since this is primarily inspection, this step is non-conversion.
   a. A fair question is why not combine the two successive conversion steps of 3 and 4 (move to exam room and take vital

signs) into one symbol? First, when a different resource is performing a job, it's a good idea to split the task into two symbols. In addition, using two symbols makes sense due to the fact that the two non-conversions are different in nature (transportation versus inspection). When the time comes to analyze the process, this improves the ability to prioritize what to work on.

5. Patient waits for 30 minutes; this element is treated as a delay.
6. Consultation is given by a doctor for five minutes. While the doctor's exam involves inspection, the main purpose of this activity is to formulate a remedy for the patient's problem. Since this does not primarily involve the four non-conversions, this task is a conversion.
7. Patient walks to the payout window. Since this activity is movement, it is considered a non-conversion.
8. Patient pays and leaves. Paying and leaving is not moving, handling, rework, or inspection. Thus, it is a conversion.

Based on the example, the PPD should look like the following diagram (see Figure 4.5).

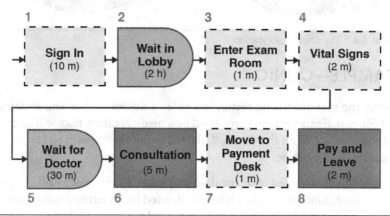

Figure 4.5   PPD: clinic

In addition, the time-in-system breaks down as seen in the following chart (see Figure 4.6).

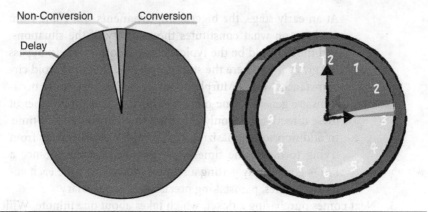

Figure 4.6   Pie chart: clinic

EXAMPLE—FILM

Beyond the office and the factory floor, a PPD can be used to diagram practically any operation. To underscore this point, it can even be used to describe going to the movies. For preliminaries, the moviegoer will be the product. After all, the theater's mission is entertaining the customer. For starters, assume that this person has gotten out of the car, locked it, and is ready to walk in. With this in mind:

1. The first step is taking one minute to walk to the box office. Since this primarily involves moving, assign a non-conversion symbol. Why? Because moving, inspection, rework, and handling are non-conversion processes. While a resource isn't involved, this example will take advantage of poetic license.

2. What's next? Before buying a ticket, remember that the moviegoer must stand in line. Since this involves waiting, it is a delay. As far as the time required, an accurate answer would be that *it depends*:

    a. On one extreme, if a blockbuster is involved, the line might take a while.

    b. On the other hand, if the film is showing on a night when the popular local sports team is playing, there won't be a line at all!

    c. Typically, most ticket queues take about 10 minutes.

    d. The takeaway from the description of ticket purchase is that times will vary. For a PPD, aim for a typical or average figure.

At an early stage, the biggest improvements will come from working on what constitutes the majority of the situations, and those would be the typical cases. In other words, bypass the gravy jobs where the stars are aligned, but also avoid circumstances where Murphy's Law prevails. Since those occasions are generally one-offs, any efforts expended in either of these directions will only help for a small portion of the time.

  e. In addition to emphasizing typical numbers, shy away from trying to determine times with pinpoint accuracy. Since a PPD's goal is only getting a relative idea of the time each activity requires, painstaking precision is unnecessary.

3. Next comes purchasing a ticket, which takes about one minute. Which category does it fall under? First, a theater employee is serving, so it is conversion or non-conversion. Since the activity isn't predominantly moving, inspecting, rework, or handling, classify this process as conversion.

4. From here, the theatergoer walks to the snack bar. Assign a non-conversion time of one minute.

5. In most theaters, the snack bar line is longer than the line at the ticket window. Since the wait at the box office is 10 minutes, assign this delay 15 minutes.

6. After the wait, the customer buys a snack. Since the purchase isn't moving, inspecting, rework, or handling, it is conversion.

7. Once the snacks are acquired, a walk to the ticket taker expends approximately one minute.

8. Generally, the ticket taker isn't immediately available, so assign a delay of one minute.

9. Once the ticket is torn, what kind of symbol should the activity be given? Is the employee checking to see if the moviegoer is a thief? Is this not an inspection? In other words, it is a quick non-conversion that can be rounded up to one minute.

10. The next step is walking to the cinema and finding a seat. Since this is travel, assign a non-conversion time of one minute.

11. Since moviegoers often hate sitting close to the screen, this customer arrived at the theater ahead of time to avoid front-row seats. Generally, this requires showing up at least 15 minutes early. Early arrival manifests itself as a delay.

12. Now, it's time to watch the film. It's conversion (why?). Average films take around one hour and 40 minutes.

Based on this, the PPD should look like the following diagram (see Figure 4.7).

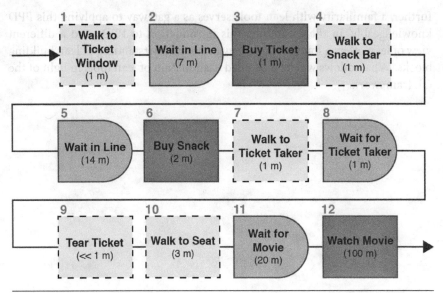

Figure 4.7 PPD: movie

In addition, the time-in-system breaks down as the following chart shows (see Figure 4.8).

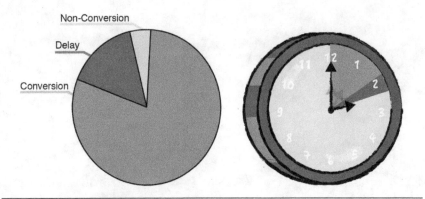

Figure 4.8 Pie chart: movie

SUMMARY

From the previous examples, it's easy to see that creating a PPD is straightforward. Soon, you will discover that a PPD is also a powerful tool for identifying and prioritizing improvement. However, before delving into this subject further, a familiarity with lean tools serves as a gateway to applying this PPD knowledgeably. In the meantime, this introduction to PPDs and a different view of lean offers a foundation to elevate your understanding of lean building blocks. What follows will be a detailed examination of lean tools in light of the QL framework.

CHAPTER 5

QUANTUM LEAN TOOLS

Many lean implementations bring cargo cults to mind. For those who haven't heard of them, cargo cults were the result of South Pacific Islands coming into contact with Western societies.[5-1, 5-2] When the civilizations met, an abundance of modern conveniences became available to people who had never seen them before. Unfortunately, once the outsiders left, the islanders had no ability to produce these wonders.

Doing their best, the island people mimicked the trappings of Western societies in the hopes that these would bring back the marvels they had grown accustomed to. For example, the natives would set up mock airports and airplanes, as well as fashioning radios from coconuts and straw. Imitating troops that visited during WWII, they even staged drills with sticks for rifles and painted military insignia on their bodies. Ultimately, due to this confusion of cause and effect, the natives came up empty because they made the common mistake of substituting protocols for proper foundations.

Many lean implementations are similar to cargo cults. Yearning for Japanese outcomes, Western companies ritualize programs like 5S, kanban, and andon. Unfortunately, it is often done with little appreciation of the deeper reasoning of these approaches. Like their South Pacific brethren, the Westerners' superficial emulations of Asian practices amounts to wasted motion.

With Quantum Lean (QL) reasoning, a company can avoid futility and eliminate a common cause of failure. As part of this, a refined understanding of frequently used lean tools will aid in this effort:[5-3]

- *Drum-buffer-rope (DBR)*—DBR is an approach for scheduling to the pace of an operation's bottleneck in order to improve shop-floor control and minimize lead time.
- *5S/workplace organization*—5S involves organizing and cleaning up the workplace. It is the foundation for a disciplined and orderly operation.
- *Product-based layout*—if the facility layout isn't right, trying to implement lean becomes a rearguard action. Where many businesses lay out their shops in a departmental fashion (i.e., lathes with lathes, mills with

mills, etc.) to maximize resource utilization, product-based layout is arranging resources so that product flow is facilitated.

- *One-piece flow*—one-piece flow (also known as *make one-move one*) is the practice where a product is immediately moved to the next stage of production once an operation is finished. This practice greatly reduces lead time.
- *Kanban*—as a way to maintain inventory levels and regulate flow, kanban signals what to buy/build, when to do it, and in what amount.
- *Andon*—andon is a method for signaling the state of the product or process so responses to breakdowns, parts outages, or slowdowns can be addressed in a timely manner.
- *Cells*—cells can be thought of as a product-based layout on steroids.
- *Quality@Source*—Quality@Source is an optimizing process to eliminate product variation and improve quality.
- *Standard work*—standard work improves work methods so variation in time and quality are minimized and speed is optimized.
- *Work balancing*—work balancing is distributing work among resources so that efforts are equalized and production rates are maximized.
- *Quick changeover*—many companies require significant time to switch production from one product to another. Quick changeover seeks setup times so low that they have no influence whatsoever on the production schedule.[5-4]
- *Quantum Lean maintenance* (QLM)—QLM harmonizes a lean tool called *total productive maintenance* (TPM) to the QL framework so that maintenance is subordinated to the needs of the product.

Despite the fact that all of these tools are mentioned, no situation requires all of them. Where the product path diagram (PPD) suggests which tool to deploy, additional insight about the use of each building block will result in better decisions.

DBR

DBR is a scheduling technique that maximizes throughput and minimizes lead time by pacing production to an operation's bottleneck. It is so central to a lean business that it's accurate to say that all roads on a lean journey lead to scheduling. In other words, improper shop-floor control is connected to practically every efficiency problem. Get this issue wrong, and achieving lean will be difficult, if not impossible. Get it right, and lean practically implements itself. Ideally, DBR should be one of the first lean tools to be deployed.

To provide you with some background information, this technique was popularized in a book entitled *The Goal*. This novel's plot was about a manager who was given three months to turn his plant around or face closure. While righting the ship, he discovered key insights, which included DBR. Although the author was brilliant, he was less than gifted at coining terms. While the phrase *drum-buffer-rope* will make sense to *The Goal*'s readers, the term confuses everyone else.

More people are able to relate to the DBR concept when it's described as *washer-dryer* (WD) scheduling. In most homes, a washer can launder clothes faster than a dryer can dry them. In this case, a person should pace laundry to the slower step in order to get the best efficiency. Since clothes can't be laundered any quicker than the speed of the dryer, pacing any faster will create piles of wet clothing. The following example using the laundering process illustrates one way to apply DBR:

- *Safety stock*—specify a safety stock to keep the dryer fed in case of hiccups such as the washer breaking down.
  - If the worst-case washer downtime is two hours, a safety stock of three hours would allow time for repair and for the washer to catch up.
- *Dryer schedule*—being the slowest step, schedule the dryer so that it is used continuously. Since laundry can only come out to the pace of the slowest machine, this maximizes throughput.
  - Dryer schedule
    - 8:00 a.m. (Load 1)
    - 9:00 a.m. (Load 2)
    - 10:00 a.m. (Load 3)
- *Release schedule*—assuming the safety stock is already in front of the dryer, release laundry to the washer so that it will arrive at the dryer in time to keep the safety stock constant. If the washer cycle takes 30 minutes, release a load thirty minutes ahead of the next dryer load.
  - Release Schedule
    - 7:30 a.m. (Load 1)
    - 8:30 a.m. (Load 2)
    - 9:30 a.m. (Load 3)

Since only the bottleneck should be constantly busy, it's okay if the washer is idle sometimes. As the schedule runs, monitor the safety stock. If the safety stock grows, throttle back the release of laundry. If it shrinks, speed up the release.

While this example is simpler than most production situations, scheduling the washer to the pace of the dryer demonstrates what will be true for more complex situations. Ironically, by throttling most equipment back, DBR maximizes throughput and minimizes lead time. After all, since any business can't produce faster than its *dryer*, elevating this constraint maximizes production. Anything running faster is wasted and increases work in process (WIP) and the product's time on the floor.

5S/WORKPLACE ORGANIZATION

In addition to DBR, 5S is one of the most important lean tools. In terms of facilitating flow, consistency, and discipline, 5S's importance cannot be overstated. With that being said, any effort at workplace organization should start with the product and determine if significant delays are traceable to a lack of organization. From there, the following questions should be asked:

- Materials
  - Are all necessary materials available:
    - When needed?
    - In the right quantity?
    - At the right quality?
  - Can materials be found and obtained quickly?
  - Could an outsider find and get materials quickly?
- Tools
  - Are all required tools available?
  - Are the tools functional?
  - Can tools be found and obtained quickly?
  - Could an outsider find and get tools quickly?
- Information
  - Is necessary information available?
  - Is the information accurate?
  - Is the information complete?
  - Can the information be found and obtained quickly?
    - Can the documentation itself be found and obtained quickly?
    - Can the information that is contained in the documentation be found and obtained quickly?
  - Could an outsider find and get the information quickly?

If the answer to any of above questions is *no*, 5S is a good tool to use. Each *S* signifies critical steps and occurs in the following order:

- *Sort* (*supply*)—this step involves equipping production strictly to the product's needs, which means screening out unnecessary clutter and supplying missing essentials. Since work areas often accumulate excess, significant effort will probably be needed to clean house. In addition, since employees often lack the tools they need to properly serve the product, chances are high that resources will need to be provided or fixed.

- *Set in order*—organize what's left. Provide a designated and identified place for everything and make sure everything is returned to its place after use. Think of it as: every tool has a home and no visitors are allowed.
- *Shine*—clean the workplace. The benefits are manyfold:
  - *Durability*—since dirt undermines machine durability, cleanliness extends equipment life.
  - *Detection*—in an immaculate environment, it's easier to detect problems like leaks.
  - *Morale*—if you've ever felt like your car runs better after it's washed, you're not alone. A shop floor will experience the same kind of psychological boost after cleanup.
  - *Behavior*—based on an idea called the *broken windows theory*, behavior improves with increasing order. The idea is that minor breaches like litter and broken windows precipitate bigger problems in societal conduct. By taking care of details up front, behavioral issues can be headed off. In an industrial setting, a cleaner and more orderly environment sets the stage for a more disciplined workforce.
- *Standardize (suppress)*—standardize 5S to ensure consistency. The Japanese use the word *suppress* to mean preventing the conditions that caused the original lack of cleanliness and organization. While the absence of a standard approach is a culprit for uncontrolled conditions, the Japanese term challenges us to attack all of the potential reasons for workplace chaos.
- *Sustain (support)*—sustain the previous five steps. A good reason to substitute the word *support* is that too many companies think *sustain* means riding employees hard to maintain housekeeping. While leaders must sometimes lay down the law, making support a first resort is the more effective long-term approach.

ONE-PIECE FLOW

Batch is intentionally building up more than one item at a station before moving it to the next process. In a plant with long distances between equipment, this approach will rule the day. Instead of running one part at a time across a large facility, any sensible person would accumulate a buildup first. However, what typically happens on a rush order? Like the atheist in a foxhole who finds religion, a person who ordinarily practices batch will run one part at a time across the plant. Why? Because the single most effective way to reduce lead time is to move a part to the next operation as soon as it is finished. Consider Figure 5.1 where each piece requires one minute at each of three stations.

Batch Processing
(Processing a batch of pieces before sending to the next step)

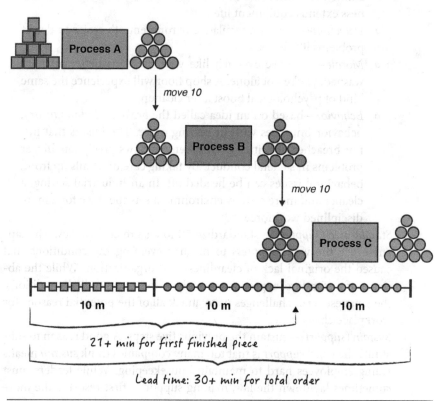

Figure 5.1   Batch versus make one-move one

Processing 30 pieces in batches of 10 will require 30 minutes to complete the order. By contrast, if a piece is sent to the next station immediately upon completion, the entire order will only take 12 minutes. That's why rush orders drive one-piece flow.

An additional benefit from one-piece flow is the quicker detection of quality problems. For example, if station 1 made a mistake that could be caught by station 2, a batch size of 10 means that 10 pieces have to be made at station 1 before station 2 has any chance of catching the problem. That is to say, at least 10 pieces will be scrapped. In one-piece flow, as little as one piece might be lost. That's a 10-to-one benefit.

A common misconception with one-piece flow is that some think that means that only one part at a time can be released to the floor. In fact, a million pieces can be released to the floor and this says nothing about whether batching is taking place. It's a question of what is done with a product once it is finished at a station. If that item is immediately sent on, one-piece flow is taking place. If it is intentionally impounded until subsequent pieces catch up, batch is occurring.

The only good reason batch occurs is due to long distances between processes. Get the operations close together and one-piece flow will have a way of automatically happening. It's that simple.

PRODUCT-BASED LAYOUT

In many shops, equipment is expensive and management wants to be sure those investments are put to work. In these situations, a departmental-resource-based layout, where like equipment is grouped with like equipment, is common (see Figure 5.2).

As a specific example, a machine shop might have lathes in one designated area and mills in another. While this layout helps keep the equipment running, it also results in idle product. Some implications of the departmental layout include:

- WIP has to be maintained to ensure that resources are keeping busy. More WIP = more lead time.
- With different resource types often located far from each other, material handling equipment is necessary to cover the distances between processes. More distance = more time.
- In addition, significant distance between resource types makes one-piece flow inconvenient. To conserve travel, batches are generally built up before products are moved to another operation. More batch = more delay.
- Since material handling equipment is typically busy, the product has to wait for this resource to become available.
- With all the built-in delays, a plethora of machine combinations, and the added challenge of maximizing utilization, scheduling is complicated and prone to constant revision. Estimating accurate delivery dates becomes much more challenging than it needs to be.

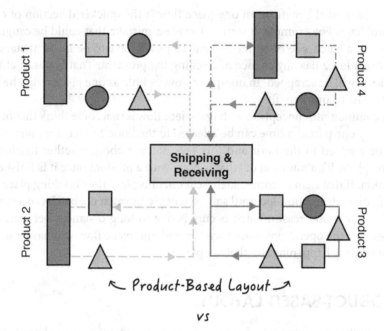

~ Product-Based Layout ~

vs

~ Resource-Based Layout ~

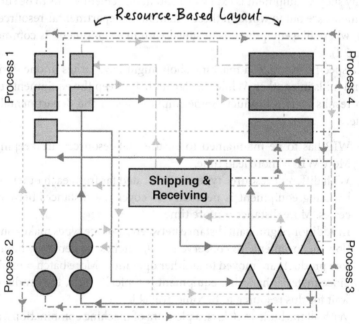

Figure 5.2   Product-based layout

With all the built-in delays, resource-based layouts can increase lead time manyfold. To improve turnaround, a product-based layout arranges equipment according to product flow and places workstations close together. By achieving proximity:

- One-piece flow is possible.
- Minimal material handling = minimal travel distance = minimal delay waiting for material handling equipment.
- WIP not only becomes largely unnecessary, but actually becomes something to be avoided.
- Dedicated equipment is possible, which minimizes delay. As a result, scheduling and on-time delivery are much simpler.

Of course, a downside of this approach is that capital investment may increase. However, Japanese companies are frequently willing to have a machine sit idle in order to facilitate flow. Given the Japanese track record for efficiency, companies would be well-advised to think about this the next time they insist that a resource be shared among many product lines.

An additional foundation for proper facility layout is storing material at its point of use—aka point of use storage (POUS). While it's obvious that parts should be placed where they will be used, this issue has a little more depth than meets the eye. Where POUS is important to lean, a lean operation is also a must for POUS to be possible. To avoid a gargantuan shop floor, true POUS requires keeping little to no inventory. Otherwise, floor space needs can easily multiply. As simple as the concept is, making it a reality can be quite difficult. In fact, getting inventory so low that all of it can be out in the shop is so challenging that few companies have actually done it. Nevertheless, it is an ideal that organizations should strive toward.

KANBAN

Like wars that are lost from depleted supply lines, winning at production means the line must be fed. One way to do this is with kanban, a system that gives simple signals on what to buy or build, when to do it, and in what amount. The main point is that demand gets filled with minimum outage and optimal inventory levels. Although it can take many forms, classic kanban involves two bins (see Figure 5.3).

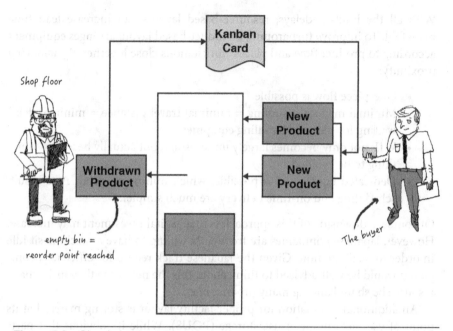

Figure 5.3 Classic kanban scenario

When one bin is emptied, an operator takes a card and sends it to purchasing. During the time required for an order to be placed and delivered, production can use material from the second bin. If the kanban is properly sized, the second bin should be emptying just as the first bin is being replenished. While this is the ideal, actual events should come close. In the classic scenario, a kanban card might look like the card in the following sample (see Figure 5.4).

Notice that all of the information needed to place an order is on this card. Obviously, this enables faster ordering and reduces turnaround time. With product, vendor, and reorder information, it's so complete that orders can be initiated from the shop floor. As it turns out, many plants do this.

In the real world, a kanban can work as previously explained. However, that doesn't mean that all kanbans are based on a signal from a card. Other methods to convey the need for reorder include:

- *Containers*—an empty tote, cart, or bin might be the signal to reorder
- *Physical location*—like painted squares on a floor or otherwise designated spaces
- *Physical triggers*—like golf balls or pins

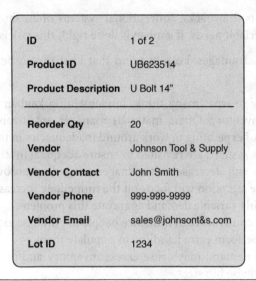

ID	1 of 2
Product ID	UB623514
Product Description	U Bolt 14"
Reorder Qty	20
Vendor	Johnson Tool & Supply
Vendor Contact	John Smith
Vendor Phone	999-999-9999
Vendor Email	sales@johnsont&s.com
Lot ID	1234

Figure 5.4 Kanban card example

- *Kanban boards*—a visualization tool to manage workflow that typically uses sticky notes or magnets on a whiteboard to communicate status, progress, and issues
- *Electronic* (*barcode, spreadsheet, database*)—there is a permanent code with a barcode that is scanned.

When first learning all of the details of a kanban system, some might wonder where the benefits are. A few benefits include the following:

- In a conventional control system, each withdrawal and replenishment must be recorded for timely reorders to occur. By contrast, kanban uses an occasional visual cue to trigger replenishment and doesn't need transactions to be documented. By comparison, the conventional approach is labor intensive.
- In addition to maintaining updates, conventional techniques must have personnel who are double-checking the counts.
- Traditional systems are error-prone. It's easy to enter a number wrong or overlook a transaction altogether. This is not idle speculation. When an auto parts store says they have a particular part in stock, an experienced shopper will make sure that the store attendant has actually laid hands on that part. Otherwise, there is a good chance of driving to a store that doesn't actually have the product. All too often, a computer will not reflect the reality on the shelf.

- Due to its drawbacks, conventional systems often short production of the material it needs. If kanban is done right, this risk is mitigated.

With all of its advantages, keep in mind that kanban can be a double-edged sword:

- Contrary to what many think, implementing kanban can actually increase inventory. Often, materials management involves a significant amount of expediting to work around inadequacies in the system. When min/max systems are revisited to ensure adequate inventory, expediting expenses will decrease, but management will often overlook this. Instead, the attention will focus on the immediate increase in stock. Parts with highly variable demand aggravate this problem.
- Two-bin constructs can influence people to purchase expensive containers and perform extra handling to populate them.
- Seasonal demand may cause excess inventory and/or the need to frequently revise bin sizes.
- Cards can be inconvenient. Employees often dislike them. If cards are used, there's a good chance many of them will end up on the floor.

Based on the pros and cons, kanban is best for low-cost parts with consistent demand and low volatility. Conventional systems are often advisable in other cases. Overall, kanban is not about bins or cards. Like everything else in lean, it is about getting the product what it needs when it needs it. Ultimately, kanban's form doesn't matter as long as it consistently fulfills demand with minimal inventory.

ANDON

I once worked for a company that did almost everything wrong and it taught me a lot about the right way to do things. Since then, I try to do the opposite of anything they did. And that is only a slight exaggeration. Despite a production rate of one assembly every twelve seconds, raw material was riddled with defects, equipment broke down continuously, and employee turnover and absenteeism were off the charts. This much I could stand. What really took the cake was the lack of urgency when anything went wrong. The general sequence of events when a machine malfunctioned was:

- Machine breaks down
- Employee finds and informs supervisor

- Supervisor pages maintenance
- Maintenance technician calls supervisor back
- Supervisor and technician confer
- Maintenance comes out to address problem

Keeping in mind that the line was supposed to produce something every twelve seconds, how much production was lost during the malfunction? A lot! Fortunately, there is a better way called *andon*. Since andon is diametrically opposed to the approach that was just described, it's safe to say it's a winner.

In general terms, andon is about notifying the appropriate people sooner so they can act sooner. In production settings, it's about notifying support functions (like maintenance) of problems that threaten production. These might include inventory outages, breakdowns, slowdowns, or quality issues. Much of the time, the centerpiece of andon is a sign incorporating signal lights to indicate process issues (see Figure 5.5).

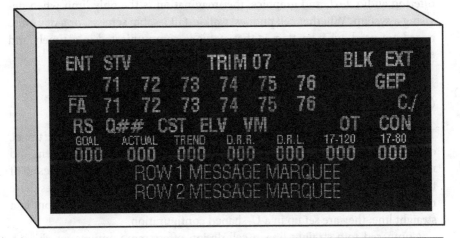

Figure 5.5 Andon example (courtesy of Static Controls Corporation)

To assist the support staff, blinking patterns or sound enhancements might be used to clarify the problem. Although an andon is often a lighted sign, it doesn't have to be. Since the fundamental point is to proactively provide notification, the challenge is deciding how to do it. Ultimately, the simplest way is generally best.

As Exhibit A that andon can take on many forms, Houston, Texas, in the 1980s provides a case in point. During that time, the city had a problem with buses not running on time. While sophisticated technology was unavailable back then, that didn't keep the city from considering elaborate fixes. While all this was going on, someone noticed that most of the bus drivers didn't wear watches on the job. Due to this perceptive observation, the expensive options were tabled in favor of a much simpler answer. By requiring bus drivers to wear watches on the job, Houston was able to increase on-time performance. Although few Americans knew the term back then, this solution was an object lesson in andon. It provided timely notification of problems to the people who could fix them.

Again, the idea is to provide timely and sufficient information so that support functions are prepared to address them. The emphasis is on the word *timely*. In high-speed manufacturing, bypassing layers saves minutes, which translates into a lot of production. In a slower-paced operation, saving hours might be sufficient. The real challenge is formatting the signals to fit the situation.

With technological advancements, numerous means for information transmission are possible. When the Japanese created andon in the 1950s, they were limited to simple technologies like light bulbs and relays. With today's systems offering audio, text, and graphics, the imagination is the only limit when devising a system. Whether cell phones, walkie-talkies, big screens, or a dry erase board are used, what matters is that status is communicated in a timely and effective way.

CELLS

To accommodate one-piece flow and minimize operator and product travel, cellular manufacturing is an approach that is used to arrange equipment and materials to best fulfill the needs of the product. Specifically, a cell includes all of the equipment and tools that are necessary to complete a job and arranges these resources like an assembly line. However, instead of stations being laid out in a straight line, they are set up in a U-shaped configuration.

Compared to a straight line, a cell design offers more options for sharing tasks. To illustrate, if a cell was arranged in single file, it would be virtually impossible for one employee to cut and pack (see Figure 5.6).

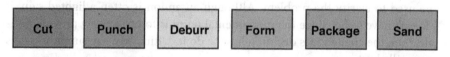

Figure 5.6   Straight-line diagram

Conversely, the *U-shaped* arrangement allows one employee to cut and to pack (see Figure 5.7).

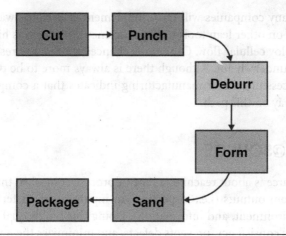

Figure 5.7 U-shaped cell diagram

By adding this wrinkle, cells not only serve the product but allow for optimal resource utilization.

A superficial glance might cause someone to overlook how profoundly lean cellular manufacturing is. On the shop floor, it's the ultimate fulfillment of a lean vision. In fact, properly implementing cells requires mastering every factor that affects production. At the same time, it synergizes these elements for overwhelming impact. Since a cell is a chain that is only as strong as its weakest link, execution is key. With minimal floor space requiring minimal WIP, any problem at one spot becomes a problem across the whole cell. If an issue is not quickly resolved, successive stations are rapidly drained of material and the cell is dead in the water. Consequently, achieving the following conditions is crucial:

- *Quality*—defect levels must be insignificant
- *Uptime*—equipment reliability is a must
- *Setup*—changeover times must be reduced to an inconsequential level
- *Personnel*—absenteeism and attrition must be minimal
- *Signaling*—since problems are inevitable, systems to rapidly address issues must be in place

When the conditions on the previous list are accomplished, these additional benefits flow:

- *Scheduling*—scheduling is simple and paced to the capacity of the cell
- *Work balancing*—with the challenge of keeping the product busy met, a U-cell arrangement facilitates the sharing of work so it is as balanced as possible, whereas, in a straight-line configuration, there are fewer tasks that can be divvied

Although many companies will try to implement cells right away, it is a good idea to work on other lean tools until proficiency with them is high enough to properly deploy cellular flow. Otherwise, chances are that the results will overwhelmingly underwhelm. Although there is always more to be done on a lean journey, successful cellular manufacturing indicates that a company has traveled a long way on this path.

QUALITY@SOURCE

Quality@Source is about reaching a state of process control so that monitoring can move from outputs (i.e., inspection) to inputs (men, material, machines, method, environment, and information). Doing this builds quality into a process, achieves consistency, prevents defects, and minimizes the need for inspection. The key foundations are:

- *Understanding a process so that outcomes can be accurately predicted.* If this is not possible, there is no hope for proactive control. Conversely, mastering cause and effect allows the establishment of controlled conditions that can be monitored. This ensures quality better than inspections after-the-fact.
- *Typical methods involve measuring the results of a process and recording the inputs that produced them.* From there, results are correlated against these inputs to determine any relationships. The goal is understanding which settings will create consistent product. In particular, statistical tools called *Six Sigma* are commonly used for this.
- *Six Sigma methods require a statistics background.* While it should be one of the later stages in a lean effort, several methods are very useful and software can help with the math.
- *Once the required process inputs are understood, empower, equip, and train employees to monitor the process in order to ensure consistency.*

Although Quality@Source has a great deal of potential benefit, the time to implement this lean tool will depend on where a company is positioned on the QL hierarchy. For example, if the product is not meeting quality standards, Quality@Source may be the most efficient solution to address this deficiency. However, if increasing throughput or decreasing cycle time is more pressing, it is probably wise to postpone the use of Quality@Source. While many companies are not in a good position to put these techniques to work right away, a company that continues on a lean path will come to a point where the techniques' implementations are called for and will bring significant benefits.

STANDARD WORK

Standard work is similar to quality at the source. In lean implementations where delay and non-conversion occupy the lion's share of time-in-system, improving work consistency may still offer significant opportunity for the following reasons:

- As quality affects cycle time and time-in-system profoundly, inconsistency can disproportionately cripple efficiency and effectiveness.
- Decreasing cycle-time magnitude and variability has its merits. However, as most process steps are non-constraints, making activities faster or more consistent can have negligible effects on overall performance in the early going.
  - At the same time, it can be argued that imposing restrictions on work can stymie innovation. Tread carefully.

When a company reaches a point where the product has minimal idle time, standard work can be an indispensable means to accomplish increased resource utilization.

As part of this effort, work methods should be analyzed using PPD. In other words, conversion steps can be broken down into a series of conversions, delays, and non-conversions. Like the improvement process for a business, jobs can be streamlined in the same manner. For example, if the majority of a task is non-conversion, these steps would be prioritized for minimization. Likewise, the same would be done for delays and conversions when they constitute the bulk of a job.

WORK BALANCING

As part of the effort to make resources busier, work balancing can be used to equalize work distribution. In addition to minimizing direct labor cost, work balancing helps morale by fostering the perception that everyone is pulling their weight. The most promising time to deploy this tool is during the implementation of an assembly line or cell. Frequently, line-balancing techniques are used to allocate tasks among personnel so that their workloads are evened to the greatest extent possible. In addition, work balancing includes strategies to redeploy personnel and other resources when products get delayed during production.

QUICK CHANGEOVER

In the 1950s, Japan was building its manufacturing base, but was faced with many barriers to becoming an industrial power. Among those barriers, the lack

of usable space was particularly dire. With setup times in the automotive industry taking several hours, the necessary buildup was staggering. As typical plants
produce finished cars at a rate of one per minute, this implied a massive WIP
level was needed to keep production running. When a country of 100 million
people only has the usable area of an American county, the space requirements
this entails are unacceptable. Something had to give—and it wasn't going to
be the Japanese auto industry. In response to this challenge, a major effort was
undertaken to get setup times under control. As part of this endeavor, many of
the tasks were shifted to a time when production wasn't taking place. Although
it required investment, doing this turned a process that took hours away from
production into a delay that only took minutes. Now that's improvement!

QLM

Most lean programs use the building block called TPM to enlist operators
and technicians to improve equipment performance. Where TPM is primarily resource-focused, QLM harmonizes this tool to the QL framework so that
maintenance is fully subordinated to the needs of the product. There are several
pillars of TPM, but QL configures them to align to the QL framework. What
results is called QLM, whose components include:

- *Maintaining equipment function*—like QL, maintenance's first priority should be assuring that the product gets what it needs. In turn,
  this means that keeping processes capable is the first order of business.
  Specifically, the ability to produce parts at the specified rate and quality
  should be maintenance's first priority.
- *Minimize repair time*—regardless of equipment condition, the next priority should be minimizing the time it takes to fix production breakdowns. In the near term, maintenance's biggest impact on timely
  deliveries can be made by minimizing the time it takes to repair equipment. While preventing breakdowns is preferable, achieving significant reductions in failure rates often requires a great deal of time and
  investment.
- *Minimize equipment failure*—while prevention carries a lower priority in
  QLM than streamlining corrective action, this point carries a caveat. If
  working on prevention has a greater near-term impact on product delivery than optimizing repair time does, make prevention a higher priority.
- *Extend equipment life*—once the previous objectives are being addressed,
  the financial impact from extending equipment life is significant and
  warrants attention.

- *Improve maintenance efficiency*—since pursuing this objective can easily undermine higher-priority objectives, tread carefully. However, if maintenance can be done with less outlay and still serve the product, continue at full speed ahead.
- *Feedback mechanisms*—a viable program should gauge efficiency, effectiveness, and fidelity.

In the final analysis, the goal for any maintenance program should be keeping equipment functional and running. With a lot of lean principles, sound business practice, and a little common sense, QLM's prospects in this regard are quite promising.

SUMMARY

Despite the fact that all the lean tools are useful, no company requires them all. However, when the PPD does suggest a tool to deploy, an awareness of the methods and what they offer comes in handy:

- *DBR*—an approach for scheduling to the pace of an operation's bottleneck to improve shop-floor control and minimize lead time.
- *5S/workplace organization*—organizing and cleaning up the workplace. It is the foundation for a disciplined and orderly workplace.
- *Product-based layout*—if the facility layout isn't right, trying to implement lean becomes a rearguard action. While many businesses lay out their shops in a departmental fashion (lathes with lathes, mills with mills, etc.) in order to maximize resource utilization, a product-based layout will arrange resources so that product flow is facilitated.
- *One-piece flow*—also known as *make one-move one*, is the practice where a product is immediately moved to the next stage of production once an operation is finished. This greatly reduces lead time.
- *Kanban*—as a way to maintain inventory levels and regulate flow, kanban signals what to buy/build, when to do it, and in what amount.
- *Andon*—a method for signaling the state of the product or process so responses to breakdowns, parts outages, or slowdowns can be addressed in a timely manner.
- *Cells*—product-based layout on steroids.
- *Quality@Source*—optimizing processes to eliminate product variation and improve quality.
- *Standard work*—improving work methods so variation in time and quality are minimized and speed is optimized.

- *Work balancing*—distributing work among resources so that efforts are equalized.
- *Quick changeover*—many companies require significant time to switch production from one product to another. Quick changeover seeks setup times so low that they have no influence whatsoever on the production schedule.
- *QLM*—harmonizes the lean tool TPM to the QL framework so that maintenance is subordinated to the needs of the product.

Although all of the lean tools existed long before QL ever entered the picture, viewing these methods through a QL lens allows for a more refined understanding of their power and improves their chances of being deployed for maximum benefit. At the same time, never restrict lean efforts to just these tools. If there are other methods that can streamline a business better than these 12 lean tools, use them. At the end of the day, the bottom line to QL is to improve a system in the most effective way.

CHAPTER 6

APPLYING A PRODUCT PATH DIAGRAM

With lean tools and the product path diagram (PPD) introduced, the next step is gaining insight into using the PPD to determine which lean tools to deploy.

" Aye Master. Whoso pulleth out these swords of this stone
is rightwise king of product path diagramming "

Figure 6.1 Product path diagram cartoon

GUIDELINES

When making improvements using a PPD, the order of attack should be dictated by the amount of time that each activity type occupies. In the early stage of most implementations, the order of attack will most likely be:

- Delay
- Non-conversion
- Conversion

To address delays, it helps to consider the reason they exist. From there, the tools to use are much easier to determine. The following list contains some common reasons for delays and the lean tools that often apply:

- Waiting for support staff (maintenance, materials, engineering) when something goes wrong
    - *Andon*—reduces the wait for these resources
    - *Kanban*—reduces outages that create the need for support
    - *Quantum Lean maintenance (QLM)*—reduces breakdowns that create the need for support
    - *Quality@Source*—reduces the need for quality control staff
- Waiting on material handling equipment
    - *Product-based layout*—reduces the distances that necessitate material-handling equipment
- Employee looking for tools/materials/information
    - *5S*
- Machine downtime
    - *QLM*—prevents malfunctions and decreases repair time
    - *Andon*—decreases response/repair time
    - *5S*—decreases the portion of repair time spent retrieving tools and parts
- Setup time
    - *Quick changeover*
- Work-in-process (WIP) inventory grows when arrival rate increases compared to the service rate. The issue can be addressed by working on the arrival rate and/or service rate.
    - *Arrival rate*
        - Drum-buffer-rope (DBR) throttles arrivals to better match the service rate and results in minimal WIP
    - *Service rate*
        - Standard work decreases cycle time to better match arrival rate

- Batch
  - *Product-based layout eliminates distances which necessitates batches*
  - *One-piece flow*
- Material outages
  - *Kanban*
- Information unavailable
  - *5S*

In addition, the following are common reasons for non-conversions and the lean tools that often apply:

- Handling
  - *One-piece flow*—reduces stacking, unstacking, and temporary packing
- Movement
  - *Product-based layout*—reduces distance and transportation
- Rework/inspection
  - *Quality@Source*
  - *Standard work*—improves consistency/quality

When conversions occupy the lion's share of a product's time, the following tools can streamline operations and increase resource utilization:

- Standard work
- Work balancing
- Cells

In addition to utilizing lean tools, remain open to methods that can help where lean building blocks aren't useful. Even though they aren't explicitly lean, software solutions, industrial psychology, and inventory-control techniques are a few possibilities that can aid improvement efforts. Although the listed tools are not the only ones that must be used to address inefficiencies, they should be initially considered since they are frequently called for. Of course, whether or not it's a lean tool doesn't matter as long as it helps.

EXAMPLE—THEATER: DETERMINING PRIORITIES

Returning to a diagram that was developed earlier in this book, the following figure is a PPD for going to the movies (see Figure 6.2).

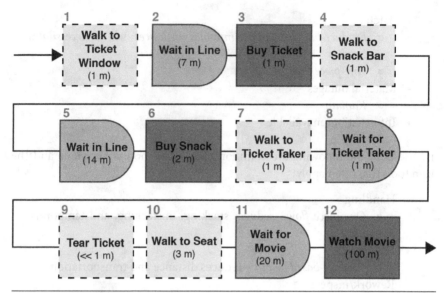

Figure 6.2   PPD: movie

There are several actions that can make the theater more efficient. Outside of watching the film itself, the majority of the customer's time is spent in delay. Using the logic of attacking delays first, here are some opportunities and potential tools that might be used to reduce the time.

Ticket Booth Queue

This is WIP that is a result of a mismatch between the arrival and service rate.

- Service rate
  - *More servers/automated kiosks*—these will work. However, since these options increase cost, these avenues should only be considered after less expensive alternatives are ruled out.
  - *Cycle time*—candidates to sell tickets faster:
    - *Standard work*—optimizing methods and bringing greater consistency to a job never hurts. However, is it the customer or the employee who accounts for most of the time?
    - *Andon/visual*—have you ever been behind some jerk in line who doesn't know which movie he wants to watch? First, let me apologize since I've been one of these guys. In my defense, the reason I didn't know which film to watch was that my original show time was sold out and

the reflection on the ticket window made it impossible to see the *sold out* notice until I was at the window. In addition to status, film offerings and times are often not visible from a ticket line. Information about showings can be located and configured so that customers are as informed as possible before reaching the ticket window.

- Arrival rate
  - *Staggered showings*—as a variation on DBR, one possibility is staggering showings so that the theater doesn't get overwhelmed at any one time.
  - *Online sales*—will reduce the number of arrivals to the ticket booth.

Snack Bar Line

Many of the solutions for the ticket line will work for the snack bar. In addition to the previously mentioned solutions, options to decrease delay include the following:

- Service rate
  - *Layout*—concession-stand layouts often maximize employee travel distance. Rearranging the work area can result in faster service.
  - *Cells*—could the snack bar be arranged like a cafeteria where the customer can be served with minimal travel?

Queue at the Ticket Taker

- Quality@Source is used when there are theaters where the ticket sale and ticket inspection are done at the same time before a customer is allowed to enter the main theater area.

Waiting for Movie

- Reserved seating may help since the main reason people show up early is that they want to avoid sitting close to the big screen. While it isn't a lean tool, reserved seating eliminates the reason for this delay. Since reserved seating is available in theaters throughout the world and increasingly in North America, it's possible.

Some of the aforementioned solutions aren't lean tools and the need to depart from lean building blocks should be expected at times. Ultimately, effectiveness is what counts. Although there isn't a cut-and-dried formula to apply lean tools, the principles and guidelines will carry a practitioner most (if not all) of the way. Although non-conversions and conversions were not covered in this example, the same kind of thinking that is used for delays can be applied to the other types of activities as well. The main idea is that the reason for any activity should be carefully evaluated before pondering ways to minimize time.

SUMMARY

From the previous example, it is easy to see that creating and using a PPD is pretty simple. The PPD advantages add up to a powerful method for visualizing a product's path. With PPD as a foundation, the steps for implementing QL include:

- Develop a PPD to account for the time that a product spends in fulfillment.
- Once a PPD is created, use QL's guidelines to help identify and prioritize the issues to be worked on.
- For each action item, apply guidelines to help determine which lean tool(s) to deploy.
- Based on findings from previous steps, implement and validate improvements.
- Once action items are implemented and validated, start over and repeat these steps.

With QL reasoning and PPD, a foundation exists to apply lean tools effectively and efficiently. With this under your belt, the groundwork is laid for additional information that offers the prospect of taking implementations to an even higher level.

SIDEBAR — PPD BENEFITS

When any effort is expended, it is important to establish the benefits that accrue from the work. PPD should not be exempt from this determination. After all, it really is an issue about the power of time-in-system and whether reducing it will improve a company's finances. In the case of the theater, what would the gains be from implementing the improvements suggested by the

Continued

PPD? Since a shorter time at the movies means that fewer people are there at any one time, the following benefits are possible:

- A smaller theater since the square footage can be reduced without crowding customers. A smaller building means decreased:
  - *Capital investment*—a smaller building means less monetary outlay. In turn, this enables a reduction in HVAC sizing and a decreased area for parking.
  - *Utility bills*—the smaller the dwelling, the less it costs to heat, cool, and illuminate.
  - *Staffing*—fewer people in a business at any one time means that fewer employees must attend to them.
  - *Taxes and insurance*—the less money that is tied up in property, the lower the property tax and insurance.
- Additional benefits include:
  - *Less waiting time*—may increase the number of customers. It can't hurt.
  - *Less balking*—whether it's the box office or snack bar, potential customers often turn away when there are long lines. Decreasing the odds of a long line decreases the chance of a guest balking.

Although some might object that a theater is nothing like a production facility, the elaborated principles apply regardless of setting. When American automakers first reviewed Japanese techniques, they were stunned by how the Japanese could achieve Detroit-levels of production while utilizing far less space and capital—by draining time from an operation, that's exactly what they did. When the fuel for waste is eliminated, it is impossible for inefficiency to thrive.

SIDEBAR—NEXT-LEVEL IMPROVEMENT

Suppose it were possible to optimize the film-going experience to the point that the time-in-system only involved watching the movie. What should the next step be?

- *Do nothing*? The experience of watching the film is what the customer is paying for.
- *Improve the movie*? Work on acquiring films that will attract an increasing share of the viewing public.
- *Reduce the length of the movie*?
- *Do something else*?

Continued

In conventional lean systems, the typical response would be to do nothing since viewing the film is considered to be *value added*. However, a QL approach would suggest that shortening the length of the film should at least be considered. Before protesting that the film's quality would be shortchanged, consider a couple of angles:

- Several years ago, actor Kevin Costner starred in a movie entitled *Dances with Wolves*. Back in the day, the movie officially ran for just over three hours. Since I watched this motion picture at the time, I can vouch that some films could stand to go on a diet.
- Is the customer really paying to watch a film or are they seeking diversion and amusement? To make a point, if it was possible to give the viewer a download to their brain that imparted the memories of viewing the film and the positive feelings that accompany it, would this be desirable? Maybe. Before dismissing this thought out of hand, consider that:
  - *The costs of delivery would plummet*—there would be no need for a building, movie rentals, and all kinds of other costs. Although a facility would probably be needed to manufacture and deliver the downloads, it's a safe bet that the alternative of multiple theater buildings would greatly dwarf this cost.
  - *The externalities would be just as impeccable*—there would be a significantly reduced environmental footprint, fatalities associated with driving to a theater would plummet, and viewers would have about two hours of life freed up that would have otherwise been spent getting to the theater and watching the show.
  - *Customer satisfaction would remain the same*.

Of course, such an idea would require technical advances that aren't likely to happen anytime soon. However, this scenario is presently useful in that it drives home the idea that reducing time-in-system should always be considered. In many instances, it will force a business to think *outside-the-box*. On top of this, it offers the potential for inspiring improved offerings and increased value to customers and society.

This book has free material available for download from the
Web Added Value™ resource center at *www.jrosspub.com*

CHAPTER 7

A FINAL REVIEW OF QUANTUM LEAN

In the previous pages, a good number of ideas were shared. Although Quantum Lean's (QL's) principles are valid in any setting, the differences among organizations will mean that some elements apply and others won't. Ultimately, properly deploying the QL framework will reveal the right answers for your environment. Although it is great when this book provides the answers, it's far better when readers internalize the QL system so that solutions can be developed as they're needed. All in all, this system provides a foundation that will guide a business to sound decisions that serve the long-term interests of customers, employees, and shareholders. To recap this system:

- QL goals are:
  - □ Provide the product's needs completely and correctly
    - ○ Quality
    - ○ Delivery
  - □ Minimize the product's time-in-system
- Product path diagramming (PPD) is the tool that reveals the constituents of a product's time-in-system and facilitates a systematic attack on waste. These three components are:
  - □ *Conversion*—activity that requires a man's or machine's time and effects progress toward fulfilling a product's finished form.
  - □ *Non-conversion*—activity that requires a man's or machine's time and does not advance a product toward its finished form. For efficiency's sake, this category is generally limited to moving, inspection, rework, or handling.
  - □ *Delay*—activity (or lack of it) that occupies time, but does not require a man's or machine's attention.
- QL prioritizes the category that comprises the greatest portion of a product's time. Since many companies are in the infancy of lean implementation, the typical order of attack is:
  - □ Delay

□ Non-conversion
□ Conversion

- QL lean tools include, but are not limited to:
  □ *Drum-buffer-rope (DBR)*—an approach for scheduling to the pace of an operation's bottleneck in order to improve shop-floor control and minimize lead time.
  □ *5S/workplace organization*—organizing and cleaning up the workplace. It is the foundation for a disciplined and non-chaotic operation.
  □ *Product-based layout*—if the facility layout isn't right, trying to implement lean becomes a rearguard action. Where many businesses lay out their shops in a departmental fashion (lathes with lathes, mills with mills, etc.) to maximize resource utilization, product-based layout is arranging resources so that product flow is facilitated.
  □ *One-piece flow*—also known as *make one-move one*, this is the practice where a product is immediately moved to the next stage of production once an operation is finished. This practice greatly reduces lead time.
  □ *Kanban*—as a way to maintain inventory levels and regulate production flow, kanban signals what to buy/build, when to do it, and in what amount.
  □ *Andon*—a method for signaling the state of the product or process so responses to breakdowns, parts outages, or slowdowns can be addressed in a timely manner.
  □ *Cells*—product-based layout on steroids
  □ *Quality@Source*—optimizing processes to eliminate product variation and improve quality.
  □ *Standard work*—improving work methods so variation in time and quality are minimized and speed is optimized.
  □ *Work balancing*—distributing work among resources so that efforts are equalized.
  □ *Quick changeover*—many companies require significant time to switch production from one product to another. Quick changeover seeks setup times that are so low that they have no influence whatsoever on the production schedule.
    ○ *Quantum Lean maintenance (QLM)*— harmonizes a lean tool called total productive maintenance (TPM) to the QL framework so that maintenance is subordinated to the needs of the product.

While QL is a simple system, a great deal of detail underlies each element. In addition, these elements are inexhaustible. The basics don't take long to learn, but the finer details associated with QL require significant time to master. As a package, they will make the technical side of your work shine more and more as you continue to learn and improve. Like all learning, this aspect of lean should be a lifelong journey. However, it's the easiest part of the task in some ways. The phase that involves getting people to work toward a common goal is a challenge that has bested many talented people. While general principles have been previously shared on making implementations work, you will have to mix and match these approaches so they fit with your style and personality. As a next step, some ideal traits for a practitioner are enumerated below. Although no individual can possess all of these traits, they are qualities anyone can aspire to.

For starters, you know that people resist change. However, since you are offering something totally positive, will everyone accept what you offer? Of course not! Why not? Because most change is bad. Even yours. Consider that all human beings have limited knowledge and capacities—and information is just as deficient. Even with perfect knowledge and complete information, everyone will make mistakes.

When you make peace with this reality, you stand a chance to change things for the better. Ironically, knowing that you will fail makes success more likely. Understanding that work must be continually revised allows for the repetition needed to get things right. The most crucial point of all is that despite the fact that positive change faces so many barriers, the biggest reason that change is viewed negatively is that human limitations make first-time success rare. As a result, there is a reluctance to revisit our work or continue to attempt to implement change. This unwillingness to try again ensures that the change will be eyed skeptically, particularly by those who suffered through the first pass.

Keeping in mind the chaos you will bring, here are some actions to take that can build rapport and get others on board:

- *Create the picture*—emphasize QL's product centricity. Making it easy to serve the product appeals to those who deal with the product on a daily basis. The win/win/win scenarios for employees, customers, and shareholders speak to common sense.
- *Shift the focus*—highlighting the product instead of resources (i.e., them) minimizes defensiveness. In any change, people often feel the need to defend their actions. For these people, the fact that most inefficiency is management-induced adds insult to injury.
- *Make your intention clear*—the undercurrent to the project should be eliminating barriers to people doing their jobs. An analogy that works

is asking participants to remember a day that left them refreshed versus another day that drained them. From there, ask which day was more productive. Nine out of 10 will agree the productive day refreshed them. Someone who thinks superficially about this issue might ask, "How can you feel more rested, but get more done?" The irony is that unproductive days require the most effort. Barriers are high and extra work is required. Being highly productive requires minimal barriers. It is the difference between swimming upstream versus downstream. One is definitely harder, but the other one takes you farther.

- *Properly define success*—as productivity gains require easier tasks, emphasize that the project will be a failure if jobs get harder.
- *Acknowledge the inevitable*—communicate that you will mess up. The idea that there is no such thing as one trip to the hardware store makes this point.
- *Reassure*—if you have the power, make it plain that any changes that the group considers a bust will be dropped unconditionally.

Beyond the previous actions, consider working on the following list of qualities to gain the confidence of others:

- *Competence*—if you can't demonstrate that you know what you are talking about, how can you help others? Get the necessary education, experience, or knowledge before doing anything else.
- *Authenticity*—you must stay true to yourself. While you might want to emulate someone you admire, only do this if it aligns with your personality. If it doesn't reflect who you really are, people tend to see through it. Whatever you are, own it.
- *Belief*—related to authenticity is the fact that you must believe what you say. If you are hesitant about the message, modify it until you can get behind it. Like being your true self, people will sense a lack of confidence where conviction is wanting.
- *Intention*—at the end of the day, your intention should be that others get more from you than you get from them.
- *Swagger*—you must be the lean authority. Period. If you don't believe it, why are you asking people to follow you? Assume that everyone else knows nothing about this subject—because most of the time, they don't.
- *Humility*—aside from being the lean authority, be humble. The people at the plant know their situation 10 times better than you do. While it's okay to challenge them, respect their knowledge and experience. There is serious talent of all kinds. For every time you tell, ask four times.

There is a saying that the soft side of a business is the hard side. With most of the principles being pretty simple, this is especially true in lean. While perfecting yourself will help, don't have any illusions about the challenge.

There is a famous song with the lyrics: "So close and yet so far." At many companies, it is this way. They are like water at 211°F, which is just one degree from boiling. While there is often talent and a strong desire to excel, man-made impediments can make the journey arduous. It's like two towns that are only one mile apart as the bird flies, but considerably farther along the highway. While the cities are inherently close, man-made paths vastly increase the distance. It shouldn't discourage you, but it pays to always keep it in mind.

SIDEBAR—HUMAN VERSUS AUTOMATED

Returning to the issue of whether an automated or human-based system is lean (see Figure 7.1), it is sometimes suggested that the answer depends on whether the standpoint is the company's or the customer's. That is essentially saying that the interests of the company and their customers are opposed. How screwed up is that? Since a relationship between a business

"It's for you again ... and they're angry"

Figure 7.1 Human versus automated

Continued

and customer can be thought of like a marriage, it is similar to suggesting that a husband's and wife's interests are at odds. If true, how successful can this union be?

From a QL viewpoint, concluding that the operator-assisted call center is the lean option is totally obvious. With the customer as the product, a human touch will get customers through the system more quickly. With better service and a minimum time-in-system, it takes the prize. If you are still convinced that the automated option is better, consider the costs of:

- Investment in software and computers
- Investment in additional phone lines (more time-in-system = more customers in system = more phone lines)
- More minutes on phone lines
- Decreased customer satisfaction

Obviously, all of these burdens are real. If you still believe that it is possible that the automated scenario is lean, consider one final point. Where does a customer end up after all of the rigmarole? With a person!

CHAPTER 8

QUANTUM LEAN VERSUS
OTHER APPROACHES

There are two kinds of people: (1) those who have been exposed to lean and (2) everyone else. For the most part, those who are uninitiated in lean immediately understand and see Quantum Lean's (QL's) power. By contrast, QL elicits the following response from those who are well-versed in other systems:

- *They understand*—an epiphany may be experienced. Where typical lean has left them wanting, QL's elegance is embraced.
- *They don't understand*—some will insist that there isn't any difference between QL and other approaches. More often, this belief is an unconscious one and is evidenced by someone treating QL and other systems as though they're interchangeable. For example, they might use the terms *value added* and *conversion* in the same breath.

In fact, it's the *experts* who are the slowest to catch on. Even when the response is overwhelmingly positive, implementing QL requires being prepared to handle misperceptions and to slowly persuade the holdouts. Although facts are overrated as a means of settling disputes, having them at your disposal remains useful. In that vein, being able to demonstrate that QL is different and better requires being familiar with other schools of thought.

A LEAN BACKGROUND

Although Henry Ford and the Japanese pioneered many of the lean ideas we see today, the term *lean production* was popularized by James Womack, Daniel Jones, and Daniel Roos in their 1990 book, *The Machine That Changed the World*. In this work, the authors articulated the methods that the Japanese used to achieve dominance in the auto industry. From there, Womack and Jones published a book called *Lean Thinking* that propounded the principles of what is now known as *lean systems*. Today, these ideas are promoted at the Lean Enterprise Institute (LEI).

From this beginning, businesses around the world started implementing lean concepts. However, the fidelity to the model espoused by Womack and company was mixed. On the ground, many programs depart from their ideas. While all of these implementations have their own flavors, the ones I've observed generally share common elements that can be characterized as *Lean as Mainly Experienced* [8-2]—or LAME. [8-2, 8-3]

To give a better idea of the differences between QL and the other approaches, *comparisons and contrasts* between QL and each system will follow. From there, these points will be expanded on, along with the reasoning behind them. However, before doing this, a quick review of each system is needed so that QL and the others can be properly compared.

LEI LEAN [8-1]

The original *lean* is built around the following five precepts.

1. Value

According to the book *Lean Thinking*, value is defined as: "the capability provided to the customer at the right time at an appropriate price, as defined in each case by the customer." This idea of value is the starting point for any lean effort. As a point of emphasis in this system, value can only be defined by the ultimate customer.

2. Identifying Value Streams

Value streams are all of the actions required to bring a product from concept to completion. Once the tasks are defined, they are classified as follows:

- *Value added*—activities that clearly create value
- *Type one muda* (*waste*)—activities that create no value but are unavoidable
- *Type two muda*—activities that create no value and are avoidable, preferably sooner rather than later

Examples of waste/muda include:

- Rework
- Idle workers
- Defects

3. Flow

Flow is defined as: "the progressive achievement of tasks along the value stream so that a product proceeds from design to launch, order to delivery, and raw materials into the hands of the customer with no stoppages, scrap, or back-flows." Specific examples of achieving flow include eliminating:

- Work-in-process (WIP) inventory
- Batches

4. Pull

Pull is defined as: "a system of cascading production and delivery instructions from downstream to upstream in which nothing is produced by the upstream supplier until the downstream customer signals a need." Instead of building up product in the hopes that it will eventually be bought, pull is initiating fulfillment only after an order is placed.

5. Perfection

Perfection is defined as: "the complete elimination of muda so that all activities along a value stream create value." As a concession to practicality, a totally waste-free operation is held as the ideal situation. Ultimately, this means that lean efforts should remain ongoing.

All in all, the LEI system is a coherent and commendable system. However, QL is formulated to retain the LEI Lean's virtues while avoiding its pitfalls.

QL VERSUS LEI LEAN

Clearly, LEI Lean is powerful or it wouldn't have the staying power that it does. In addition, many criticisms are leveled against lean concern systems that depart from LEI principles. In other words, many of the downsides witnessed in the field have nothing to do with LEI Lean. In fact, the broad outlines of LEI Lean and QL share common ground and offer the goal of wins for customers, owners, and employees. The problems with LEI Lean mostly result from principles that become ambiguous when they have to be applied. Put another way, what looks well-defined from a high level ends up murky when the rubber meets the road. This lack of clarity probably contributes to the improper implementations of *Lean Thinking*'s teachings.

Some of the downsides to LEI Lean are rooted in its fundamental concepts, while others flow from suboptimal approaches to implementation. The good news is that QL uniquely addresses these problems. The reasons for this will be expounded upon in detail later, but for now, the major advantages that QL offers can be summarized as follows:

- *QL is streamlined*—a major portion of LEI Lean is identifying all the specific actions that are required to bring a product to completion. This entails considerable legwork to collect and document all of these details. By contrast, QL's product focus requires significantly less effort.
- *QL is more thorough*—ironically, QL's narrower scope results in a broader elimination of waste. By focusing on outcomes (aka, product experience) first, and then drilling down on upstream factors on an as-needed basis, QL ensures that inefficiencies are addressed comprehensively without getting bogged down in details. By contrast, investigating all of the actions needed to fulfill a product is similar to not seeing the forest for the trees.
- *QL is quicker*—where QL's product-centric analysis quickly zeros in on high-impact problems, LEI Lean's broad-brush approach requires more time to collect information and draw conclusions.
- *QL is easier*—value stream mapping, a frequently used LEI analysis tool, has several icons that require training in order to learn and use. With only three symbols and straightforward rules for determining priorities, QL's techniques are easier to understand and apply.
- *QL facilitates deeper understanding*—even though QL doesn't require an ability to see waste, QL facilitates this capability. Whereas people trained in other approaches often struggle to recognize waste, QL's framework facilitates an ability to identify multitudes of inefficiencies, even without the aid of diagrams.
- *QL achieves buy-in*—product-centricity is highly appealing to people who work on the floor.
- *QL unifies*—by focusing on an idea as subjective as value, it is difficult to impart a consistent understanding using an LEI framework. In other words, how can a workforce be unified if a significant number of employees are not on the same page?
- *QL uses unambiguous markers*—by contrast, QL's use of unambiguous markers like time and product specifications ensures that everyone can get on the same page.
- *QL gets results faster*—all other things being equal, an approach that is quicker, easier, and more unifying should get results faster.

QL VERSUS LEI LEAN—CONCEPTUAL DIFFERENCES

"Value can only be defined by the ultimate customer."

James Womack

"If I had asked people what they wanted, they would have said faster horses."

Henry Ford

"A word that can mean anything doesn't mean anything."

Weldon Steele

On a fundamental level, centering efforts around value is starting on the wrong foot, and multiple issues will spring from this. Of course, value is extremely important. In fact, it's so critical that a company must provide it if it wants to stay in business. In theory, it's a great organizing principle for a lean effort. But in practice, not so much!

Value Is Ambiguous

Every person is familiar with the idea of value and has definite beliefs about it. At the same time, no two opinions on it are alike. And no matter how carefully value is spelled out, preconceived notions can't help but override even a precise definition. Practically speaking, this creates a situation where no one is on the same page. If you doubt this, witness a debate over whether a task is considered *value-added*. Although conclusions are eventually drawn, it is decided less on the merits and more by who had the emptiest bladder.

Value Leads to Inconsistency

Sound analysis requires a consistent frame of reference. With value as the nominal focal point, this key requirement can't be met because value's ambiguity makes it a moving goalpost. Even for one product, there's a slim chance that every customer defines value the same way. For a luxury car, Jack may love technology while being indifferent to styling. For Jill, it might be the opposite. If the car manufacturer takes Jill's viewpoint, efforts to incorporate bells and whistles would be considered non-value-added. If they adopt John's thinking, the opposite conclusion will be drawn. In other words, optimizing a value stream around one customer's definition of value implies the shortchanging of others.

Although completely customized products would be ideal, most products need standard features that will please some and disappoint others. In such situations, trying to reach a goal using value as a yardstick can be difficult. Even for simple products, what's value-added for one customer might be muda to another. Increase the number of features and the contradictions skyrocket.

Value Is Impractical

Even if value could be consistently understood, explicitly relating an operation's inputs to value can be difficult, if not impossible. Often, it is speculation. Even if a relationship can be established, there's still a good chance that opinions will differ over how well a process meets customer needs. For example, at what point does preventing the waste of variation become the waste of excess processing? If completely eliminating one waste could possibly cause any of the following, would value be enhanced?

- Reduce product reliability by 1%
- Reduce production uptime by 1%
- Result in a flaw that only 1% of customers would notice?

While a lean guru might reply that everything should get better at the same time, such a possibility is often out of reach. In a world where tradeoffs are a reality, an improvement process focused on value can't help but break down.

LEI Lean's definition of value is questionable. It specifically states that only a customer can define value. Practically speaking, this insistence is debatable. While the end user has the last word on this subject, they often have little to initially offer on the topic. That's why companies have sales departments. Outside of extremely simple cases, an end user who completely understands their needs is virtually nonexistent. From cars to software, the knowledge necessary for this is beyond anyone's capabilities. To expand on this point:

- Features that delight customers the most are often ones that were never requested.
    - How many iPhone users know all of its virtues before they buy one?
    - If the customer solely defined value, it would be impossible to under promise and over deliver.

- Some tradeoffs are best left to experts.
  - How unsafe are you willing for your car to be? Anything safer is non-value-added.
  - How much pollution do you want your car to spew? Anything cleaner is non-value-added.

The reality is that customers can and should rely heavily on providers to fill in the blanks. Ideally, the determination of requirements should be a joint venture between a company and customer.

In contrast to value, QL's product-centricity offers a framework that is consistent, clear, and easy to align to. This results in a workforce with a common understanding of what is being sought. In turn, everyone pulling in the same direction facilitates faster conclusions. By avoiding conceptual dead ends, QL is also able to offer significant advantages on a practical level.

SIDEBAR—VALUE AS DEFINED BY THE CUSTOMER?

I have a friend who used to work as a transmission mechanic. When the transmissions were pulled, the engines from which they were removed would often have corroded freeze plugs. If they weren't replaced, future leaks were virtually guaranteed. With transmission work being so expensive, customers were in no mood to spend a penny more than required. When my friend would suggest replacing the freeze plugs for a few dollars, most customers would indignantly refuse. Complying with those customer's wishes, my friend left the freeze plugs alone. By the LEI definition of the word, he delivered value to the customer. But did he do so by any other standard?

QL VERSUS LEI LEAN—PRACTICAL DIFFERENCES

On a nuts-and-bolts level, LEI Lean's techniques have problems that impair efficiency and effectiveness. These include:

- *LEI Lean's efforts are front-loaded and benefits are back-loaded*—before attacking any problems, LEI Lean's first step is enumerating every task involved in the creation of value, the associated information and material flows, and the timelines. Up front, this entails considerable legwork before any benefits can start to be realized. By contrast, QL first focuses on outcomes to the product and prioritizing targets based on this. From there, upstream factors that are relevant to the selected targets, and only those targets, are investigated. This focuses initial efforts on high-impact issues to yield the greatest results quickly. This results in less up-front work and in a better balance between efforts and results.

- *LEI Lean methods are complicated*—although value stream mapping (VSM) isn't explicitly promoted in the book *Lean Thinking*, LEI prominently features it as one of their tools. For those who aren't familiar with VSM, it is a flowcharting technique that is used to identify activities and waste. Its biggest downside is its complication. For starters, it uses so many icons that it can get pretty esoteric. As one example, VSM has an icon for seat-of-the-pants scheduling called "go see production scheduling" that looks like a pair of glasses (see Figure 8.1). By contrast, with only three symbols, QL's product path diagram (PPD) is much easier to understand and apply.

Go See Production Scheduling

Figure 8.1   Go see production scheduling

- *The LEI Lean improvement path is unclear*—a claim about VSM is that it teaches how to clearly see waste. However, the opposite can be strongly argued. By recording anything and everything (including *go see production scheduling*), a VSM ends up cluttered and can confuse more than clarify. And beyond admonitions to achieve flow, implement pull, and abolish waste, LEI Lean offers few specifics on how to accomplish these things. In contrast to VSM, PPDs are simple and visual. In addition, QL undergirds this simplicity with specific and straightforward guidance to identify problems and determine priority.

Although the differences between PPD and VSM have been elaborated in theory, one example is worth a thousand explanations.

Example—PPD versus VSM

Returning to an example of the fabrication shop from Chapter 4:

A. An operator waits 30 minutes to get access to a crane so he can remove sheet metal from a rack.

B. Using the crane, sheet metal is removed from a shelf and moved to a computer-controlled cutting table in 10 minutes.

C. Due to a lack of coordination between production control and the shop floor, the program needed to run the table will not be available for an hour.

D. Once a program is available to run the cutting table, setup operations require 30 minutes.

E. After setup, the sheet metal is cut into 30 pieces at a rate of two minutes per piece.

F. After cutting is finished, a forklift arrives in 15 minutes and the parts are moved to assembly in five minutes.

G. Since assembly is working on another order, the parts are placed in queue.

H. After 100 minutes in queue, assembly is ready to process the cut pieces.

For this sequence of events, a VSM would look similar to the one in the following figure (see Figure 8.2).

Looking at the VSM, what needs to be worked on? According to the LEI Lean plan of attack, the achievement of flow is the first order of business. Looking at the timeline, you would want to attack one of the bars where no value is being added. Beyond that, the rest is up to you. A few points should probably come to mind:

- The VSM is pretty busy.
- Since the first priority is achieving flow, only the timeline is relevant. Why does everything else need to be compiled? Once barriers to flow are addressed, the VSM will change and the one that was just developed becomes obsolete anyway.

QL avoids these pitfalls. The PPD for the fabrication shop looks similar to Figure 8.3.

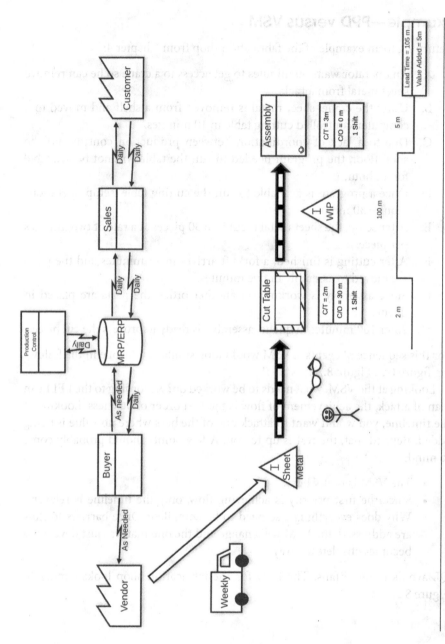

Figure 8.2 Value stream map: fabrication

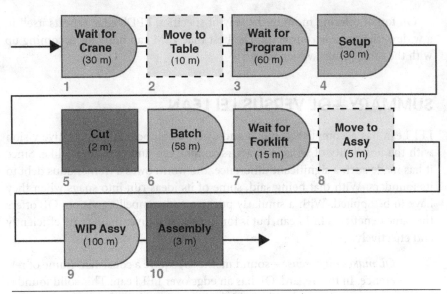

Figure 8.3 PPD: fabrication

Since the bottleneck is not in the portion of the shop being diagrammed (why?), the PPD indicates that the upcoming targets should be considered in the following priority order:

1. WIP—assembly
2. Wait for program
3. Batch
4a. Wait for crane
4b. Setup
5. Wait for forklift
6. Move to table
7. Move to assembly
8. Assembly
9. Cut

Ultimately, the PPD reveals a target-rich environment. As each element is considered, the reasons behind the time are considered and lean tools are deployed to minimize or even eliminate the time. By contrast, the VSM shows a lot, yet reveals little. Despite the clutter, wastes like *wait for a crane, wait for forklift,* or *wait for a program* are missing from a VSM. In such a case, the saying: "Data rich, information poor" comes to mind.

On top of offering more in the way of specifics, PPD's edge repeats itself in a wide variety of environments. The best that VSM can hope for is coming up with the same results, which it won't.

SUMMARY—QL VERSUS LEI LEAN

LEI Lean has accomplished much and offers a compelling and positive vision with the possibility of wins for owners, employees, and customers alike. Since it has made such a significant difference, the world owes a tremendous debt to its founders. With that being said, some of its ideas run into snags when they have to be applied. With a similarly positive and compelling vision, QL offers the same benefits as LEI Lean, but is formulated to deliver them more efficiently and effectively:

- *QL makes more sense*—sound methods require a consistent frame of reference. In this regard, QL has an edge over LEI Lean. This solid foundation paves the road with multiple downstream benefits.
- *QL unifies better*—in many ways, QL builds the unity needed for successful implementations including:
  - *Respect*—value is a positive idea, but the flip side is that matters can turn negative when activities get classified as *non-value-added*. No matter how it is handled, characterizing work this way carries a connotation that will alienate those doing the work. By maintaining a product-centric frame and avoiding recriminations, the QL approach is blame-free and imbued with respect for all.
  - *Buy-in*—bypassing implied insults is a good start, but employees must believe in the means and goals for there to be any chance of gaining their support. Based on experience, product-centricity squares with common sense and is highly appealing to people who work on the floor.
  - *Alignment*—buy-in is one thing, but getting a workforce aligned is another. For employees to pull in the same direction, a common understanding of goals is a must. By centering efforts on a fluid idea like value, it is virtually impossible for an LEI framework to get everyone on the same page. QL's anchoring to the product makes for an easily understood and consistent focal point.

- *QL is streamlined*—instead of first identifying all the specific actions that are required to bring a product to completion, QL restricts the efforts in determining what actually happens to the product, and only drills down on associated details once priorities are identified. This focus prevents a lot of unnecessary data collection by performing legwork only when it will contribute to eliminating waste.
- *QL is easier*—QL's techniques are easier to understand and apply than LEI Lean's tools.
  - *Simplicity*—VSM, the most frequently used LEI Lean analysis tool, has several icons and they differ for production, office, and consumption. With only three symbols that work in any setting, creating a PPD is simpler.
  - *Clarity*—by trying to record anything and everything, a VSM ends up with a bunch of clutter that confuses more than clarifies. And beyond general admonitions to achieve flow, implement pull, and abolish waste, LEI Lean offers few actionable specifics. Along with the simplicity of PPD, QL facilitates application with specific and uncomplicated guidance for identifying problems and determining priority.
- *QL is faster*—in addition to front-loading benefits, QL is streamlined, easier to use, and better at achieving buy-in. It should stand to reason that QL can get results faster.

While QL offers advantages over LEI Lean, it's when LAME enters the picture that QL is not only a better alternative, but an overwhelmingly superior one.

SIDEBAR—DUALITY

In the world of math, there is a principle called duality that holds that an optimization problem can be looked at in two ways. These two views are called the primal and dual. In the primal case, the issue is maximizing a goal subject to a set of limits that act like a ceiling. Conversely, the dual problem involves minimizing a goal with a set of constraints that act like a floor. When solving problems, the fact that primal and dual formulations converge around the same solution can be very useful. If the arithmetic needed to solve the primal version is difficult, the math associated with the dual might be a lot simpler. If so, solving the problem becomes short work since the dual and primal converge toward the same answer (see Figure 8.4).

Continued

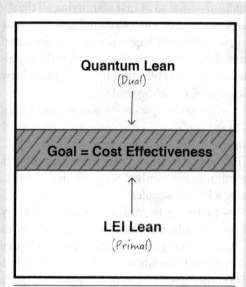

Figure 8.4   Primal-dual relationship: QL versus LEI Lean

If LEI Lean could be characterized as a primal problem, QL could be thought of as its dual. While both approaches work toward the same objective, QL is the simpler formulation that makes solving the lean problem easier and quicker.

LAME

While the book *Lean Thinking* inspired many companies to pursue lean initiatives, much got lost in translation. It's a lot like the gossip game at birthday parties that's also known as *Telephone*. For those who haven't heard of it, this game involves gathering kids in a circle. The birthday child thinks of a message and whispers it to the kid on the right. From there, the child that heard the message passes it along to the kid who is to the right. This process repeats until the child to the left of the birthday kid hears the message. At this point, the birthday kid's original message is compared to what the last child heard. For anyone who's participated in this game, the two messages are never alike. Along the chain, much gets lost in translation.

Like the gossip game, LAME draws from LEI Lean, but substantially departs from it based on the inevitable misinterpretations that come with preconceived notions and poor communication. In addition, due to companies wanting to put their own flavor to it, there are a fair number of LAME variations. Despite this, many lean implementations have enough in common that they can be called LAME:

- *Financial obsession*—where QL is product-centric and LEI Lean is centered on value, monetary considerations are generally the focus for typical lean programs. A variation on this is resource obsession where management considers resource utilization a proxy for good financial performance.
- *Toyota Production System (TPS)*—although TPS inspired most of what is disseminated by LEI Lean, some elements of TPS, like Taiichi Ohno's 7 wastes, are not explicitly included in *Lean Thinking*. However, most lean implementations use these to guide efforts.
- *Tool obsession*—in most lean implementations, obsession with lean building blocks runs a close 2nd to financial considerations. The lack of coherence manifests in tool fixation where a company decides to deploy lean tools like 5S and hope that there is a benefit. If the company is large enough, cost savings will be found whether or not they exist.
- *Cosmetic*—in LAME, appearances are often more important than achievement. Evidence of this tendency can be seen in one-point lessons that aren't needed, A3s blanketing the workplace, and 5S efforts that extend into personal effects.

Beyond the enumerated points, companies may add their own touches. However, these elements that were just outlined are commonly shared by many programs.

QL VERSUS LAME

"You know all about companies trying to get 'lean and mean'? A friend says her company has now transcended lean and mean. Now it's 'skinny and pissed.'"

Anonymous email to Scott Adams,
author of the "Dilbert" comic strip

While LAME shares a few of LEI Lean's weaknesses, it has many significant problems of its own. In the following comparisons, QL is contrasted with LAME.

LAME Is Haphazard; QL Is Systematic

As an extension of its tool fixation, LAME implementations frequently start with lean building blocks and search for places to apply them. In such cases, little analysis takes place. Correspondingly, real benefits can be haphazard. QL follows a logical and systematic approach that prioritizes actions according to impact, which results in faster and bigger gains. By extension, QL is systematic and optimizes an operation in a consistent and logical sequence.

LAME Invites Conflict; QL Unifies

Not being animated by a consistent vision, LAME does nothing to minimize the inherent conflicts that come with any organization. Some of these conflicts include:

- *Department versus department*—an example of this would be a purchasing department that sources lower cost parts, but creates significant downstream quality problems for production.
- *Customer versus company*—from automated customer service to self checkout at the grocery store, companies inconveniencing customers to save money is all too frequent.
- *Employer versus employee*—in the path to *lean and mean,* many companies are easy prey for the *skinny and pissed* model where employees are penalized by cost-cutting efforts.
- *Employee versus employee*—LAME has nothing to offer that can offset the natural friction that can occur among people whose perceived interests are in conflict.

Hearing these types of questions is a telltale sign of a company that's prone to these types of problems:

- Are we looking at this issue from the viewpoint of the company or its customers?
- Are we looking at this issue from the viewpoint of the company or its employees?

Although conflict is inevitable, QL minimizes it like no other approach can. When discussions are limited to the product's needs and not what management, departments, or employees want, it is much easier to prevent conflicting objectives. In addition, QL's approach appeals to common sense, is easy to understand, and approaches lean in a way that benefits all involved.

QL Has Better Buy-In

Shop-floor employees who work with the product tend to be highly receptive to QL's product-centric message. In contrast, the financially driven motivations behind LAME leave hourly workers cold.

QL Is Faster

By using systematic rather than scattershot approaches, QL will arrive at decisions more quickly. In addition, these decisions will have a higher impact sooner since actions are prioritized accordingly. And because the QL approach is systematic, logical, and unifying, it stands to reason that it will get results faster than LAME.

SUMMARY

Whether it's a question of better, faster, or cheaper, QL beats LEI Lean and LAME. And if anybody says there's no difference, make them read this chapter as many times as it takes until they say otherwise!

CHAPTER 9

INVENTORY

For want of a nail the shoe was lost.
For want of a shoe the horse was lost.
For want of a horse the rider was lost.
For want of a rider the message was lost.
For want of a message the battle was lost.
For want of a battle the kingdom was lost.
And all for the want of a nail.

Proverb—Source Unknown

While many facets of an operation are critical, inventory is a literal showstopper. In other words, where other functions are important, an inability to supply material stops an order in its tracks. And despite the perception that lean means eliminating inventory, few have the kind of control over vendors to make that a reality. Outside of a few Fortune 500 companies, who does? Although this might seem like a major barrier to a lean operation, Quantum Lean (QL) defies conventional wisdom by treating inventory as a resource rather than a liability. As unlikely as that might seem, the QL framework makes this possible.

QL INVENTORY MANAGEMENT

A QL inventory management system seeks to fulfill QL objectives and consists of the following elements:

- *Aligned objectives*—some goals of inventory management systems are detrimental to a QL operation. Assuring that objectives are compatible for both materials management and an overall operation is the first order of business.
- *System parameters*—for optimal results, an approach to estimate inventory control parameters is needed.

- *Maximizing inventory accuracy*
  - *ABC analysis*—this analysis is a method of prioritizing inventory counts by focusing on the items that have an outsized influence on company performance. While this method often revolves around financial criteria, QL tweaks this approach to achieve QL goals.
  - *Cycle counting*—instead of counting every stock-keeping unit (SKU) annually, cycle counting schedules inventory checks throughout the year for better accuracy and less operational disruption.
  - *Kanban*—Kanban's visuality can be used as a fail-safe against improper updates.
- *Early warning system*—a system to detect potential shortages to allow early countermeasures.

In total, every element of this system integrates into one indispensable piece of the QL puzzle.

OBJECTIVES

Properly applying inventory management techniques means harmonizing them to the QL framework. Keeping in mind that QL's top priority is giving the product everything it needs in a timely way: where do typical inventory goals stand against this objective?

- *Inventory turns*—the idea behind this objective is to decrease inventory levels. At the least, this won't increase the odds that an order is fulfilled. Much of the time, it will even decrease the chances of serving the product in a timely way.
- *Man-hours*—all things being equal, decreasing the man-hours involved in materials management will lower the cost. In the QL hierarchy, this is important, but has a lower priority than serving the product.
- *Accuracy*—accurate counts increase the probability that shortages will be caught and addressed. By extension, this improves the ability to serve the product.
- *Fulfillment*—fulfilling an order when the need occurs is a textbook definition of serving the product in a timely way.

Out of these goals, fulfillment is the top priority for QL, with accuracy coming in second. As long as these top two aren't undermined, decreasing man-hours and increasing turns is desirable. On the other hand, considerable havoc is possible when inventory and man-hours are decreased. As a case in point, inventory turns are a poster child for the amount of damage one metric can do.

Inventory Turns

Although there is a consensus that maximizing inventory turns is an important objective, this widespread belief is seriously detrimental to QL goals. Knowing why requires drilling down on this metric's implications. As a refresher, inventory turns are defined as:

Annual sales (in cost of goods sold)/average inventory (in $)

When the effects of this measurement are mulled over, they aren't pretty. Although the outcomes of prioritizing inventory turns are similar in any economic climate, consider an average situation when sales are flat. In this scenario, minimizing inventory is the only way to improve turns. And therein lies the problem. Most of the time, maximizing turns will translate into minimizing stock levels. In turn, the negative downstream consequences include:

- *Increased outages*—under equal customer demand, lowering inventory increases the chance of outages.
- *Increased lead time*—if parts aren't on the shelf, the best-case scenario is that lead time isn't compromised—but, more often than not, it is.
- *Increased cost*—shortages trigger increased expediting, overnight shipments, overtime, and tender loving care (TLC) for irate customers.
- *Decreased sales*—increasing lead time never improves a company's sales prospects. While a market boom can paper over this problem, how much higher could sales be if a company maintained or improved turnaround time?

Returning to the formula:

Inventory turns = annual sales
(in cost of goods sold)/average inventory (in $)

What happens to inventory turns if sales decrease? Ironically, turns go down and the goal is undermined. The asymmetric nature of business can mean that the decrease in sales will more than offset any reduction in inventory. Put another way, the efforts to increase turns stands a good chance of decreasing turns instead!

A common workaround to this problem is balancing sales against material levels and arriving at reorder points and quantities that compromise the two. The problems with this approach include:

- Balancing inventory versus sales is often a time-consuming, ad hoc exercise due to the fact that SKUs must be evaluated (and reevaluated) on a case-by-case basis.
- Despite the effort, the results will probably be inaccurate, and successful decisions will possibly be due to luck.

Often enough, the cycle that was just described continues without resolution. Instead of rethinking assumptions when experience dashes hope, the common response is to keep trying to refine a system that rests on invalid foundations. Fortunately, QL provides a way out of this spiral:

- Given QL's goal of minimizing a product's time-in-system, a company must minimize outages to keep lead time under control. By implication, this means that the key objective of an inventory control system should be minimizing outages (or maximizing fulfillment).
- A secondary objective, like accuracy, can be used to bolster fulfillment.
- From there, minimizing stock levels and cost reduction can be tertiary goals as long as higher priorities aren't compromised.

That's it. By focusing on fulfillment, the benefits are manyfold:

- *Decreased outages*—maintaining inventory by focusing on fulfillment decreases the chance of shortages.
- *Minimum lead time*—parts on the shelf facilitate rapid turnaround.
- *Decreased cost*—an environment with fewer shortages means that expediting, overnight shipments, overtime, and customer TLC are largely unnecessary.
- *Retained sales*—maintaining or reducing lead time never hurts a company's sales prospects. In a booming market, maintaining or improving lead time synergizes this.
- *Increased inventory turns*—interestingly, increasing fulfillment by increasing stock levels often increases inventory turns because:
  - Minimizing outages minimizes lead time
  - Maintaining turnaround time preserves or improves sales
  - Right-sized stock levels tend to increase sales disproportionately to any increase in inventory

In other words, chasing inventory turns frequently results in fewer turns, but prioritizing fulfillment increases them. Ironic, isn't it?

SYSTEM PARAMETERS

To maximize order fulfillment, properly estimated reorder points (ROPs) and reorder quantities (ROQs) are critical. Even though minimizing outages may require increasing some stock levels, a sound approach to estimating ROPs and ROQs can maximize fulfillment without getting too carried away on inventory quantities.

ROP

Without a decent estimate of the ROP, fulfillment has little chance of consistently occurring. At the same time, a fair question is how to determine the proper parameters. As a start, models are often developed based on ideal assumptions with modifications made later to accommodate reality. With this in mind, an ROP-based system under the ideal conditions of uniform demand of 200 per day and a constant lead time of three days would work as indicated in the following chart (see Figure 9.1).

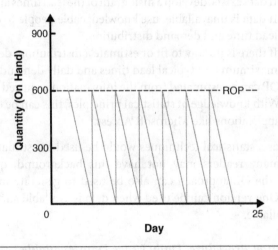

Figure 9.1 Ideal reorder system

Since the lead time is three days and the daily usage is 200, this means that 600 pieces must be on hand to keep operations going while waiting on a shipment. Thus, every time the on-hand quantity drops to 600, a purchase order (PO) must be issued. Since there will also be nothing left once an order arrives, this also implies that the ROQ must be at least 600. However, since there is no point in having more than necessary, the ROQ should also be no more than 600. So, 600 it is. Not coincidentally, 600 is also the ROP.

While this scenario of constant demand and lead time is ideal, the logic behind this approach is highly instructive when developing techniques to deal with more complex and realistic situations. The key takeaways are that:

- An operation needs enough material on hand to last during the vendor's lead time.
- The ROP and ROQ will be dictated by how much risk an organization is willing to bear. For an SKU that can be acquired quickly, a company may be comfortable with outages and the ROP and ROQ can be kept relatively low. For a long-lead item, this comfort level should be lower. As a result, the numbers should increase.

In a nutshell, the primary challenge for QL inventory management is specifying reasonable numbers that give assurance that outages won't occur. The general approach to calculating these parameters is as follows:

- Determine the range of lead times (in days) and the range of daily demands. In both cases:
  - If data exists, develop a histogram of the lead times and demands.
  - If data is unavailable, use knowledgeable people to estimate the lead time and demand distribution.
  - If there is no way to fit or estimate a distribution, determine the maximum and typical lead times and daily demands.
- An ROP can be estimated from the information acquired in the previous step. With knowledge of statistical principles, this can be done efficiently with applications like Microsoft Access.

In the best case, statistical techniques would be used to estimate ROPs. However, since many readers may not have this background, quick-and-dirty variations of the QL approach can also be used to generate initial inventory parameters. One version can be used when data is available and another when data is unavailable.

ROP Estimation Procedure: Daily Usage Data Available

- *Estimate maximum lead time*—if data is available to estimate lead time, use it. If such information is lacking, ask a knowledgeable person. Within reason, estimate the maximum lead time for a part. For example, if one shipment out of many took six weeks, but all of the others were under four weeks, use four weeks as the maximum lead time.

- *Denominate lead times in workdays*—for a five-days-per-week operation, a six-week lead time means thirty days. For a six-day week, the same turnaround would translate to thirty-six days.
- *Demand*—as shown in Figure 9.2, load the daily usage data into a spreadsheet.

Product ID	Qty	Day	Demand	Period of Demand
1234	39	1		
1234	100	2	139	1 through 2
1234	23	3	123	2 through 3
1234	21	4	44	3 through 4
1234	88	5	109	4 through 5
1234	8	8	96	5 through 6

Figure 9.2 Demand estimation

- *Determine maximum usage*—over the date range for a part, use the spreadsheet's functions to determine the maximum usage over the worst-case lead time.
- *The result is a starting solution for the ROP*—while conservative, it works. Although statistics can be used to arrive at a more refined answer, more advanced approaches are often based on this technique.

Example—ROP Estimation: Daily Usage Information Available

The spreadsheet contains information on part identification, date, and day. Notice that the day column is formatted as an integer and each day's sequence reflects the order on where the day falls in the date range. To clearly show the method, a short lead time of three days will be used to estimate an ROP for the SKU ABCD (almost half of the alphabet went into those acronyms!):

- To the right of the usage column, proceed to the fourth day and use the formula that adds the usages from the days one through three (see Figure 9.3).
- Copy the formula down to the row corresponding to the last day (see Figure 9.4).
- Enter the formula to capture the maximum usage for every three-day period in the date range (see Figure 9.5).
- For this spreadsheet, the ROP is 544.

If the lead time remains three days or less, this will represent a worst-case usage for the date range and should keep a company supplied if it is used as a reorder

Product ID	Day	Qty
1234	1	39
1234	2	100
1234	3	23	= SUM(C2:C4)
1234	4	21
1234	5	88
1234	6	8
1234	7	61
1234	8	236
1234	9	30
1234	10	154
1234	11	48
1234	12	34
1234	13	252
1234	14	100
1234	15	99
1234	16	56
1234	17	10
1234	18	82
1234	19	119
1234	20	245
1234	21	180

Figure 9.3   Usage estimation 1

Product ID	Day	Qty	Usage Over Lead Time
1234	1	39	-
1234	2	100	-
1234	3	23	162
1234	4	21	144
1234	5	88	132
1234	6	8	117
1234	7	61	157
1234	8	236	305
1234	9	30	327
1234	10	154	420
1234	11	48	232
1234	12	34	236
1234	13	252	334
1234	14	100	386
1234	15	99	451
1234	16	56	255
1234	17	10	165
1234	18	82	148
1234	19	119	211
1234	20	245	446
1234	21	180	544

Figure 9.4   Usage estimation 2

Product ID	Day	Qty	Usage Over Lead Time	
1234	1	39	-	
1234	2	100	-	
1234	3	23	162	= MAX(D4:D2:
1234	4	21	144	
1234	5	88	132	
1234	6	8	117	
1234	7	61	157	
1234	8	236	305	
1234	9	30	327	
1234	10	154	420	
1234	11	48	232	
1234	12	34	236	
1234	13	252	334	
1234	14	100	386	
1234	15	99	451	
1234	16	56	255	
1234	17	10	165	
1234	18	82	148	
1234	19	119	211	
1234	20	245	446	
1234	21	180	544	

Figure 9.5   Usage estimation 3

point and quantity. Does this method work? The following spreadsheet starts
with 544 units in stock and the same usage data. Since the ROP for ABCD has
been reached, an order will be placed for 544 parts right at the beginning. Note
some points about this spreadsheet and chart (see Figures 9.6 and 9.7):

- The *On Hand* column shows the quantity of parts on hand as of the end
  of day.
- The *On Order* column shows the quantity of parts that are on order.
- The *Note* column indicates:
  - When an order is placed and when it will arrive.
  - When an order has arrived and which order it is.

From the spreadsheet, the *On Hand* column never fell below zero. The lowest it
got was 230. In other words, the ROP worked. Although lower ROP levels may
work, this method rapidly generates an estimate that's close to ideal. In addition, a lower ROP runs the risk of continually decreasing inventory levels where
outages become the norm. While past performance doesn't guarantee future
results, accounting for daily fluctuations when estimating ROPs will improve
the odds of fulfillment.

Product ID	Day	Qty	On Hand	On Order	Note
1234	1	39	544	544	Order Placed - Purchase order initiated. Will Arrive on Day 4
1234	2	100	444	0	
1234	3	23	421	0	
1234	4	21	944	0	Arrival - Purchase Order from Day 1
1234	5	88	856	0	
1234	6	8	848	0	
1234	7	61	787	0	
1234	8	236	551	0	
1234	9	30	521	544	Order Placed - Purchase order initiated. Will Arrive on Day 12
1234	10	154	367	0	
1234	11	48	319	0	
1234	12	34	829	0	Arrival - Purchase Order from Day 9
1234	13	252	577	0	
1234	14	100	477	544	Order Placed - Purchase order initiated. Will Arrive on Day 17
1234	15	99	378	0	
1234	16	56	322	0	
1234	17	10	856	0	Arrival - Purchase Order from Day 14
1234	18	82	774	0	
1234	19	119	655	0	
1234	20	245	410	544	Order Placed - Purchase order initiated. Will Arrive on Day 23
1234	21	180	230	0	

Figure 9.6   Usage part 1 spreadsheet

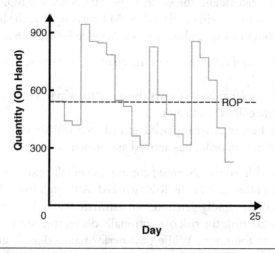

Figure 9.7   Usage part 1 chart

ROP Procedure: Data-Challenged

If daily usage isn't available, a spreadsheet's randomization functions can be used to create scenarios so that the *data-available* procedure can be used.

- Estimate a range for daily usage. Within reason, provide a minimum, typical, and maximum estimate. For instance, if an extreme demand occurred once in the last 10 years, leave this out. Also, if a disproportionate number of days have no usage at all, estimate the percent of the time that this would be the case.
- Using a spreadsheet's statistical functions and random number generation capabilities, a scenario for daily usage can be created. Formulas and details are illustrated in the associated example.
- Create at least 100 daily demands to get a good sample.
- Use the data-available procedure to estimate the ROP.

Example—ROP Procedure: Data-Challenged Case

A spreadsheet has been created (see Figure 9.8).

SKU	Random #	Triangular Random #	Day	Probability of Zero Demand	Min	Typ	Max	Triangular Demand	Demand
1234	0.927	0.903	1	0.25	1	50	75	62	62
1234	0.947	0.929	2	0.25	1	50	75	64	64
1234	0.680	0.573	3	0.25	1	50	75	47	47
1234	0.078	0.000	4	0.25	1	50	75	1	0
1234	0.158	0.000	5	0.25	1	50	75	1	0
1234	0.732	0.643	6	0.25	1	50	75	49	49
1234	0.539	0.385	7	0.25	1	50	75	38	38
1234	0.449	0.266	8	0.25	1	50	75	32	32
1234	0.421	0.227	9	0.25	1	50	75	30	30
1234	0.073	0.000	10	0.25	1	50	75	1	0
1234	0.550	0.400	11	0.25	1	50	75	39	39
1234	0.275	0.033	12	0.25	1	50	75	12	12
1234	0.097	0.000	13	0.25	1	50	75	1	0
1234	0.958	0.943	14	0.25	1	50	75	65	65
1234	0.979	0.972	15	0.25	1	50	75	68	68
1234	0.025	0.000	16	0.25	1	50	75	1	0
1234	0.608	0.477	17	0.25	1	50	75	43	43
1234	0.301	0.068	18	0.25	1	50	75	17	17
1234	0.018	0.000	19	0.25	1	50	75	1	0
1234	0.532	0.376	20	0.25	1	50	75	38	38
1234	0.566	0.422	21	0.25	1	50	75	40	40
1234	0.871	0.828	22	0.25	1	50	75	57	57
1234	0.584	0.445	23	0.25	1	50	75	41	41
1234	0.104	0.000	24	0.25	1	50	75	1	0
1234	0.702	0.603	25	0.25	1	50	75	48	48
1234	0.944	0.926	26	0.25	1	50	75	63	63
1234	0.998	0.998	27	0.25	1	50	75	73	73

Figure 9.8   Usage: randomly generated

- While creating at least 100 entries for daily use will give more certainty to an answer, this example only uses 25 for brevity.
- Columns are set aside for minimum, typical, and maximum daily usage and this information is populated for every daily entry. Although there are more efficient ways to utilize the worksheet space, this approach makes the job easier for spreadsheets with several SKUs.
- A column is set aside to generate a simulated demand for each day and uses a formula as shown in Figure 9.9:
  - ▫ This formula is based on the triangular statistical distribution. This distribution is typically very moldable to approximate many situations.
  - ▫ Ultimately, as an actual demand history is built, generated data can be replaced with actual data.
- Apply the *data-available* method to the results.

For the spreadsheet, the ROP is 176. While an ROP that would work in this case could be lower, consider how fast the ROP can be generated with the

SKU	Random #	Triangular Random #	Day	Probability of Zero Demand	Min	Typ	Max	Triangular Demand	Demand
1234	0.927	0.903	1	0.25	1	50	75	62	62
1234	0.947	0.929	2	0.25	1	50	75	64	64
1234	0.680	0.573	3	0.25	1	50	75	47	47
1234	0.078	0.000	4						0
1234	0.158	0.000	5						0
1234	0.732	0.643	6						49
1234	0.539	0.385	7						38
1234	0.449	0.266	8	0.25	1	50	75	32	32
1234	0.421	0.227	9	0.25	1	50	75	30	30
1234	0.073	0.000	10	0.25	1	50	75	1	0
1234	0.550	0.400	11	0.25	1	50	75	39	39
1234	0.275	0.033	12	0.25	1	50	75	12	12
1234	0.097	0.000	13	0.25	1	50	75	1	0
1234	0.958	0.943	14	0.25	1	50	75	65	65
1234	0.979	0.972	15	0.25	1	50	75	68	68
1234	0.025	0.000	16	0.25	1	50	75	1	0
1234	0.608	0.477	17	0.25	1	50	75	43	43
1234	0.301	0.068	18	0.25	1	50	75	17	17
1234	0.018	0.000	19	0.25	1	50	75	1	0
1234	0.532	0.376	20	0.25	1	50	75	38	38
1234	0.566	0.422	21	0.25	1	50	75	40	40
1234	0.871	0.828	22	0.25	1	50	75	57	57
1234	0.584	0.445	23	0.25	1	50	75	41	41
1234	0.104	0.000	24	0.25	1	50	75	1	0
1234	0.702	0.603	25	0.25	1	50	75	48	48
1234	0.944	0.926	26	0.25	1	50	75	63	63
1234	0.998	0.998	27	0.25	1	50	75	73	73

Formula (shown in box overlaying days 4–8):

```
=ROUND(IF(C2<=(G2-F2)/(H2-F2),
    F2+SQRT(C2*(H2-F2)*(G2-F2)),
    H2-SQRT((1-C2)*(H2-F2)*(-G2+H2))),
0)
```

Figure 9.9　Triangular formula

spreadsheet. Also, the higher number is close and allows for a margin of safety (see Figures 9.10 and 9.11).

Product ID	Day	Qty	On Hand	On Order	Note
1234	1	62	176	176	Order Placed - Purchase order initiated. Will Arrive on Day 4
1234	2	64	112	0	
1234	3	47	65	0	
1234	4	0	241	0	Arrival - Purchase Order from Day 1
1234	5	0	241	0	
1234	6	49	192	0	
1234	7	38	154	176	Order Placed - Purchase order initiated. Will Arrive on Day 10
1234	8	32	122	0	
1234	9	30	92	0	
1234	10	0	268	0	Arrival - Purchase Order from Day 7
1234	11	39	229	0	
1234	12	12	217	0	
1234	13	0	217	0	
1234	14	65	152	176	Order Placed - Purchase order initiated. Will Arrive on Day 17
1234	15	68	84	0	
1234	16	0	84	0	
1234	17	43	217	0	Arrival - Purchase Order from Day 14
1234	18	17	200	0	
1234	19	0	200	0	
1234	20	38	162	176	Order Placed - Purchase order initiated. Will Arrive on Day 23
1234	21	40	122	0	
1234	22	57	65	0	
1234	23	41	200	0	Arrival - Purchase Order from Day 20
1234	24	0	200	0	
1234	25	48	152	176	Order Placed - Purchase Order initiated will arrive on Day 28

Figure 9.10   Usage part 2 spreadsheet

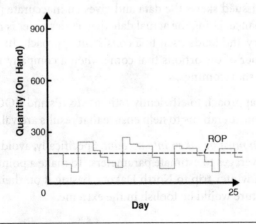

Figure 9.11   Usage part 2 chart

Since these methods are at least partly based on estimates, it is important to frequently update ROPs as more data is collected. At the same time, these approaches provide a starting point and framework for estimating system parameters. As a disclaimer and to keep the sticklers at bay, the data-challenged example isn't mathematically pure. However, it works pretty well and the approaches are grounded on sound ideas. Regardless of how the initial estimates are arrived at, be sure to:

- Inspect the results to see if they look reasonable. If they don't, reexamine the spreadsheet and data carefully to be sure there aren't mistakes with the entries or formulas. If the spreadsheet is free of data-entry errors, this may mean that estimation techniques you used aren't valid for your situation. Consider a different approach.
- Record usage by the day as soon as possible. Information gathered in this manner will prove indispensable in future efforts to produce good ROP estimates and will help you adjust and refine the inventory control system.
- Apply a consistent definition for the day on which the material is *used*. Some possibilities:
  - Is it the day it is issued to production?
  - Is it the day the order is placed?
  - Is it the day an order ships?
  - Is it the day an order is literally consumed by production?

  The recommendation is to treat the date on which a customer submits an order as the date of demand. Because order initiation is typically adjusted based on material availability, basing usage dates on the day material is issued skews the data and gives an inaccurate picture of system performance. Using the actual date that a sales order is received is a hard boundary and lends itself to a consistent approach. In turn, it forestalls all manner of distortions that come when a company works around its system's shortcomings.

With an initial approach to efficiently estimate ROPs and ROQs, keep in mind the following considerations to help ensure that results are valid:

- *Variation must be taken into account.* Specifically, avoid exclusively relying on averages to estimate parameters. To make a point, consider packing for a winter trip to North Dakota; basing it on their average annual temperature would be foolish in the extreme.

- *Determining ROPs requires estimating ranges for lead time and daily use.* If this information is available, use a spreadsheet. If not, there are data-challenged ways to deal with the situation. While a mathematician might cluck at the methods, they often work reasonably well and refinements can be made over time.
- *Inventory parameters should be based on daily usage.* Unfortunately, there are software packages and companies that aggregate usage data by the month and base inventory parameters on this information. Since using aggregated monthly data means that a substantial amount of insight is lost, make every effort to track parts usage by the day. Even if previous daily demand is unavailable, collect daily figures as soon as possible.
- *When estimating ROPs,* day *means* workday *or only days when the business is open*—holidays, weekends, and shutdown days need not apply. For example, if a facility is closed on weekends, Saturday and Sunday should be excluded from the data.
- *In QL, ROQs and ROPs are equal.*

The methods to determine ROPs may need to vary to account for company specifics. At the same time, the principles elaborated on in this section will apply regardless of the setting. Once a quick and accurate approach is implemented for specifying ROPs (and by extension, ROQs), a system to ensure accuracy will help ensure proper execution of a material control system.

ACCURACY

No matter how accurate reorder points and quantities are, inaccurate material counts can derail the best-laid plans. To combat this, QL draws on these tools:

- *ABC inventory*—when performing inventory counts, it makes sense to prioritize SKUs that present the greatest risks when outages occur. For instance, the longer a lead time gets, the more difficult it is to recover when a shortage occurs. ABC classification facilitates more frequent checks of high-risk products. Like other tools, QL applies a variation on typical approaches in order to align ABC analysis to the QL framework.
- *Cycle counts*—as opposed to counting every SKU annually, cycle counting schedules inventory checks throughout the year. Specifically, SKUs are allotted to each cycle count so that every SKU ends up being checked

at least as frequently as its ABC classification requires. Using cycle counts in place of comprehensive annual checks has been shown to be more accurate and less disruptive.

- *Kanban*—whether it's partially or totally implemented, kanban can be used to fail-safe operations against counting mistakes that can lead to outages.

From here, ABC analysis, cycle counts, and kanban will be explored further.

ABC Analysis

ABC analysis is a prioritization technique that divides stock into three categories:

- A—critical to organization. Requires the tightest control and accuracy.
- B—less critical than A, but more critical than C. Needs less control and accuracy than A items.
- C—least critical. Minimal control and accuracy necessary.

While there are no official criteria for defining these categories, they are frequently subject to financial considerations. For example, the highest scrutiny is generally applied to parts with the greatest dollar volume. Unless the most expensive items are equally critical to production flow, this approach works at cross purposes to QL. By ignoring critical factors like lead time and usage, money-driven materials management virtually ensures that efforts will focus on parts that are unlikely to shut down production. Instead, ABC categories should be based on lead time or usage. Conceptually, the criteria could involve the following:

- A—outage likely to result in late delivery or customer canceling the order. This is likely to occur regardless of expediting and overtime.
- B—outage likely to require expediting and overtime to achieve on-time delivery.
- C—outage unlikely to result in late delivery or the need for expediting and overtime to achieve on-time delivery.

Practically speaking, a numeric proxy for the aforementioned classification allows for automatic and efficient category assignment. In one instance, it could be based on lead time. In another, it might be based on (lead time) × (average daily usage) and could look something like this:

- A—(maximum lead time) × (average daily usage) ≥ 100
- B—$100 >$ (maximum lead time) × (average daily usage) ≥ 10
- C—(maximum lead time) × (average daily usage) < 10

- In addition to this high-level explanation, the following example shows how an ABC analysis might work based on the ABC criteria that was just detailed (see Figure 9.12):

SKU	Avg Daily Usage	Lead Time	Lead Time x Demand	Classification (Lead Time x Usage)	Classification (Lead Time)
1	10	50	500	A	A
2	5	3	15	C	B
3	3	7	21	B	B
4	20	5	100	C	A
5	1	20	20	A	B
6	0.25	1	0.25	C	C
7	10	3	30	C	B

Figure 9.12   ABC analysis

As something to chew on, notice how significantly the classifications vary when the criterion changes from (maximum lead time) × (average daily usage) to just lead time. How a company would want to do this depends on their risk profile. The point is to configure this tool to minimize the risks from shortage. While ABC analysis doesn't mean much on its own, incorporating it into cycle counting allows both tools to achieve QL goals.

Cycle Counting

As opposed to counting every SKU once per year, cycle counting schedules inventory checks throughout the year. Specifically, a portion of SKUs are allotted to each cycle count so that every SKU ends up being checked at least as frequently as its ABC classification requires. With this in mind, cycle counting offers the following advantages over annual physical inventories:

- *Less disruptive*—due to the need to check every inventory item, annual physical inventories are generally labor intensive, time consuming, and disruptive to operations. Since fewer SKUs are involved in an individual cycle count, this method requires fewer people, is quicker, and is less disruptive.
- *More accurate*—all things being equal, cycle counting has been shown to be significantly more accurate than annual physical checks.
- *More timely*—by updating inventory numbers on an ongoing basis rather than annually, inventory data is timelier.

Although cycle counting is in no way unique to QL, this tool is so important to QL objectives that it warrants coverage. In addition, the intersection of

ABC analysis and cycle counting is when these tools are specifically harnessed for QL.

Cycle Counting Process

The following steps are typical for a successful cycle counting program:

- *Determine how many times a year to check each category of inventory*—typically, a company shouldn't count every SKU with the same frequency. Some items may be highly critical while others are less so. For example, a high-demand part with a long lead time can make or break a plant. On the other hand, an off-the-shelf bolt shouldn't leave an operation quite so vulnerable. Likewise, scrutiny should vary as well.
- *Setting frequency*—typically, an ABC system for classifying inventory is used to assign inventory check frequencies. Since the A category is most critical, it makes sense to apply extra attention and check more often. Conversely, C items aren't as urgent, so less control is in order (see Figure 9.13). In the example, A items would be checked six times per year while C items would be checked once annually.

Category	Annual Frequency
A	6
B	3
C	1

Figure 9.13　ABC frequency

Although a properly prioritized cycle counting program can achieve extremely accurate inventory counts, mistakes are always possible. To elevate performance, a trusty lean tool merits consideration.

Kanban

Kanban is a visual system that can serve as a supplement to cycle counting. In a company with conventional inventory control, kanban's visual cues can serve as a line of defense in case inventory numbers have been improperly updated. By the same token, this can enable a larger portion of the workforce to report potential problems. To illustrate, consider a classic two-bin kanban system (see Figure 9.14).

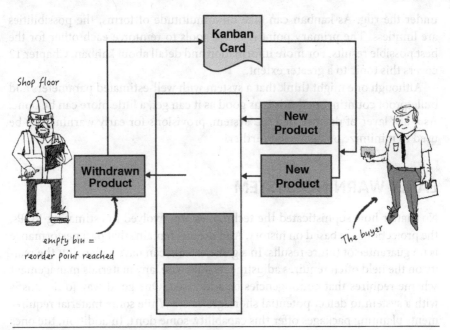

Figure 9.14 Classic kanban scenario

When one bin is emptied, an operator removes the attached card from the bin and sends it to purchasing to initiate replenishment. During the time required for an order to be placed and delivered, material can be drawn from the second bin. If all goes according to plan, this cycle repeats continuously and operations are supplied. If this concept is used in conjunction with conventional practices, the two can reinforce each other for near-perfect results.

As part of a regular cycle count, scanning for kanbans showing the need for reorder could be added to the duties. Where there are visual cues indicating a need, the cycle counter can record and communicate the need to purchasing. By noting this condition, a determination can be made for whether kanban procedures have been followed (e.g., was the supplier notified?). A blending of these methods allows for a powerful check and balance:

- Cycle counts can serve as a backstop against kanban-related failures.
- Conversely, in case of inaccurate cycle counts, kanban's signaling is a line of defense to ensure that reorders occur in case of such oversights.

In either case, by taking immediate action to address shortcomings but still putting failures on record, expediency is allowed without sweeping problems under the rug. As kanban can take on a multitude of forms, the possibilities are limitless. The primary point is to use tools to reinforce each other for the best possible results. For more information and detail about kanban, Chapter 12 covers this topic to a greater extent.

Although one might think that a system with well-estimated parameters and bulletproof counting methods is as good as it can get, a little more can be done. As a last layer of defense in a QL system, provisions for early warning can be used to minimize outages even further.

EARLY WARNING SYSTEM

No matter how sophisticated the techniques are involved in estimating ROPs, the projections are based on history. And the fact remains that past performance is no guarantee of future results. In a game, a team can have a plan, but the reality on the field often requires adjustments. Likewise, any materials management scheme requires that contingencies be addressed. One good way to do this is with a system to detect potential shortages early. While some material requirements planning packages offer this capability, some don't. In addition, the ones that do can be cumbersome when dealing with a multitude of SKUs. Although specific software recommendations are beyond the scope of this book, there are essential elements:

- For each SKU, there needs to be a procedure to efficiently estimate material usage for each period between material arrivals and the amount of material that will be available. This procedure needs to be initiated when:
  - New orders are accepted or canceled
  - Production schedules are shifted
  - POs are delayed or quantities are revised
  - New POs are initiated
  - Quality problems or missing products are detected

  The reason it's important to check the supply/demand balance for the periods between material arrivals is that it's possible to fulfill aggregate demand over a large time horizon but experience outages within constituent periods. As one example, consider these scheduled purchases (see Figure 9.15).

Source	Qty	Material Available Date
Inventory	100	Now
PO 1	200	Day 10
PO 2	200	Day 20
PO 3	50	Day 30
PO 4	275	Day 40
Total	**825**	

Figure 9.15 Early detection POs

If each period has the following consumptions, the supply will exceed aggregate demand over the entire period. However, a few of the intervening intervals will fall short (see Figure 9.16):

Period	Material Received	[Leftover from Previous Period] LPP	[Material Received + LPP] Available Material	Demand	[Available Material - Demand] Leftover	Enough Material?
Day 0 - Day 10	0	0	100	100	0	Yes
Day 10 - Day 20	200	0	200	500	-300	No
Day 20 - Day 30	200	-300	-100	21	-121	No
Day 30 - Day 40	50	-121	-71	100	-171	No
Day 40 - Date of Last Sales Order	275	-171	104	100	4	Yes
Now - Date of Last Sales Order			825	821		

Figure 9.16 Early detection

- It is crucial to have the ability to identify the shortages for all SKUs in one step. If inquiries have to be done for one part at a time, the task of detecting shortfalls will probably be neglected.

When the method is well-defined, a report of missing parts, affected orders, and quantities is achievable with the right software. In most cases, an application like Microsoft Access is capable of this.

SUMMARY

While many facets of an operation are critical, inventory is a literal showstopper. In other words, where other functions are important, an inability to supply material stops an order in its tracks. Despite the perception that lean requires the elimination of inventory, QL flips the conventional equation by transforming inventory into a resource rather than a liability. As unlikely as that might seem, the QL framework makes this possible by harmonizing inventory management to QL objectives. A QL inventory management system seeks to maximize order fulfillment and consists of:

- *Sound objectives*—first and foremost, inventory should be about fulfillment.
- *Proper ROP and ROQ*—even though minimizing outages may require increasing some stock levels, a sound approach to estimating ROPs and ROQs can enable getting the best of both worlds.
- *Maximizing inventory accuracy*
  - *ABC analysis*—ABC analysis is a method of prioritizing inventory counts by focusing on the items that have an outsized influence on company performance. Instead of revolving around financial criteria, QL bases this classification on the risk of outage.
  - *Cycle counting*—instead of counting every SKU annually, cycle counting schedules inventory checks throughout the year for better accuracy and less operational disruption.
  - *Kanban*—kanban's visuality can be used as a fail-safe against improper updates in an inventory control system.
- *Early warning system*—an early warning system detects potential shortages early and allows maximum time for countermeasures.

Taken together, the elements of this system integrate into an indispensable piece of the QL puzzle. And the efficiency gains and positive effects that such a system can bring will astound.

CHAPTER 10

SHOP-FLOOR
CONTROL/LOGISTICS/SCHEDULING

"The line between disorder and order lies in logistics."

Sun Tzu

"Behind every great leader, there was an even greater logistician."

James M. Cox

"In the lean journey, all roads lead to scheduling."

Weldon Steele

Ninety-nine times out of 100, businesses begin lean initiatives with workplace organization. In 98 of those cases, they're leading with the wrong foot. Often, companies schedule work in a way that inadvertently increases work-in-process (WIP), stretches out lead time, and initiates a chain reaction of chaos. In this environment, 5S amounts to rearranging deck chairs on the Titanic. While there are businesses where starting with workplace organization is the better bet, the smart money is on shop-floor control.

LOGISTICS AND LEAN

In facilities with ad hoc coordination, WIP inventory will be stranded due to material shortage or waiting on busy resources. Although both causes are typically present, just one of them is enough to move scheduling to the top priority. It is so central to efficient operations that there's a phrase: "On the lean journey, all roads lead to scheduling." Put another way, improper shop-floor control aggravates virtually every efficiency problem an operation will encounter (see Figure 10.1).

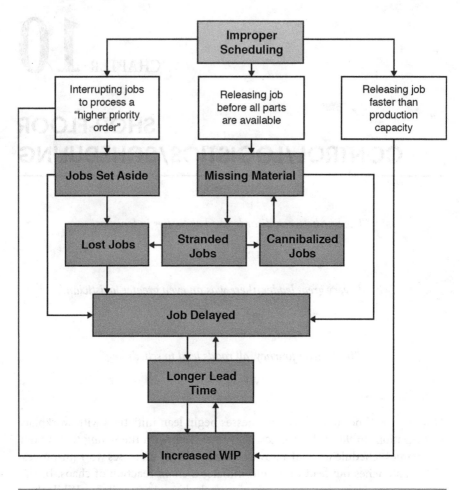

Figure 10.1 Scheduling feedback loops

To expand on this diagram, there are three common mistakes and the corresponding ways they create and compound waste:

- *Releasing jobs before all materials are available*—frequently, jobs are intentionally released without all the necessary materials. In anticipation that the missing pieces will arrive in the nick of time, it's thought that useful work can be accomplished while waiting for shipments to come in. While it may seem like starting a job sooner will result in it being finished sooner, doing so rarely has a positive effect. The pie chart for a product's time-in-system shows why (see Figure 10.2).

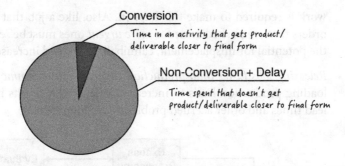

Figure 10.2 Time-in-system pie chart

When only 5% of a product's time on the floor is in conversion, how much time can really be saved by beginning early? No more than 5%. On top of this, premature starts create or aggravate all kinds of problems that feed off of each other:

- *Delayed orders*—while the expectation is that ordered parts will arrive just in time to keep things moving, this rarely happens and a job will often stall out. In addition to the delayed order, other side effects come with it.

- *Lost jobs*—when an order is dead in the water, it generally has to be moved out of the way. Those who haven't worked in manufacturing might be surprised at how often jobs get lost. In addition to the extra work tracking a misplaced order, the delivery date gets further delayed.

- *Cannibalizing parts*—since a stalled job isn't going anywhere, it's a tempting target to raid. It brings to mind the cliché about robbing Peter to pay Paul. As an example, parts from Job 1 are robbed because Job 2 needs them. All too often, insult is added to injury because no one is notified that Job 1 was robbed. When it's time to reinitiate Job 1, the shortage is belatedly discovered and a scramble for material begins. Often, this manifests itself in the form of cannibalizing another order with the concomitant lack of notification. That is, if there is another order with material to rob.

- *Breaking into jobs that are already under way to accommodate an expedited order*—this entails interrupting one order's production run to process another. For the interrupted order, this means that any previous setup work has to be repeated when the remaining pieces must be produced. In addition to inconveniencing production, a great deal of extra work is required to make this happen. Also, like a job that lacks parts, orders that are pushed aside for *more urgent* ones must be set aside with the potential for misplacement, cannibalization, and increased delays.

- *Releasing jobs faster than production capacity can accommodate*—overloading production leads to increased WIP, which results in increased lead times and other accrued problems (see Figure 10.3):

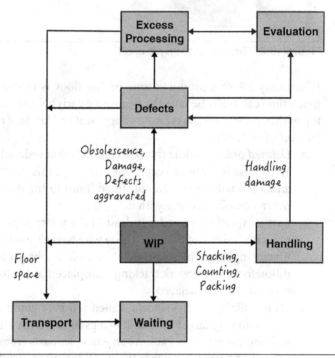

Figure 10.3   WIP and waste

In short, improper scheduling makes Quantum Lean (QL) almost impossible. By contrast, get this issue right, and lean practically implements itself. With that being said, there is much more to proper shop-floor control than scheduling resources using drum-buffer-rope (DBR).

LOGISTICS FOUNDATIONS

Proper groundwork is needed for DBR to work smoothly. It's like a team that plays one game a week, but spends the rest of the time practicing. There is a similar ratio of up-front work with scheduling as well. All of these elements work together and rest on one another.

This pyramid (see Figure 10.4) can be characterized as logistics, which involves the coordination of scheduling, procurement, sales, production, shop-floor control, and inventory control. From these facets spring several fronts that must be nailed down for the greatest success.

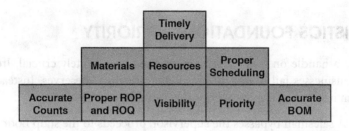

Figure 10.4   Scheduling pyramid

Materials

For scheduling to work, a job must have enough material to be completed. Potential barriers to having sufficient material include:

- *Adequate material in stock*—this subject is covered in the chapter about QL inventory control techniques.
- *Cannibalizing*—while orders can be prematurely released as a matter of intention, it's also possible for this to occur by accident (as will be explained later). When this occurs, the problem of cannibalizing can creep in, setting off a daisy chain of pilfering, expedites, and late deliveries. Fundamentally, this vicious cycle is rooted in two issues:
  - *Priority*—frequently, companies take an ad hoc approach to determine what to work on first, second, and third. Often, the outcome depends on who screams the loudest. Because of unclear lines of authority, it's even possible for multiple orders to have top priority at the same time. Even worse, priorities can change from moment to moment. Without a consistent approach to priority, it's difficult to accurately predict delivery dates.
  - *Visibility*—if more than one person handles sales orders, it's common for employees to lack knowledge of each other's commitments. If several orders draw from the same inventory, it's possible that the supply can be overcommitted. Like inconsistent priority, an inability to address this issue will also make hash out of the most carefully formulated production schedule.

Taken separately, any one of these problems will undo the best laid plans. Together, they create a negative synergy that reduces a company to chasing its tail. Since adequate inventory is addressed in a separate chapter, the task that remains is addressing the cannibalization of parts. Although it's frequent for all of its culprits to exist simultaneously, these problems will be expounded upon individually.

LOGISTICS FOUNDATIONS—PRIORITY

Getting a handle on how priority is assigned is absolutely crucial. Ironically, many businesses fail to give this issue the priority it deserves. Instead, many perform half-baked improvisations that can take many forms:

- A salesman bypasses the supervisor, proceeds to the shop floor, and orders employees to expedite his or her job. Lo and behold, this order is put at the front of the line! And those who think a typical hourly employee can refuse a salesman (who often has the owner's ear) haven't been to very many shops.
- In a warehouse with multiple employees issuing parts, the sequence in which jobs are issued can change depending on who receives requisitions, who issues them, and the persuasiveness of the individuals involved.
- On shop floors, there will often be multiple orders sitting around with no clearly assigned priority. Arrange ten jobs in order of difficulty and which one will people tackle first? Of course, the easiest. If priority is not clearly communicated to the shop floor, the de facto priority will fall this way. It's human nature.
- In many companies, all of the above are happening at the same time.

Due to the haphazard way priority can be handled, chaos and volatility are the norm at too many facilities. As critical as it is for many companies, the idea of prioritizing a priority scheme never seems to make the list. Although millions of *to do* lists are being created right now, it's unlikely that any have prioritized the task of specifying an approach for determining priority. While it may not make a big difference for an individual, it's often make-or-break for a company that hopes for efficient and timely deliveries. For those who think that a due date is good enough for defining priority, the next section is especially for you.

Defining a Priority Scheme

Why is a priority scheme so important? In many situations, orders draw from the same material supply. If there aren't enough parts to go around, which order takes the penalty? It's like a checking account that's about to bounce. Which bill gets paid? Without a consistently understood priority, the answers will be all over the map. As an example, one family member might want to pay for pet grooming first, while another person may think that the gas bill should get the first dollar (this is going somewhere). In such a divided home, the provider that gets paid will be the first to deposit the payment. What's worse is there is no good way to predict the outcome. In short, chaos is ensured. In a business, this problem grows exponentially as the number of employees and customers increase. This is where a priority scheme is so important. By creating consistent and logical rules for determining what comes first, second, and third, greater alignment can be achieved. Here are a few guidelines:

- Develop and document a scheme that defines who, what, when, where, and how for assigning priority.
- For best results, factor in the need for flexibility and provide a mechanism for overriding the rules.
- Due date is a great starting point for priority. In principle, orders that are needed sooner should be put at the front of the line. However, stopping there leaves vulnerabilities. As one simple case, what about two orders with the same due date? Which one comes first?
- A priority code is essential for flexibility. A company that services the oil field might specify one like this:
  1. *Broken arrow: an oil rig is down*—no matter what the due date is for other orders, first claim on parts must go to an order that involves an emergency like a rig being down. Whatever parts have been allocated to other orders will be redirected to this one.
  2. *High*—a number of reasons, such as a returned order that needs to be fixed, an important customer, or an expedite could result in management assigning *high* to the priority.
  3. *Default*—all sales orders are assigned this priority automatically. Escalating this code requires management authorization.
  4. *Stock order*—job orders that are not directly tied to a sales order. Typically, orders to stock the shelves should be accommodated when production capacity allows it.
- On top of a priority code and due date, it's ideal to specify an additional override code to allow management an extra level of flexibility to best

serve the customer (or themselves). As there are always ifs, ands, and buts, such a provision allows for the fact that rules may need to be broken. However, this should only occur as part of a process. Like priority codes, a default value would be assigned to every override code and only management may assign a different value.

Example

In a scenario where all orders have normal priority and management hasn't issued any overrides, the following sales orders will have the default override and priority codes assigned to all jobs (see Figure 10.5).

Sales Order Number	Override Code	Priority Code	Due Date	Order Placed	Time at Bottleneck
1	10	3	12/09/24	11/1/2024	10
2	10	3	12/17/24	11/1/2024	11
3	10	3	12/26/24	11/1/2024	11
4	10	3	12/01/24	11/4/2024	18
5	10	3	12/09/24	11/7/2024	8
6	10	3	12/15/24	11/9/2024	21
7	10	3	12/30/24	11/10/2024	11

Figure 10.5 Priority scheme 0

Applying the example priority scheme will sort these jobs in the following order (see Figure 10.6):

Sales Order Number	Override Code	Priority Code	Due Date	Order Placed	Time at Bottleneck
4	10	3	12/01/24	11/4/2024	18
1	10	3	12/09/24	11/1/2024	10
5	10	3	12/09/24	11/7/2024	8
6	10	3	12/15/24	11/9/2024	21
2	10	3	12/17/24	11/1/2024	11
3	10	3	12/26/24	11/1/2024	11
7	10	3	12/30/24	11/10/2024	11

Figure 10.6 Priority scheme 1

- Override code, then
- Priority code, then
- Due date, and then
- First come, first served

In other words, the first job the shop should allocate material to is Job 4. From there, Job 1 follows, then Job 5, then Job 6, then Job 2, then Job 3, and then Job 7. When Job 8 comes in with a due date of 12/09/24, the new priority order will look like the spreadsheet in Figure 10.7.

Sales Order Number	Override Code	Priority Code	Due Date	Order Placed	Time at Bottleneck
4	10	3	12/01/24	11/4/2024	18
1	10	3	12/09/24	11/1/2024	10
5	10	3	12/09/24	11/7/2024	8
8	10	3	12/09/24	11/13/2024	6
6	10	3	12/15/24	11/9/2024	21
2	10	3	12/17/24	11/1/2024	11
3	10	3	12/26/24	11/1/2024	11
7	10	3	12/30/24	11/10/2024	11

Figure 10.7 Priority scheme 2

Based on the rules, Job 8's earlier due date puts it in front of prior orders with later due dates. At the same time, it falls below the orders with the same due date but that were received by the company at an earlier time.

What if the clerk who negotiated the sales order for Job 8 thinks her order justifies special treatment? She can appeal to management and propose raising the priority code from 3—default to 2—high. If management accepts her reasoning, the new priority order for material allotment would be Figure 10.8.

Sales Order Number	Override Code	Priority Code	Due Date	Order Placed	Time at Bottleneck
8	10	2	12/09/24	11/13/2024	6
4	10	3	12/01/24	11/4/2024	18
1	10	3	12/09/24	11/1/2024	10
5	10	3	12/09/24	11/7/2024	8
6	10	3	12/15/24	11/9/2024	21
2	10	3	12/17/24	11/1/2024	11
3	10	3	12/26/24	11/1/2024	11
7	10	3	12/30/24	11/10/2024	11

Figure 10.8 Priority scheme 3

Suppose upper management has misgivings about Job 8 getting first consideration over Job 4. They could adjust the override code to fine tune Job 8's position in the hierarchy (see Figure 10.9).

Sales Order Number	Override Code	Priority Code	Due Date	Order Placed	Time at Bottleneck
4	10	3	12/01/24	11/4/2024	18
8	10	2	12/09/24	11/13/2024	6
1	10	3	12/09/24	11/1/2024	10
5	10	3	12/09/24	11/7/2024	8
6	10	3	12/15/24	11/9/2024	21
2	10	3	12/17/24	11/1/2024	11
3	10	3	12/26/24	11/1/2024	11
7	10	3	12/30/24	11/10/2024	11

Figure 10.9 Priority scheme 4

While a priority scheme is only limited by the imagination, it is wise to make priority assignment rules closely match what the company actually values. Although it's preferable to be consistent with QL, it is more practical to create an approach that will generate what management wants. For example, if management wants high-dollar jobs to get the first shot at materials, it will prevent a lot of fine tuning if this desire is accommodated up front. Otherwise, the schedule will be tampered with endlessly and the pandemonium that follows will derail QL anyway. Of course, every effort should be made to talk upper management into the QL system, but remember that the powers-that-be will skeptically view any scheme that they constantly feel the need to overrule.

While the rules for determining priority should fit the company, understanding the necessity of a scheme is the vital first step. Once a consistent approach is developed, there is a good chance that political challenges will remain.

In some cases, the chaos that occurs serves the purposes of higher-ups. Put another way, accountability can be avoided when lines of authority are blurred. As the thinking goes, the ability to shift blame maintains job security. This is especially true in corporate settings. While the organizational aspects of priority setting are beyond the scope of this book, they warrant consideration.

Even where motivations are pure, deploying a priority scheme will require the cooperation of sales, purchasing, planning, and inventory. In addition, thorough training and follow-up will be needed to ensure that people understand the system and that execution is proper. However, while this task isn't easy, the rewards from success will far outweigh the efforts required.

LOGISTICS FOUNDATIONS—TRANSPARENCY

Over 100 years ago, the famous story *Gift of the Magi* was written. In this tale, a husband and wife were searching for Christmas gifts for each other. The wife cut her hair and sold it in order to buy a chain for her husband's prized pocket watch. Not knowing what his wife had done, the husband sold his pocket watch in order to afford a set of combs for his wife's treasured hair. On Christmas Day, the couple exchanged gifts only to find that neither had what they needed to enjoy their gifts. Despite the silver lining that they loved each other, the logistical takeaway is that a lack of transparency can result in everyone getting the short end.

Companies are not immune to this. To illustrate this point, think of the checking account analogy that was alluded to earlier in this chapter. Dad believes the pet grooming bill should be paid no matter what. By contrast, Mom thinks the gas bill should get first dibs. If the account balance is $200 and the bills total $280, both simply cannot be paid. To get a better idea of the problem, imagine bill collectors calling and with a different person answering the phone each time. In the first call, Dad picks up:

> *Pet Grooming Business*: This is Harry Dunne from Mutt Cutts and your account is $120 past due.
>
> *Dad*: Actually, I was just paid, and I will send you a check immediately (note: the balance decreased to $80, but since this is only logged in Dad's check register, Mom is unaware of this).

On the next call, Mom happens to be closest to the phone:

> *Gas Company*: This is your gas man Joe Mentalino calling. You owe us $160 and we will have to charge a service fee if you don't pay.
>
> *Mom*: I have $200 in my account. If I send a check right now, can I avoid late fees?

Obviously, the checking account is going to be overdrawn and there is no way to predict which service will be suspended. In a household, one hand not knowing what the other hand is doing is no way to do business. If a lack of transparency is such a problem on this level, how much worse is it for a company to lack visibility? Actually, it's much worse. When more money and personnel are involved, the complications skyrocket.

At many businesses, salespeople make commitments without knowing what other salespeople have agreed to. It's not a matter of neglect. It's built into a system where there is no timely way to find out what others are doing. In addition, even systems with this capability can make the task so time-consuming that timely verification is impractical. The upshot is that sales runs an elevated risk of overcommitting materials and causing orders to run late when inventory comes up short. To prevent this from happening, organizations must anticipate the problem and take measures to provide visibility. A vital first step is determining what is needed to establish transparency.

Transparency Ingredients

A good system will have the capability of quickly providing an up-to-date snapshot of a company's commitments relative to its inventory and purchase orders (POs). Since even the best-laid plans can go awry, such a system can also determine the effect of late deliveries so that countermeasures can be taken as soon as possible. This system can be thought of as two crystal balls, with one clearly seeing the present and the other glimpsing into the future.

Transparency Requirements

Assuring transparency to commitments requires the following:

- As detailed earlier, a consistent and effective priority assignment scheme.
- An automated method that allocates inventory and POs to sales orders in priority order and detects shortages and late deliveries. In turn, this requires up-to-date and accurate:
  - *Inventory*—inventory counts
  - *PO information*—in particular, delivery date estimates are essential.
  - *Bill of material (BOM) (or equivalent)*—BOM defines the parts that comprise a product and the quantity of pieces per finished unit. Ideally, the ability to identify substitute parts would be nice, but is not absolutely required. If a system is very simple or non-repetitive, a BOM may not be necessary.
  - *Software*—unless a situation is extremely basic, software will probably be needed for this procedure to be practical. Performing the process manually will be too time-consuming and error-prone. For those who assume that software will be cost-prohibitive, this procedure is very doable with Microsoft Office.

□ *Timeliness*—to function effectively, the ability to generate the current system snapshot must be quick and painless. While *quick* is in the eye of the beholder, anything beyond a few minutes will probably not be used. Hence, the reason software is recommended.

□ *Multiple line-item capability*—while there are enterprise resource planning packages that perform this routine, it's often for only one line item at a time. In such cases, verifying material availability for an order with several line items will be cumbersome and time consuming. By contrast, a routine where an employee can verify every line item in one mouse click will be quicker, easier, and much more likely to be used. Again, Microsoft Office is often equal to the task.

Although a particular company may have requirements that go beyond the list, the above will suffice in many cases. Once these ingredients are provided, a procedure to achieve transparency is the next step.

Transparency Method

This procedure to determine a company's outstanding commitments needs to be initiated when:

- A new order/quote is being created
- Priority changes are being considered
- Inaccurate inventory counts are caught
- Late PO delivery is anticipated

As far as the procedure is concerned, the following needs to occur in the order of priority that the company has assigned to each sales order:

- One at a time, scroll through each order/product/part combination in priority order.
- Allocate the required material to each order according to product quantity and the quantity per unit as specified by the BOM.
   □ Draw first from inventory, and then from POs according to the closest anticipated delivery date.
   □ Record whether the part in question is short or in sufficient supply.
   □ If material is drawn from a PO, also record the arrival dates from the associated POs; this information will be used to indicate the earliest start date for an entire job.

- □ For each allocation, update the available material for the inventory and/or POs from which it was drawn.

Once the procedure is complete, there is enough information to determine which orders have shortages and by how much. For orders that can be completely fulfilled, the earliest possible start date can be projected based on the associated PO's delivery dates. Of course, orders drawing exclusively from stock can be released immediately. Describing a procedure is one thing, but there is nothing like an example to clarify.

Example: Transparency

This section offers a step-by-step example of the transparency process using the priority scheme that was elaborated on in the previous section. To start, materials will be allocated to the jobs listed on the following spreadsheet (see Figure 10.10).

Sales Order Number	Override Code	Priority Code	Due Date	Order Placed	Quantity
A	10	3	12/09/19	11/1/2019	15
B	10	3	12/14/19	11/1/2019	15
C	10	3	12/17/19	11/1/2019	15
D	10	3	12/01/19	11/4/2019	15

Figure 10.10   Sales orders

To make this example easier to follow, the priority and override codes will start out identical among jobs. Given this, material will be allotted by due date first, and then on a first-come, first-served basis. To keep matters simple, the jobs in this example all use the same part. While the principles work just as well in complicated situations, the points are much easier to follow in a simple example. For allocation, a quantity of 20 will be available in inventory and the following POs and associated quantities are scheduled to arrive as seen on the PO spreadsheet (see Figure 10.11).

PO	Quantity	Due Date
1	20	12/01/19
2	20	12/15/19

Figure 10.11   POs

Based on the priorities, this spreadsheet shows how the parts allocate to the jobs (see Figure 10.12).

Material Source	Date of Availability	Starting Qty	Qty Allocated to Job	Remaining Stock	Qty Remaining to Issue to Job	Job	Override Code	Job Priority	Due Date (Job)	Order Date
Inventory	-	20	15	5	0	D	10	3	12/01/2019	11/4/2019
Inventory	-	5	5	0	10	A	10	3	12/09/2019	11/1/2019
PO1 - 12/01/2019	12/1/2019	15	10	5	0	A	10	3	12/09/2019	11/1/2019
PO1 - 12/01/2019	12/1/2019	5	5	0	10	B	10	3	12/17/2019	11/1/2019
PO2 - 12/15/2019	12/15/2019	20	10	10	0	B	10	3	12/17/2019	11/1/2019
PO2 - 12/15/2019	12/15/2019	10	10	0	5	C	10	3	12/26/2019	11/1/2019

Figure 10.12   Material allocation 1

The allocation proceeds as follows:

- Since Job D has the earliest due date, it is the first in line to get parts. Even though this order arrived after several others, its earlier due date gives it precedence. Since the inventory quantity is 20, 15 pieces can be issued to Job D, leaving five in stock. Since Job D can be fulfilled from stock, it can be released to the shop right away.
- From there, Job A needs 15 pieces. Since there are only five in stock, these will be issued to Job A. However, since 10 pieces are still needed, this job will have to wait on PO 1 to arrive on 12/1/19 before the entire order is ready to start. By withdrawing 10 pieces from PO 1's purchase quantity of 15, five pieces remain available from this PO.
- Job B will claim the remaining 5 pieces from PO 1. Since 10 are still needed, Job B will need to wait for 10 pieces from a shipment due on 12/15/19. Similar to Job A, Job B will have to wait until 12/15/19 for the entire order to be ready to start. Since PO 2 started with a quantity of 20, pulling 10 from this PO will leave 10 available for Job C.
- With inventory already depleted and only 10 parts still available from POs, Job C can't be completed unless another shipment is scheduled.

What if the salesman who negotiated the order for Job C thinks his order justifies special treatment? He can appeal to management and propose raising the priority code from 3—default to 2—high. If management concurs, the resulting material allotment would be as shown in Figure 10.13:

Material Source	Date of Availability	Starting Qty	Qty Allocated to Job	Remaining Stock	Qty Remaining to Issue to Job	Job	Override Code	Job Priority	Due Date (Job)	Order Date
Inventory	-	20	15	5	0	C	10	2	12/26/2019	11/1/2019
Inventory	-	5	5	0	10	D	10	3	12/01/2019	11/4/2019
PO1 - 12/01/2019	12/1/2019	15	10	5	0	D	10	3	12/01/2019	11/1/2019
PO1 - 12/01/2019	12/1/2019	5	5	0	10	A	10	3	12/09/2019	11/1/2019
PO2 - 12/15/2019	12/15/2019	20	10	10	0	A	10	3	12/09/2019	11/1/2019
PO2 - 12/15/2019	12/15/2019	10	10	0	5	B	10	3	12/17/2019	11/1/2019

Figure 10.13   Material allocation 2

Although Job *C* can now be completed, two orders that were previously in good shape are now in jeopardy:

- Job *A* has a due date of 12/9, but some of the material arrives on 12/15. It's impossible for the entire order to ship on time.
- Job *B* can no longer be fulfilled from the existing lineup of inventory and shipments.

With this seemingly innocent move, the company went from one order in trouble to two. If this decision is made knowingly, that is fine. However, many companies blindly move priorities around because there is no efficient way to determine the overall effects from small decisions. And the effects are often huge. Using the findings from this process identifies the problems and shows where countermeasures are needed. Since real-world situations will add some complications, software like Microsoft Access can be customized to accommodate them and still perform this process efficiently.

SIDEBAR—DEDICATING MATERIAL TO ORDERS

To ensure that particular orders are fulfilled on time, materials management will commonly reserve inventory for a particular job. A one-word recommendation for this practice would be:

Don't!

If priority is properly set and followed, allotting according to priority will automatically send material where it should go. At best, reserving materials to a job will only ratify what the system is already doing. More likely, it will result in higher-priority jobs being denied parts unless additional steps are taken to reroute material from another job. Often enough, mistakes will happen with jobs getting starved for material and extra handling occurring simultaneously. Don't go there.

LOGISTICS FOUNDATIONS RECAP

Regardless of the scheduling method deployed, it's critical to avoid common pitfalls that bedevil many systems including:

- Releasing jobs to the floor before all materials are available
- Interrupting jobs that are being processed to accommodate an expedited delivery
- Releasing jobs faster than production capacity can accommodate

In addition, addressing the following issues will prevent unnecessary delays due to material shortages:

- *Priority*—a consistent approach to priority will help to identify and prevent material shortages.
- *Transparency*—providing customer service employees with visibility to material commitments will prevent overdrawing materials and inadvertently leaving orders dry.

In the long run, avoiding pitfalls and reliably providing material will lay a solid foundation that any scheduling system can rest on.

SCHEDULING

With effective materials management underway, the challenge of scheduling remains. Although there are several techniques to do this, QL emphasizes DBR scheduling, due to its elegance and the fact that its principles are highly aligned with QL's. As a refresher, DBR is a scheduling technique that maximizes throughput and minimizes lead time by pacing production to an operation's bottleneck. This idea was popularized in a book entitled *The Goal*. This novel's plot was about a manager who was given three months to turn his plant around or face closure. While righting the ship, he discovered key insights which included the principles of DBR. With the fundamental ideas behind this concept covered in the chapter on lean tools, there are some additional points to consider when implementing this method.

DBR TIPS

Point 1

One critical task for DBR is determining a constraint. While calculations are warranted, avoid falling into the trap of too much analysis. Since the first suspect will often be wrong, it's generally faster to take an educated guess and validate after implementation. Three things can happen:

- *The bottleneck was correctly identified*—WIP will only accumulate in front of this constraint. Other work centers will be mostly free of buildup and only the constraint will be consistently busy.
- *The real bottleneck is upstream*—the constraint that was identified will be starved for material while the real bottleneck will be busy and backed up.

- *The real bottleneck is downstream*—the constraint that was identified will be fed, but the real bottleneck will also be busy and its WIP should be increasing.

Keep trying out bottlenecks until arriving at the right one.

Point 2

People often think that bottlenecks can change from day to day. While anything's possible, this is not likely. Like shifting winds, there is still a prevailing direction. Constraints can be this way. Although fluctuations are possible, there is generally a prevailing constraint and it is best to stay the course until another bottleneck presents itself for several days. Only trim the sails at that time.

Point 3

To repeat a point made earlier, release orders once all the necessary materials are available. Issuing jobs any other way might starve the bottleneck of material. After all, if an order gets stranded, there's a chance that this will also happen to the constraint. In addition, if a bottleneck needs the material that is missing from a job, what happens if the order arrives at the constraint without the right material? Clearly, there's going to be lost production capacity.

When no order has all the materials but there is a need to capture production capacity that will otherwise be lost, rely on the following principles:

- What will serve the product best?
- What will minimize the time-in-system?

The ultimate goal is that the last minute can become the first resort. In scheduling, a robust system allows last-minute starts and still delivers impeccably. In turn, last-minute releases minimize WIP. Assuring all materials are ready before release is imperative to achieving this.

Point 4

When the customer is the constraint, theory states that orders should be released based on due date. However, due to demand variability, production that is faster than the average demand rate can still be overwhelmed when demand is spiky. In turn, late orders result. When setting up a scheduling system, releasing jobs to a faux constraint and setting the pace to the average demand rate will help work around this problem. While this doesn't entirely line up with the theory, it's a concession you may need to make.

Complications

In addition to aligning inventory and purchasing with the production schedule, there may be additional issues that come up when implementing DBR:

- *Product that runs through a bottleneck more than once*—as one example, it is quite common for machine shops to have products that are processed by a bottleneck resource more than once. As most production scheduling requires a computer, workarounds for this need to be thought through before developing or purchasing software. This problem is solvable, but needs to be considered ahead of time.
- *Outsourcing*—outsourced processes like heat treat, coating, and other specialized processes must be factored in to be able to estimate delivery dates accurately.
- *One-piece flow*—for job shops, many scheduling packages assume batch processing. For the sake of QL, make sure your scheduling package can accommodate the assumption of one-piece flow. It will make a big difference in predicting delivery dates accurately.
- *Break-ins*—expedited orders are a fact of life. And they should be. In a dynamic environment, an organization must have the flexibility to change its mind. The issue isn't whether priorities change, but how it's done. In other words, allow a job to cut in line, but don't interrupt a job in mid-process. Let the order that is in process finish, and then accommodate the expedited order.

SUMMARY

There are several things that are required when establishing effective shop-floor logistics:

- *Materials*—a well-functioning system that maintains accurate inventory counts and specifies accurate reorder points will keep a business fueled. Where BOMs are used, accurately allocating materials is a must.
- *Priority*—a logical, consistent, and universally understood approach to assigning priority ensures that accurate delivery dates can be projected when there is not enough material to go around.
- *Transparency*—before new agreements are forged, visibility to all commitments and their allotted materials prevents the inadvertent dedication of resources that are already spoken for. In turn, this prevents jobs from being stranded on the shop floor and preserves on-time delivery to the greatest extent possible. Even better, the need for corrective

action can be determined in a timely way and allow maximum time for countermeasures.

- *Scheduling*—divvying work to the pace of the shop floor minimizes WIP, turnaround time, and cost. Coupled with a good scheme to assign priority and maintain visibility, methods like DBR have a great chance to shine.

Together, these elements will provide highly effective production scheduling. However, once these technical issues are ironed out, there is a good chance that political challenges will remain. In a corporate setting, implementing such a scheme will require the cooperation of sales, purchasing, planning, and inventory. While this task isn't easy, the rewards from success are too overwhelming to ignore.

This book has free material available for download from the
Web Added Value™ resource center at *www.jrosspub.com*

CHAPTER 11

5S—WORKPLACE ORGANIZATION

Good order is the foundation of all things.
Edmund Burke

For every minute spent organizing, an hour is earned.
Benjamin Franklin

The organization of information actually creates new information.
Richard Saul Wurman

Although all of the words in 5S begin with an S, reading between the lines is key. Limiting yourself to the 5S script can leave you with equally limited results. Where the steps—*sort, set in order, shine, standardize,* and *sustain*—are primarily technical in nature, the personal and political can also be decisive. Without the buy-in of management and rank-and-file alike, the deployment won't last. If failing to satisfy the boardroom doesn't get an implementation's plug pulled, a lack of employee enthusiasm will achieve a similar outcome. The upside is that there are a thousand ways to handle the soft side of implementations, and getting creative will make all the difference.

However, before addressing the human element, assuring technical soundness first will lay the groundwork for securing buy-in later. Doing this will prevent problems that crop up when 5S is deployed, with little consideration of where, when, or why it is being done:

- *Management*—lack of fundamental soundness runs the risk of ineffective outcomes. Depending on management styles, this can be lethal in the short term.
- *Employees*—just as serious as the management angle, shop-floor employees can generally detect a lack of forethought in a heartbeat. On top

of disappointing results, the diminished respect for lean damages every aspect of the program. Sad!

5S—WHEN

Like any other lean tool, 5S should be deployed when an organization's capacity constraint lies within its own operations. Beyond that, it's necessary when the product path diagram (PPD) indicates a need. Ideally, this should be when the biggest contributor to a product's time-in-system can be traced to the inability to find tools, information, or materials. With that being said, a lean practitioner must weigh the issue of management buy-in. If upper management is absolutely sold, let the product be the absolute authority for determining what you should be working on. However, if instant gratification is necessary to forestall flagging interest in lean, 5S might be brought out of the box early due to its high visibility. While 5S should be about getting product out more quickly, its potential as eye candy can't be ignored. Since humans are visual by nature, this promotes buy-in and the perception of a quick win. In the final analysis, strictly adhering to principles won't do a company any good if it gets an initiative canceled. The trick is restoring the product's priority after any compromises have been made.

5S—WHERE

Whether the decision to implement 5S is based on principle or expediency, the priority for initiating 5S should be (with a couple of caveats to follow):

- *Bottleneck*—if a bottleneck for an organization lies within the operation, this constraint should be optimized first. In other words, any barrier to utilizing every minute of a bottleneck's time needs to be minimized. Even if there aren't significant delays that are traceable to searching for information, tools, or materials, even a slight performance improvement offers outsized gains.
- *Delay*—if major progress has been achieved on bottlenecks, start where the greatest time penalty can be traced to a lack of workplace organization.

Like the initial decision to deploy 5S, these guidelines carry a couple of caveats:

- *Pushback*—if there is one work area that will resist 5S and another where the acceptance will be greater, consider the path of least resistance.

- *Difficulty*—similar to pushback, if the technical difficulty or legwork for one area far outweighs another department's, you might start with the other department. This is especially true if the impacts are similar.

Such adjustments can be extremely helpful when there is a lack of awareness of the need for order. One example would be situations where employees are so conditioned to their surroundings that they don't even notice the chaos that engulfs them. In such cases, having a tangible example in a less resistant area offers a stark contrast that shows doubters what's possible. In addition, success in one area can build momentum and lead to quicker and easier results down the line.

EXTENT—HOW MUCH 5S IS ENOUGH?

In many facilities, a lean *sensei* (i.e., teacher) can get carried away with workplace organization. In turn, employees are constantly nagged when nits aren't picked. Often, exasperated rank-and-file are left wondering if 5S will ever have a stopping point. While other versions of lean evade this question, Quantum Lean (QL) offers a clear answer. At a minimum, 5S should be applied to the extent that it benefits the product. Also, any additional 5S must not undermine this. For example, there might be bells and whistles that have little to do with the product's needs, but they don't hurt anything either. In addition, they help build a discipline that will ultimately pay off in other ways. Such measures would be compatible with QL:

- *Polished/painted floors*—most of the time, polishing or painting the floors is for the sake of appearance. Sometimes, it's helpful.
- *Shadow boards for cleaning supplies*—although useful for expediting cleanup, shadow boards for cleaning supplies have little explicit effect on deliverables.
- *Signs identifying work areas*—while it's nice for getting newcomers acquainted with the workplace, signs identifying work areas probably don't serve the product.

By contrast, ideas like the following may or may not be beneficial:

- *Standardization*—if it makes serving the product better, faster, or cheaper, full speed ahead with standardization. On the other hand, if different areas of a plant have different needs, what's good for one department might be detrimental to another. In that case, standardization would actually impair performance.

- *5S audits*—follow-up is important. Even more critical is how the audit is done. Commonly, companies commit significant man-hours to audit 5S compliance. If it is to improve the 5S program, that's one thing. However, if it ends up harassing the workforce, that's another. At the end of the day, it's impossible to police a company into being lean.

In addition, there are provisions that are counterproductive and obnoxious. Some examples of organizations running amok with 5S include:

- *Personal effects*—some companies will specify minutiae like beverage placement and where employees can hang their coats. Some places even prohibit family photos!
- *Obvious points*—beyond personal effects, the zeal to organize can be so great that even obvious issues fall within the 5S net. Some pitfalls with this include:
  - *Redundancy*—if an issue is manifestly obvious, it might be best to leave this out of the organization's efforts. For example:
    - A machine tool's chip bin can only be in one place. In many 5S efforts, the location of this chip bin would probably be marked off and labeled. However, since any operator knows exactly where the bin should go, no useful information is conveyed. In addition, a memory jogger isn't needed because nobody in his right mind would fail to put the chip bin back. At least, that would not happen more than once. On top of that, blueprinting what's obvious is subtly insulting.
    - It's not unheard of for universally known and permanent equipment (that can't get misplaced) to be marked and labeled. While it won't hurt the product, it doesn't help.

To reiterate, pick your battles when organizing objects that don't affect a deliverable's flow. Try to limit this effort to issues that will help or allow employees to prioritize their primary duty, which is serving the product. If this isn't done, attention gets taken away from more urgent tasks, not to mention exasperating people.

5S SPECIFICS

Once 5S is selected for the right targets at the right time, the next challenge is deploying the right methods to get the most from this lean tool. As an aid when doing this, the following subsections include some details to take into account when applying 5S.

Shadow Boards

Shadow boards should play an outsized role in any 5S implementation. They are so essential that they could be thought of as one of the five S's. For those who wonder why, another approach's vices can demonstrate a shadow board's virtues.

As an example of folly, one company was so concerned with pilferage that they insisted that tools be kept in lockboxes and issued to employees each day. At the beginning of a shift, a long check sheet that enumerated the toolbox's contents would be reviewed and an employee had to sign off that everything was there. Making matters worse, tool placement in the box was haphazard. What isn't wrong with this picture?

- How long does it take to verify tools are in the box and in proper condition? Remember that the tools are stored haphazardly.
- If a tool is missing, how long will an employee spend with the tool crib attendant verifying this?
- When the tools are returned, how much time will the tool crib attendant spend verifying everything is back?
- Who tracks the paperwork?
- On the job itself, how efficient can a worker be when tools are in a disorganized pile?

Needless to say, what was just described is inefficient, cumbersome, and time-consuming. When a system is this unwieldy, it's certain that employees are largely ignoring it with additional side effects that include:

- When rules are being ignored anywhere in a company, it fosters a disregard for rules everywhere in the company. Over time, this aggravates the chaos that everyone wants to avoid.
- Ironically, a system that is ignored is susceptible to the pilferage that terrified management in the first place.

The only silver lining to this dark cloud is that the management at this company is no longer there. Compare what was just described to a shadow board (see Figure 11.1).

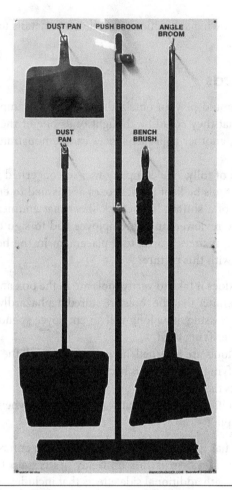

Figure 11.1 Shadow board

Advantages of shadow boards include:

- Since a missing tool can be instantly spotted, lengthy inspections are not needed
- Unmistakable tool locations mean quick retrieval and efficient work
- The board's innate visibility makes pilferage more challenging
- Since missing tools can be immediately identified and accountability can be demanded, a standard that all tools are returned to the board at shift's end is now enforceable

- Fewer misplaced tools mean greater tool availability, which means more efficient work
- Fewer misplaced tools mean less outlay

When creating a shadow board, keep these points in mind:

- Use background colors keyed to work areas to prevent one work area from cannibalizing another's tools.
- In addition to outlines, add written descriptions of the tools for even greater specificity.

Despite all the praise just showered on this manner of organizing tools, keep in mind that shadow boards are a means and not an end. Like any other method, use them when they are the best option for serving the product.

Office 5S

While 5S on the shop floor can underachieve, it is in the office where matters can get really woeful. Most of the time, organizing at the front end translates into labeling every cabinet and establishing a standardized location for items like office supplies, phones, and computers. Although it isn't harmful, it is anti-thetical to QL. Since an office serves a different product than the shop floor, lean in the office must reflect this:

- The product that the office serves is information. Specifically, the office processes the information that serves the product that the shop floor handles.
- Since QL is product-focused, begin where the product resides. In the office, information is in electronic and paper form. That's all there is to it.
- In other words, why obsess over pens? Instead, apply 5S to paperwork. Promising targets include:
  - *Forms*—sales orders, purchase orders, inspection sheets, etc.
  - *Blueprints*
  - *Specification sheets*
  - *Enterprise resource planning/materials requirements planning (ERP/MRP) system*
  - *Order boards*

As an example of applying 5S in the office, consider a sales order form. The 5S process might go as listed in the following sections.

Sort/Supply

- *Supply*—does the form capture all the information needed to fully specify the product? If not, revise this form to facilitate complete information capture.
- *Sort*—is any information on the form unnecessary? If so, remove the associated fields.

Set in Order

- Is there an explicit location/field for every order requirement? A telltale sign that there's a problem is when employees have to add notes in the margins and/or in a general comments field.
- Do salespeople have to remember issues that aren't explicitly called out on the order form? For example, a customer may have specific packaging requirements. Although this can be addressed in the comments field, is there a way that the documentation might include a memory jogger to be sure this issue isn't overlooked? For example, could a section be included with common special requirements as shown in Figure 11.2?

Additional Requirements/Clarifications – √ All That Apply And Elaborate Under Comments					
☐ *See Customer Order Sheet* ☐ *See Referenced Quote* ☐ *Revisions Made Below*					
None	☐	3. Labeling	☐	6. Process	☐
1. Certification(s)	☐	4. Vendor	☐	7. Confidentiality	☐
2. Traceability	☐	5. Customer Verification	☐	8. Other	☐
Comments -					

Figure 11.2   Form: special requirements

- For each element, is there sufficient space for the requirement to be completely documented? For example, have you ever filled out a form where the space for the e-mail address is far too small?
- If there isn't enough space to fit all of the information on one page, is there an efficient way to address the overflow consistently? Specifically, is there a continuation page (or equivalent) that can capture the overflow?

Shine

- Can the information be recorded in a neat and legible manner?

Standardize/Suppress

- Establish a standard approach for data collection/capture
- Verify that everyone can interpret and populate the form consistently

Sustain

- To help sustain 5S, can documentation be made easier to use and interpret?
- Can information be configured so it is easier to retrieve?
- On the example form that was developed, a few tricks were used to streamline data entry:
  - *Checkboxes*—instead of separate fields for rarely invoked requirements, a general comment box can be used in conjunction with numbered checkboxes. The comments can then be keyed to the number associated with the checkbox. Ambiguity is eliminated and space is conserved.
  - *Checkboxes: Part 2*—maximizing the use of checkboxes minimizes the amount of data entry (see Figure 11.3). In turn, this enhances legibility.

General Information				Page 1 Of 1
Customer Order ID	*Quote Reference* ☐ *Not Applicable*		*Customer*	*Buyer/Phone*
Payment Method (√ One) ☐ Account ☒ Bill ☐ On Receipt	*Terms (Bill Only)* 2% Net 10/Net 30	*Order Processed by*	*Due Date* ASAP	*Date Reviewed* ☐ *Customer Info Complete*
Bill To: (☐ *See Customer Order Sheet* ☐ *See Referenced Quote)*				

Figure 11.3 Form: checkboxes

  - Key coding—on top of numbering special requirements, every line item under product information is identified with a letter. Again, under the general comments area, notes about a particular item can be referenced using a letter rather than writing out the entire product identification (see Figure 11.4).

Product Information	☐ See Customer Order Sheet	☐ See Referenced Quote	☐ Revisions Made Below			
#	# of lbs	Hardness Requirement	Rev #	Product ID and/or Product Description	Material	Pricing
A			N/A			See pricing sheet
B			N/A			See pricing sheet
C			N/A			See pricing sheet
D			N/A			See pricing sheet
E			N/A			See pricing sheet
F			N/A			See pricing sheet

Figure 11.4   Form: keyed requirements

If the form can incorporate many of these ideas, filling out information should be a smoother affair. Being easier, it stands to reason that the odds of *sustaining* will increase. In its entirety, the form might look like the following example (see Figure 11.5).

Even though some offices are largely paperless, the approach in the previous example remains relevant. In many cases, business software gives little consideration to lean imperatives and often undermines them. As a result, such applications may cause an operation to run in a manner that is diametrically opposed to lean. In other words, since ERP/MRP can usher in so many inefficiencies, software-driven systems can offer more targets for improvement than manually-run offices.

As a business increasingly obtains correct, complete, timely, and understandable information, downstream benefits accrue exponentially. Although getting an office in proper order can be a tall order, it beats wasting time organizing pens and pencils. It would be ok to address trivia like office supplies to the extent that it affects the product. However, it doesn't.

Sales Order Form
Rev. (Original)
Filename - OrderForm.doc

Page 1 of 1
Approved by: QMS Representative
Document Type – Form

General Information				Page 1 Of 1
Customer Order ID	Quote Reference ☐ Not Applicable	Customer		Buyer/Phone

Payment Method (√ One)		Order Processed by	Due Date	Date Reviewed
☐ Account	Terms (Bill Only)		ASAP	☐ Customer Info
☒ Bill	2% Net 10/Net 30			Complete
☐ On Receipt				

Bill To: (☐ See Customer Order Sheet ☐ See Referenced Quote)

Product Information ☐ See Customer Order Sheet ☐ See Referenced Quote ☐ Revisions Made Below

#	# of lbs	Hardness Requirement	Rev #	Product ID and/or Product Description	Material	Pricing
A			N/A			See pricing sheet
B			N/A			See pricing sheet
C			N/A			See pricing sheet
D			N/A			See pricing sheet
E			N/A			See pricing sheet
F			N/A			See pricing sheet

Additional Requirements/Clarifications – √ All That Apply And Elaborate Under Comments
☐ See Customer Order Sheet ☐ See Referenced Quote ☐ Revisions Made Below

None	☐	3. Labeling	☐	6. Process	☐	
1. Certification(s)	☐	4. Vendor	☐	7. Confidentiality	☐	
2. Traceability	☐	5. Customer Verification	☐	8. Other	☐	

Comments -

Disclaimers – Order terms are subject to change. Customer will be notified of such changes. * We reserve the right to assess a 1% per month finance charge on overdue accounts * Customer is responsible for all shipping arrangements * Revisions in this document supersede any information in source documents (i.e. quotes and customer purchase orders) * Unless otherwise noted, pricing is per lb. * Min – minimum charge

AnyCo, Inc. * Any Street * Anytown, AW 99999 * **Phone**: 999-999-9999

Figure 11.5   Form after 5S

PRACTICAL TIPS

When implementing 5S, here are some specific pointers that can help when nailing down details.

Floors[11-1]

Where concrete floors are concerned, it's no coincidence that the word *paint* begins with pain. Due to its chemistry, concrete contains moisture that slowly but continually evaporates from its surface. The fly in this ointment is that moisture on coating surfaces creates adhesion problems. In fact, a floor has to be practically perfect for coatings to stick at all. Outside of new construction, most floors are old, abused, neglected, and/or soaked with hydrocarbons. Since most facilities have been around for awhile, such factors are practically a certainty. In turn, successful application requires knowledge and meticulous preparation. Unless there is in-house expertise, strongly consider retaining a well-qualified contractor to handle this process. While such help is expensive, success can be hard to achieve by amateurs. Even with extensive planning and every effort to condition the concrete, doing it yourself stands a high chance of ending up with a surface that flakes anyway. And should these problems be surmounted, traffic in many shops will make short work of a painted floor anyway.

As an alternative and if the budget allows, concrete polishing is a lower-cost option that is attractive, robust, and more durable. Simply put, this process is similar to sanding wood. However, rather than sanders, polishing machines are used to grind surfaces to a desired finish. By using different grit levels, a polished floor has a glossy finish that can vary from matte all the way up to mirror-like. In addition, a wide variety of options for color and patterns are possible. A major functional advantage is that polished floors don't absorb liquids like typical concrete surfaces do. In turn, this makes for easy maintenance that requires dust mopping and occasional use of a cleaning product. The following image is one example of a polished floor (see Figure 11.6).

With its economy, durability, minimal maintenance, and attractive appearance, polished floors are a viable option, especially considering all of the problems associated with paints and epoxies.

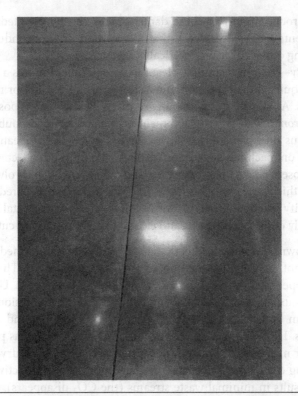

Figure 11.6   Polished floor (level 3 reflectance)

Dry Ice Blasting[11-2]

A common desire in 5S projects is to clean up equipment. Like floors that have absorbed years of oil leaks, machines can accumulate a daunting amount of crud that doesn't go away without a fight. Beyond the obvious price tag associated with downtime, count the costs:

- *Method*—the nature of the filth will determine the cleaning method and agents employed. For example, if hydrocarbons (i.e., oil) aren't involved, water-based solutions like steam or power-washing are probably called for. If oil-based sludge has formed, solvents will need to be deployed. In addition, blast media like sand or shot can be considered. Regardless of approach, preparation is in order.
- *Preparation*—water-based cleaning means that any electrical circuitry that might be in the spray range must be sealed to guard against

electrocution and machine damage. This can be very tedious. Where solvents are needed, verify that the solvents are nonconductive before opting out of covering electrical boxes.

- *Safety*—without planning, cleaning up equipment stands a high chance of requiring that operators must stand on slippery and/or unstable surfaces. Anticipate this possibility so that a workaround is possible.
- *Environmental*—when equipment is cleaned, have no doubt that a hellacious mess generally follows. For example, all that cleaning solution used on machines ends up on the floor and must be collected and legally disposed. Given that oils, grease, and metals are often involved, odds are that this waste can't be thrown in a dumpster. Be prepared to properly classify and document this waste. Although environmental laws are unevenly enforced, it's smart and ethical to comply and not cut corners.

All of the downsides associated with the previously mentioned mediums helped usher in another cleaning method called dry-ice blasting. This technique involves propelling frozen carbon dioxide pellets at high speeds. Upon impact, the pellets sublimate very quickly and produce minimal abrasion. Instead of coming from abrasion, dirt removal results from thermal and microscopic shock waves. In a wide variety of situations, this mechanism has proven superior to other methods. Although it doesn't work in every case, dry-ice blasting merits strong consideration because this medium is nonconductive, machine-safe, and results in minimal waste streams (the CO_2 disappears). In any case, cleaning is frequently a tall order that requires a lot of homework in order to do the job right.

Perspective

Despite all the social media posts portraying blissful marriages and close-knit families, the corresponding dysfunction seen in everyday life belies all of this seeming perfection. By the same token, getting bombarded by all of these ideal images from 5S implementations may leave a practitioner feeling inadequate. This is good to keep in mind when looking at other organizations' results. Like social media, there's a tendency to put the best foot forward. After all, who wants to advertise their dirty laundry?

On top of this, photography has a way of smoothing over gritty details. In other words, shop floors generally look better in photos than they do in real life. Before taking things too hard, take a photo of your shop and see if you don't feel a little better.

5S ALTERNATIVES

Before zeroing in on frequently used methods like point-of-use storage, there are ideas to consider that aren't explicitly lean, but can greatly aid your efforts. While you may not adopt these options, they are good to consider before committing too much time on a course of action that might end up being less than optimal.

Pick-to-Light

In a high-speed environment where parts can be hard to distinguish, pick-to-light may be viable. This technology uses lights and buttons at storage locations to guide manual part-picking. In a typical system, the operator scans a barcode that references the parts necessary to fulfill an order (see Figure 11.7).

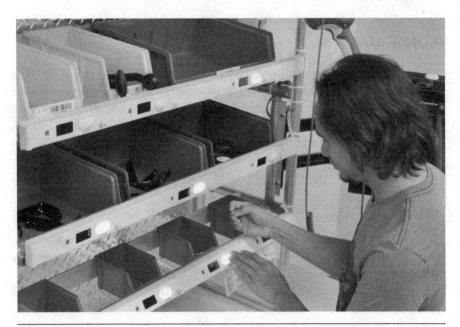

Figure 11.7 Pick to light (Courtesy of Lightning Pick)

A typical arrangement involves light-emitting diodes (LEDs) placed at applicable storage locations that light up to guide operators to the right place and indicate the number of pieces to pick. Once an operator places the items in a container, the activity is confirmed by pressing a button near the display. These displays will continue until the order is completely picked. Like any system, variations are possible, but the basic idea remains. Although investment is needed in information systems and hardware, the potential gain in error-free operation coupled with the decreased training demands can pay for itself manyfold.

Kitting

In environments with extensive bills of material (BOM) and a wide variety of parts, point-of-use storage on the shop floor can be impractical due to limitations of space and human capacity. Since a BOM with a hundred or more stock-keeping units can be overwhelming, having specialized employees assemble kits for jobs can be a compelling alternative. By focusing training on a few material handlers who will kit components, the shop floor can concentrate on serving the product. At the same time, errors can be reduced.

SUMMARY

5S is so integral to lean that its necessity is often taken as self-evident. While it is good that this tool has such widespread acceptance, thinking generally ends where consensus begins. Getting the most from 5S means revisiting this subject and questioning the who, what, where, when, and how of this method. In a QL framework, the most important consideration is applying this building block at the right time. As a result, there are certain guidelines that can help guide in the selection of 5S as a solution.

When

5S should be deployed when an organization's capacity constraint lies within its own operations. Beyond that, it should be deployed according to the priority determined when analyzing the PPD. Ideally, this should be when the biggest contributor to a product's time-in-system can be traced to the inability to find tools, information, or materials.

Where

The priority for initiating 5S should be:

- *Bottleneck*—if a bottleneck for an organization lies within the operation, this constraint should be optimized first. In other words, any barrier to utilizing every minute of a bottleneck's time needs to be minimized.

- *Delay*—5S should be applied where the greatest time penalty can be traced to a lack of workplace organization.

Extent

Companies can get so carried away with workplace organization that exasperated employees are often left wondering if 5S will ever have a stopping point. While other versions of lean evade this question, QL offers the clear answer that 5S should be applied to the extent that it benefits the product. Additional 5S is not required, but is acceptable as long as it does not undermine the prior point.

Company Politics

In addition to technical points, political issues can loom large in deciding when and where to apply 5S, and these must be taken into account. However, applying 5S in a technically sound manner will go a long way toward nailing down the soft side of the implementation. Overall, using QL principles to ensure validity will give a company the best odds of success.

While 5S takes a minute to learn, mastering it is another matter. However, using QL principles can accelerate this process and make the path to success a little smoother.

CHAPTER **12**

KANBAN

The best kanban is no kanban.

Weldon Steele

In lean organizations, kanban is used for everything from managing stock to shop-floor control. Since Quantum Lean (QL) mostly relies on drum-buffer-rope (DBR) to manage workflow, this deep dive will focus on using kanban to control inventory. In particular, the emphasis will be on configuring it to avoid a situation that I used to encounter at a former workplace. Frequently, the production line would shut down due to an outage of a single part. Employees would be sent home without pay, but no expense was spared in expediting an emergency shipment. Had a visual technique like kanban been adopted, some of these shortages might have been avoided. At the very least, it couldn't have hurt. On the other hand, it might not have helped either. Without analysis, there's no good way to tell. And before a tool such as kanban can be properly investigated, understanding its basics is key.

KANBAN BASICS

Although it comes in many forms, the classic version of kanban provides a good illustration of the principles involved. This variation uses two bins to store parts and has cards to convey information (see Figure 12.1).

When one bin is emptied, an operator takes the attached card from the bin and sends it to purchasing. During the time required for an order to be placed and delivered, material can be drawn from the second bin. If the kanban is properly sized, the second bin should be emptying as the first bin is being replenished. While this is the ideal, actual events will vary from this perfect scenario. However, the results should come close if the homework was properly done. While kanban can vary from what was just described, the principle of using

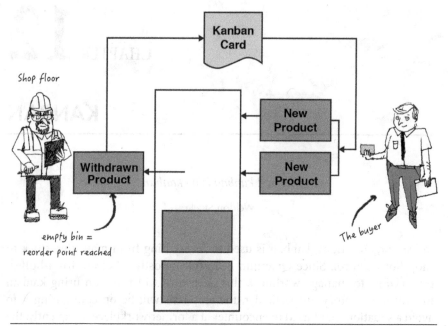

Figure 12.1   Classic kanban scenario

visual triggers to fulfill demand remains the same. Depending on the specifics of the implementation, kanban's advantages include:

- *Reduced effort*—conventional inventory-control systems require that withdrawals and replenishments be recorded. Compared to kanban, which has no such requirement, this is labor-intensive and error-prone.
- *Reduced expense*—along with reduced effort, fewer necessary updates usher a corresponding reduction in scanners, computers, and software.
- *Mitigated risk of outage*—without access to a computer, typical inventory-control systems offer no way to know when a stock-keeping unit (SKU) needs to be reordered. In other words, if there are data-entry errors, there is no easy way to tell without an inventory count. If this verification isn't timely, outages have a way of happening. By contrast, kanban's visuality improves the ability to detect when stock falls below specified levels.
- *Employee involvement*—in conventional inventory systems, knowledge of system status is generally relegated to a priesthood of planners and buyers. By contrast, kanban makes this information accessible to all

levels of a plant. In turn, the workforce can be enlisted to serve as a line of defense against system failure. On top of improving company performance, empowerment improves employee productivity.

On the flip side and depending on how it is done, kanban's disadvantages may include:

- *Increased effort*—proper information flow requires discipline, which correspondingly necessitates training and follow-up. In addition, special-purpose containers might be used, which means that parts must be moved from their original packaging to kanban bins.
- *Increased expense*—special-purpose containers are expensive. In addition, printing, tracking, and maintaining cards carry a cost.
- *Potentially increased risk of outage*—unattended cards can fly or fall away in the rough-and-tumble of a plant environment. As a result, necessary reorders may not occur and outages might ensue.
- *Employee alienation*—often, shop personnel perceive kanban's burdens to outweigh its benefits and resent the protocols. This can manifest itself in lost cards and dropped balls.

From the pros and cons, a clear takeaway is that kanban is a double-edged sword. Knowing when to use this tool will go a long way in making or breaking this method. Although it applies to a variety of cases, kanban works best when it's applied to specific types of products under specific conditions. Knowing the when, what, and why helps assure that kanban is a good fit.

KANBAN—WHEN

When managing inventory, kanban is best used for the following reasons:

- *Improved fulfillment*—if outages are due to reorders not being placed in a timely way, a kanban's visuality may improve the detection of stock falling below specified levels.
- *Reduced cost*—sometimes, companies expend considerable resources on inventory management and kanban can minimize this investment.

If either of these conditions exists, kanban should be entertained as an option. However, because this technique works better with specific product types, an additional screen should be applied to assure compatibility.

KANBAN—WHAT

In addition to fulfillment, inventory revolves around cost. To properly size kanbans, minimum stock levels often need upward revision. When this happens, management will often overlook decreased expenses like expediting. Instead, the attention will focus on the immediate increase in stock. Parts with highly variable demand aggravate this problem. Consequently, the best candidates for kanban are SKUs where implementation can be most economical:

- *Low-cost product*—because kanbans may increase inventory, using them for high-cost items risks damaging management support. Unless expensive materials are on consignment, a better alternative may be keeping inventory as low as possible and tracking it with cycle counting.
- *High-demand product*—keeping kanbans for one-off items risks the need for a substantially increased storage space. As these parts should only be needed occasionally, it may not be worth the added cost if lead times can otherwise be met.
- *Low volatility*—high demand variation greatly increases necessary on-hand levels. In this case, applying kanban may increase space requirements. Similar to low-demand product, a better option may be keeping inventory as low as possible and monitoring it with cycle counting.

Beyond the aforementioned points, another benefit of using kanbans with low-cost, high-demand, and low-volatility items is that it offers rapid feedback about the implementation. Any other combination requires more time and resource for the returns to come in. With results coming in quicker, methods can be fine-tuned faster.

By knowing the when and what of kanban, this technique can be kept in reserve and contemplated when problems are identified. When thorough analysis shows kanban as an answer, the remaining task is putting a system into play. That's when the real work begins.

KANBAN—IMPLEMENTATION

Although kanban is straightforward in principle, significant detail must be resolved to arrive at this seemingly simple arrangement. It's like a virtuoso concealing years of toil by making things look easy. Similarly, elegance is generally preceded by due diligence. To this end, a disciplined launch will typically begin with fleshing out details like quantities, means of communication (e.g., cards), and rules for triggering fulfillment. The upcoming sections include some steps to follow when making these determinations.

Containers

Try to use existing packaging or designated locations. As most people have been repeatedly exposed to two-bin systems, the tendency is to default toward special-purpose containers. However, there are downsides:

- *Expense*—containers are expensive. Due to a lack of longevity, inexpensive ones can end up being costlier in the long run. In a dynamic or seasonal environment, costs can be further compounded by a need to manage and pay for a wide variety of receptacles.
- *Lack of flexibility*—if demand or lead times change, a bin's quantity, size, and utilization are subject to revision. Besides requiring extra work, more expense will be involved.
- *Extra handling*—transferring parts from their original container to a new receptacle requires handling. On top of the handling itself, other costs flow from this:
  - *Damage*—the more a part is handled, the more likely it will be damaged.
  - *Safety*—increased handling increases the risk of injuries.
  - *Updates*—when reorder points and quantities are revised, additional handling will be required to update the bins.

The bottom line is to only invest in special-purpose receptacles if there are no other good options.

Means of Communication (aka Cards)

Like the tendency to use dedicated bins, many are biased toward cards due to oft-repeated kanban examples. As with special-purpose containers, there are downsides. Unless a card can be reliably secured and conspicuously located, it is best to tread carefully. In production environments, unattended cards tend to disappear. They are easy to misplace. When they aren't overlooked, they are ignored. Sometimes, the cards are even thrown away. The implications include:

- Dropped balls—a lost card can mean a missed or late reorder.
- Inconvenience—as demand or lead times change, new cards may need to be reprinted and distributed. In a dynamic market, this would need to be done frequently.

Regardless of the communication medium that is selected, information to consider transmitting includes:

- *ID*—sequential identification to assure that missing kanbans can be identified
- *Quantity*
- *Part ID and Part Description*
- *Dates*—date the request is sent to the buyer/date replenished/due date
- *Traceability*—if lot numbers need to be tracked, provide a way to record this information
- *Customer order details*—for finished goods, information may need to be specified, such as packaging requirements, customer ID, sales order ID, and delivery information

In addition, it pays to consider information that is constant versus that which is subject to change. A sturdy medium might be good for unchanging information while volatile data could use paper or electronic storage.

Other Tips

Additional points to think about include:

- *Triggers*—on top of the need to reorder, other potential cues could include showing purchase order information and expected delivery dates.
- *Baby steps*—while initiating reorders directly from the warehouse is ideal, consider starting with kanban as a supplement to the existing inventory control system. For example, when cycle counts take place, add a check box to the inventory count sheet for employees to fill out when a visual reorder has been triggered. In addition to serving as a backstop to improper inventory counts, it also serves to validate the effectiveness of the visual cues and whether procedures are followed.
- *Checks and balances*—kanban can serve as a check and balance. In a company with conventional inventory control, visual cues can serve as a line of defense in case inventory numbers are improperly updated. In addition, by encouraging employees to report improperly updated kanbans, workforce involvement is encouraged and buy-in can be gauged.
- *Ease*—inconvenience the floor as little as possible. Try to have purchasing do most of the legwork.
- *Withdrawal method*—kanbans won't work if materials are withdrawn in an improper sequence. For example, if employees randomly withdraw

parts from a two-bin system, it's highly likely that the reorder point will be reached without either bin emptying. To prevent this, implement methods to assure that containers are emptied in the proper sequence. If mistake-proofing isn't possible, specify, train, and verify employee understanding of the protocols for removing and replenishing material.

- *Reorder point and reorder quantity*—methods to calculate reorder point and reorder quantity are covered in this book's chapter on inventory.

With so much information being presented, there's nothing like specific cases to bring ideas to life.

Example: Kanban Elevated

Although kanban doesn't have to involve bins and cards, could the classic version of this tool be enhanced? In a classic scenario, the only thing a shop floor can easily know is whether material needs to be ordered. On the other hand, there is no visibility to the following potentially negative developments:

- The card never made it to the buyer
- The buyer never placed the order
- The order will arrive too late to keep the shop from running out of material
- The shipment gets lost

Because affected employees are out of the loop, the scheme has to work flawlessly if problems are to be avoided. Since perfection is rare, such a scheme is vulnerable. To address the gaps, the system could provide transparency to the following milestones as procurement progresses:

- The kanban card is on the way to purchasing
- Purchasing has received the card
- The supplier has accepted the order
- The order has shipped
- Best of all, the signaling would indicate the estimated delivery date

Putting specifics to this wish list might end up with signaling that works as follows:

- Once a bin is empty and a card is on the way to a buyer, the placeholder that held the kanban card can now hold a card that says, "In transit to purchasing," along with a due date for the next update. Note that the card shouldn't indicate that it has been *delivered*, but that it is *on the way*.

- Once purchasing has received the order, the buyer could generate a card that says, "Purchase request received," and the due date for the next update.
- Once the purchase order (PO) is issued, the buyer can generate a card that indicates the PO number and the expected delivery date.
- If an estimated delivery date gets revised, the placeholder can be updated to reflect this.

With provisions to assure that the updates are properly delivered, the following conditions would become visible to the shop floor:

- If the card never reaches purchasing or the request gets otherwise lost, the due date on the placeholder will expire and indicate that something went wrong.
- Once a purchase order is issued, an estimated delivery date coming without an arrival indicates that follow-up is in order.

With employee involvement, these provisions could be used to empower the shop floor as a last line of defense in case of a system breakdown. Despite potential complications, the concepts remain valid. The point is finding a way to notify of all threats to product flow.

Example: Nonstandard Shipments

A shop buys custom parts from a manufacturer that routinely produces overruns and adds them to the order. In addition, the provider likes to use any spare box it can get its hands on. Put another way, the shop gets shipments that are all over the map. On one day, an order for 120 might come in as a shipment with 127 pieces allotted in four different boxes. On another day, the same order quantity might bring 140 parts in five different containers. While there are several ways to apply kanban, here are a couple of ways this situation might be handled:

- *Option 1*—in line with conventional accounts of kanban, reconfigure the shipments according to a standard arrangement. For example, shipments could be placed in bins or designated rack spaces. If shelf space were used in lieu of containers, the equivalent of a two-bin system can be achieved without the expense of special-purpose containers. The downside is all of the extra handling.
- *Option 2*—take the shipment as it comes. To send a visual cue for reorder, the box where the reorder point falls can be marked to indicate the need for replenishment. For instance, a sticker labeled *reorder* could be affixed to this container.

Example 2: Super-Sized Orders

There are times when quantity discounts are irresistible. For example, a buyer might take advantage of a price break at a quantity that is larger than the reorder quantity. In addition, if the entire order can fit into one crate, how should kanban be handled?

At the least, force fitting a conventional approach would entail a substantial amount of handling. In some cases, containers might have to be acquired. On the other hand, accommodating the crate will decrease the costs. Depending on the numbers, some possibilities include:

- If the difference between the actual and specified order quantity is small, diverting the difference to another box/container/skid can achieve the aim of a two-bin system. For example, if 300 pieces are ordered and the reorder point is 270, 30 pieces could be diverted to another box. By drawing from the smaller container first, a replenishment would be triggered when the box is emptied.
- Depending on the nature of the product, a partition could be used to apportion one section with the reorder point quantity. A reorder can be triggered once the first portion of the crate is emptied.

While some handling would be involved with either method, the amount should be substantially lower than strictly adhering to classic arrangements.

For any of the previous examples, possible approaches to transmit the reorder signal to the buyer include:

- *Cycle counts*—as part of a regular cycle count, scanning for items needing reorder can be added to the duties. If visual cues indicate the need for replenishment, the cycle counter can record and communicate this to purchasing.
- *Cards*—a card (or the equivalent) can be used. When an employee depletes the section/container/portion that has the card, the card can be transferred to a holding point that purchasing picks up on a scheduled interval.
- *Hybrid*—a combination of cards and cycle counting might be used. In addition to noting reorder points being breached, the cycle counter records whether the placeholder for kanban cards is up-to-date (e.g., card has been sent to purchasing). This way, the cycle counter can double-check against potential oversights.

With these examples representing only a fraction of the possibilities, it is pretty clear that kanban can take on a myriad of forms and is only limited by the imagination. Ultimately, the idea is to maximize kanban's advantages while minimizing its drawbacks.

SUMMARY

Kanban is used for everything from managing stock to shop-floor control. However, since QL mostly relies on DBR to manage workflow, inventory control is the primary area where kanban will be found in a QL system. In the first place, kanban has a track record of success in preventing inventory outages. In addition, the visual concepts are useful in multiple situations. Despite this, there are potential pitfalls and this chapter is geared to optimizing this tool by preventing the most common problems. Key points to remember include:

- *Deploy kanban based on need*—tool-obsessed companies often implement kanban without determining whether it's necessary. Before making the decision to apply this method, make sure that the product is delayed due to factors that kanban can address.
- *Kanban basics*—to help properly determine when to apply this method, be sure to have a grounding in kanban's basics and know the best times and situations to use it.
- *The best kanban is no kanban*—since kanban can require training and resources, simpler alternatives that achieve the same outcome are preferable. Ideally, perfect lean is so simple that nothing extra is needed.

Although technology and methods like DBR have reduced the need for kanban, this tool is conceptually powerful and remains useful in a wide array of settings. The most important takeaway from any study of kanban should be that the form it takes is irrelevant as long as the principles are upheld. Ultimately, when demand triggers the right signal being sent to the right resources at the right time, it's kanban whether bins and cards are used or not.

SIDEBAR—WE'VE ALWAYS DONE IT THIS WAY!

Although kanban is a powerful idea and does considerable good, the manual aspects of this approach get more obsolete by the day. Since these techniques were developed long before computers became so inexpensive, it would stand to reason that today's technologies have enabled approaches that bypass the need for much of what originally came with this tool. Ironically, as often as lean practitioners disparage the phrase, "We've always done

Continued

it this way!", it could be argued that the lean community itself has become a creature of habit. At the same time, it's just human nature, as even the most astute organizations can succumb to this. If you think well-run businesses are immune to "We've always done it this way!"—even a stellar company like Southwest Airlines may have fallen prey. Where their unreserved seating was once a major edge, changes in the industry since 9/11 have obviated many of the original reasons that this idea was so powerful.

Pre-9/11

In the beginning, the Southwest approach to loading planes was to issue plastic boarding passes that were sequenced. This method was simple and economical:

- No computer system was required to regulate boarding.
- The plastic passes were reusable. There was no need for printers, paper, and ink.
- When this system was developed, unassigned seating allowed for the fastest turnaround at the gate. This supported Southwest's flow-based approach.
- Unassigned seats allowed Southwest maximum flexibility in allocating planes and maximizing seat occupancy. If a flight sold fewer tickets, a smaller plane could be scheduled.

Post 9/11

After the 9/11 disaster, security rules changed to require that every passenger be positively identified before boarding a plane. Due to this, many benefits from unassigned seating were lost:

- Plastic boarding passes could no longer be used. Printers, paper, and ink were now required in order to link a boarding pass to a particular passenger; one benefit down.
- Additionally, computer systems were now needed to generate and administer boarding passes; two benefits gone.
- Researchers have devised quicker turnarounds that are compatible with reserved seating; third benefit bites the dust.
- With software advances, could Southwest develop an approach to reserved seating that would still allow flexibility in plane allocation? Maybe so! The fourth benefit might be a draw.

Additional benefits from adopting reserved seating:

- Southwest's 24-hour check-in window is inconvenient for customers. Reserved seating at the time of purchase would be easier.
- The present system that requires standing around before boarding is an imposition. While it helps stage the passengers to speed up the turnaround, more lemonade can come from this lemon.

Continued

- Southwest's present setup for boarding (see Figure 12.2) could be leveraged to further accelerate the boarding process. The stands could be devised to help passengers enter in the proper order.

Figure 12.2   Southwest boarding

Despite vastly changed circumstances, Southwest keeps their open seating policy. Although it may be driven by the facts on the ground, perhaps it's due to habit.

CHAPTER **13**

QUICK CHANGEOVER

In Quantum Lean (QL), the criticality of proper scheduling can't be overstated. Without it, efficiency improvements will be minimal. At companies with lengthy changeovers, the same can be said about setup reduction. If nothing is done to minimize the changeover time involved, a multitude of downstream effects will stymie any lean initiative. Some of the downsides include:

- *Decreased throughput*—any changeover time on a capacity constraint will come at the expense of a plant's production rate.
- *Increased work-in-process (WIP)/finished goods inventory (FGI)*—for every minute a machine is down, at least a minute's worth of product must be built up if subsequent processes need to keep working. On top of this, companies may need to stock a significant amount of finished goods to work around the longer lead times that result from the increased WIP.
- *Longer turnaround*—on top of the added lead time due to increased WIP, lengthy setups make companies reluctant to initiate new production runs. When a new run gets delayed, orders that a customer needs sooner will be released to the shop floor later. With delayed starts and longer turnarounds, customers end up with late orders and a company's competitive position gets compromised.
- *Resource*—obviously, time spent performing changeovers is time away from serving the product.

To address the problems, setup reduction techniques are available. Although it would be ideal to eliminate changeover altogether, reducing it so that setup has no influence on business decisions is all that's needed to achieve QL and makes for a more practical goal.[13-1] For example, a company that doesn't have changeovers affecting their actions would behave in the following ways:

- If 100 pieces of part XYZ are on order, only 100 pieces will be produced. No excess will be manufactured for finished goods inventory or to reduce unit costs.

- If order *A* for 100 widgets is due in week 1, order *B* for 100 thingamabobs is due in week 2, and order *C* for 100 widgets is due in week 3, a company will process orders *A*, then *B*, then *C*. There will be no effort to combine orders *A* and *C* into one production run.

In all likelihood, the decisions in the previous two scenarios would be different if the changeovers were lengthy. As American companies have historically minimized the number of changeovers to deal with long setups, it took Japan to come up with a new way to deal with this issue.

SINGLE MINUTE EXCHANGE OF DIES (SMED)

Although the downsides of long changeovers are bad enough in a vast nation like the United States, think about how disastrous they would be for a country like Japan. After World War II, the Land of the Rising Sun was establishing itself as a manufacturing force, but faced seemingly insurmountable barriers to reaching this goal:

- *No natural resources*—lacking energy and key minerals, Japan has to import critical supplies like oil and iron ore.
- *Minuscule space*—with mountains rendering much of the landscape unusable, this country only has a serviceable area the size of the state of Connecticut. For the geographically challenged, Connecticut is very small. Also, with this tiny landmass holding 100 million people, much of the real estate is already occupied.

Among the problems, the lack of usable space was particularly dire. With setup times in the automotive industry often taking several hours, the necessary buildup was staggering. As typical plants produce finished cars at a rate of one per minute, this implied a massive WIP level was needed to keep production running. When a country of 100 million only has the effective landmass of an American state, the space requirements this entails are unacceptable. To combat this problem, the Japanese committed themselves to eliminate setup time. From there, a setup reduction technique called SMED was born and the benefits poured in.

Where previous changeovers required hours of production time, SMED techniques were able to reduce this to minutes. By leveraging the weakness of limited space into the strength of rapid changeover, the Japanese performed an act of industrial Jujitsu. By repeating these types of feats across a wide range of endeavors, dominance in the auto industry was achieved by a country that started out as a 90-pound weakling.

SETUP REDUCTION

Setup reduction in QL is similar to SMED, but configured to harmonize into the QL framework. Essentially, it's the same procedure one would perform when improving any process:

- Develop a product path diagram (PPD) of the changeover process with the affected machine being the product:
  - The equipment is being served; therefore, it is being treated as the product.
  - If the manufactured article were considered the product, most of the setup would be treated as a delay. In turn, little insight would be gained from the PPD.
- Each step is only recorded if it occurs during a production run for a new manufactured article.
- Prioritize investigation of delays, conversions, or non-conversions according to the time accounted for by each source.

In addition to these basic steps, there are a couple of variations when it's time to apply the PPD:

- *Efficiency phase*—first, the goal is decreasing the real time involved with a setup.
- *Shifting phase*—after efficiency has been maximized, the focus moves to minimizing the setup time relative to the production run. In other words, this would involve shifting changeover tasks from occurring during production (*online*) to taking place at a different time and/or location (*offline*). While this does nothing to improve the speed of the tasks, it does eliminate setup times from an *online* standpoint. This is why the steps of a PPD are timed from the beginning of a production run. If a task is moved from online to offline, it will disappear from the PPD despite the fact that the task is not eliminated in an absolute sense. However, from the standpoint of the production run, these steps no longer exist.

The reason for splitting improvements into phases is that making tasks as quick as possible is generally cheaper than moving the steps from online to offline. Although both stages can be cost-effective, why not begin with more economical options? In addition, if the efficiency phase reduces setups to the point that they have no influence on business decisions, QL conditions can be achieved at a lower cost. Although examples have been given for applying QL improvement techniques to operations, demonstrating how it can be done with changeovers will give a clearer idea of how to implement QL setup reduction techniques.

SETUP REDUCTION—EXAMPLES

Spare Tire Change

A pit crew for a race car is often given as an example of a quick changeover. What would ordinarily take several minutes is done in seconds at the track. While a pit stop isn't a true changeover, setup reduction principles are used to minimize the time.

Although this example is frequently cited, what never seems to follow is an explanation of how the tasks were analyzed and revised. Until now! Among the multiple jobs that the pit crew performs, changing a spare tire is second nature to many and a good subject for illustrating improvement methods. Using PPD as the analysis tool and with the car defined as the product (Why? Because the car is being served), changing a spare tire can be diagrammed as in Figure 13.1.

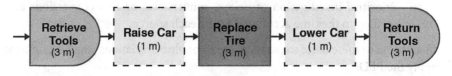

Figure 13.1   PPD: spare tire

For clarification on the steps:

- *Retrieve tools and spare tire*—although the car's trunk is opened and one might think of it as a non-conversion, the predominant nature of this element is handling tools and the spare tire. Since nothing is essentially happening to the product, this task is a delay.
- *Raise the car*—since it explicitly involves handling the car, this step is non-conversion.
- *Remove tire and put new one on*—a resource is devoting attention to the car and the task is not predominantly inspection, handling, rework, or movement. Therefore, it is conversion.
- *Lower the car*—the reverse of raising the car.
- *Put tools and flat tire in trunk*—the reverse of retrieving the tools.

Analysis

The times break down as follows:

- *Delay*—six minutes
- *Conversion*—three minutes
- *Non-conversion*—two minutes

The following sections describe possible ways to reduce the time spent doing those key tasks.

Delay

- 5S—the trunk is filled with junk and it's disorderly. Keep the trunk clean and organized.
- The bolt that locks down the spare and jacks are phenomenally long and take a while to remove. Replace with bolts that only require a few (or fewer) turns to loosen.

Conversion

- The lug-nut wrench that comes with the jack has to be taken off and re-positioned with every turn. Replacing it with a socket wrench will eliminate the need to remove and reposition the lug wrench.

Non-Conversion

- The screw jacks that comes standard with cars are as slow as Christmas. Replace it with a hydraulic jack that raises and lowers much more quickly.

With a new PPD as shown in the following diagram, the process should take about four minutes (see Figure 13.2).

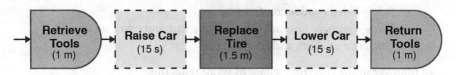

Figure 13.2   PPD: spare tire after improvements

Since it appears that the tasks are substantially minimized, the next step is analyzing tasks to be moved offline. For an example of an offline task, consider the spare tire itself. Although we are accustomed to the spare just being available, many tasks and resources are involved in their creation:

- Removing the old tire and mounting a new one to a rim. Without specialized equipment, this is a time-consuming task.
- Airing up a new tire requires a compressor.
- Balancing the tire necessitates specialized machines.

Without capital investment, these tasks would take quite a while. So much so that auto shops invest a great deal in machines to expedite the steps. Beyond this outlay, drivers tie up cash by stocking an extra tire and rim for roadside emergencies. In terms of ease and speed, moving spare tire preparation *offline* brings significant advantages. In fact, the benefits so outweigh the burdens that no one would even consider going without one. Moving tasks offline can be just as beneficial on the shop floor, but management is often reluctant to spend the money necessary to do it. Thankfully, executives aren't outfitting cars!

Example: Paint Booth

For paint booths, changeovers can be lengthy. This nonproductive time can be especially damaging as coating processes often set the pace for an entire operation. Any time lost on a bottleneck is a corresponding loss to overall plant capacity. To free up this time to serve the product, setup reduction will be deployed. With the paint equipment as the product, a PPD of a suboptimal changeover might resemble Figure 13.3.

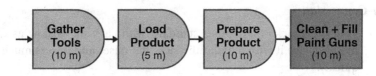

Figure 13.3   PPD: paint booth (Phase 1)

- *Delay*—gather materials and tools
- *Delay*—load product on fixtures
- *Delay*—prepare product (e.g., remove rust and mask surfaces)
- *Conversion*—clean and fill paint gun

To improve in the efficiency phase of setup reduction:

- Apply 5S to the paint area to speed up the gathering of tools and materials.

If this improvement is made, the PPD for the shifting phase will look like Figure 13.4.

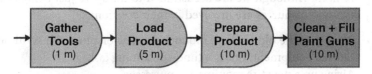

Figure 13.4   PPD: paint booth (Phase 2)

To streamline the setup in this phase, here are ideas to shift the time from online to offline:

- Have product preparation and loading performed before setup begins. This may require fabricating more fixtures.
- Have all tools and materials kitted and ready for the next setup. This will further shrink the time spent gathering tools and materials from the time that the production run begins.
- To allow the paint gun to be ready immediately for the next paint job, get a duplicate paint gun that can be cleaned and filled offline.

With these improvements, the PPD for a streamlined changeover looks like Figure 13.5.

Figure 13.5   PPD: paint booth after improvements

Essentially, by moving most tasks offline, there is virtually no setup for the paint operation. By making these tasks as efficient as possible in the first phase, the costs associated with changeover steps are also minimized.

Example (Machine Shop)[13-2]

In the machining sector, setups are a significant delay in practically every shop. However, with a QL approach and selective investments, substantial setup time reductions are possible. This example will analyze a changeover for a computer numerical control (CNC) lathe.

Phase 1

With the lathe as the product, the major highlights for a suboptimal setup might look like this (see Figure 13.6).

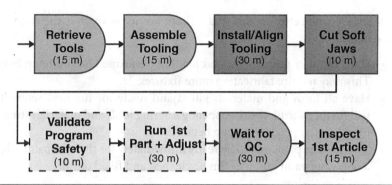

Figure 13.6   PPD: Lathe (Phase 1)

- *Retrieve tools and fixtures*—since nothing is happening to the CNC lathe, this is a delay.
- *Assemble tooling*—to allow workpieces to be turned, CNC lathes need cutting tools to be loaded. Before this loading can occur, cutting tools must be assembled. Since nothing is happening to the CNC lathe while tooling is being put together, this step is considered a delay.
- *Install tooling and align to machine*—during a setup, tooling often needs to be switched out. Once the tools are installed, they need to be aligned to the machine by measuring the tools and entering this information into the machine's computer. Since the CNC is being modified, this step is a conversion task.
- *Cut soft jaws*—to keep from marring workpiece surfaces, soft jaws may need to be used and this requires cutting softer material to prevent scratches. Since the chuck is a part of the machine and the chuck is being changed, it is a conversion step.
- *Validate program safety*—to prevent high-speed collisions of parts and cutting tools, a program is run under fail-safe conditions to verify that there aren't unforeseen errors that could cause damage to people, product, or property. This step is non-conversion due to being an inspection.
- *Run first part and adjust machine*—since there are variations in cutting forces, material stiffness, and ambient temperatures, settings on the CNC lathe must be fine-tuned so that accurate cutting can be *dialed in*. Since this is a form of *fixing* the program, this can be thought of as rework and hence it is classified as non-conversion.
- *Waiting for QC*—since this is a wait, it is a delay.
- *First-article inspection*—once a first piece is run, most shops verify that the program is producing accurate product by performing a comprehensive inspection and determining if the program needs further

adjustment. Since the manufactured article is being inspected and not the machine, this is a delay.

Although lathe changeovers may involve several steps beyond what is shown on this PPD, the ones included are common to most setups and useful for illustrating the QL setup-reduction process.

Analysis

The times break down as follows:

- *Delay*—75 minutes
- *Non-conversion*—40 minutes
- *Conversion*—40 minutes

CNC Lathe Phase 1

The possibilities for reducing the online times involved are listed here.

Delay

- Retrieve tools and fixtures—5S: have all tools and fixtures available and organized before setup is performed.
- First-article inspection
  - *Conditional approval*—create conditions where production can immediately start while first article inspections are performed. To assure that potentially defective product can't leave the facility until all specified inspections are successfully completed, implement positive recall procedures so that suspect and defective product can be retrieved and dispositioned should issues be found.
  - *Risk adjusted inspection procedures*—to minimize the need to invoke positive recall, specify first article inspections so that features most susceptible to being out of specification are verified first. If problems are found, it is most likely to be found on these dimensions. Catching them early will enable corrective action sooner and minimize the need to recall suspect product.
- Waiting for QC
  - *Visual techniques*—implementing andon (see Chapter 5 for information about andon) can improve notification of QC and improve this department's responsiveness.
  - *Quality@Source*—training and empowering production personnel to perform first article inspections will increase the

personnel available for inspections and decrease the delays associated with waiting on the QC department.

Conversion

- *Install tools and align to machine*—quick change tooling is available to significantly decrease tooling installation time. In addition, there are tool holders that are ultra-precision with absolutely certain lengths. These lengths can be entered into a machine without having to measure the tools.
- *Cut soft jaws*—many shops will cut soft jaws manually when they could be cut using a pre-developed program. In addition to cutting under superior conditions, a program will typically do it faster.

With the following ideas in place, the second phase PPD looks like Figure 13.7.

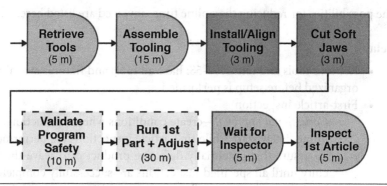

Figure 13.7 PPD: Lathe (Phase 2)

Analysis

The times break down as follows:

- *Non-conversion*—40 minutes
- *Delay*—30 minutes
- *Conversion*—6 minutes

With the times significantly reduced, moving online tasks offline offers additional time savings as follows:

- *Assemble tooling*—by acquiring duplicate tooling, cutting tools can be assembled ahead of time before a production run begins.

With this idea in place, the PPD after two phases looks like Figure 13.8.

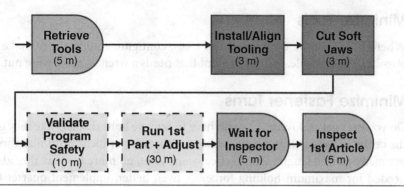

Figure 13.8   PPD: lathe after improvements

Analysis

The times break down as follows:

- *Non-conversion*—40 minutes
- *Delay*—15 minutes
- *Conversion*—6 minutes

With additional effort, training, and method improvement, setup times can be further reduced. Based on the PPD, the first priority for such efforts would be the non-conversion task of running the first part and adjusting the machine.

By pursuing QL approaches, excellent results are possible. Hopefully, the previous examples give a clearer idea of how setup reduction is done in a QL system. In addition to providing this guidance, the next section offers general tips that can help regardless of whether or not a company is lean.

SETUP REDUCTION—TIPS

In addition to a sound process, the following possibilities are available to support changeover reduction.

Quick Connects

Practically every plant has quick connects for compressed air connections. Despite this, there are occasions where setups would be significantly streamlined with them. This simply serves as a reminder to double check this possibility when investigating changeovers. This book would be remiss if this reminder were not mentioned.

Minimize Tools

Where hands can be used instead of tools, configure equipment to make this possible. For example, instead of a nut that needs a wrench, use a wing nut.

Minimize Fastener Turns

Do you ever get annoyed when you have to remove bolts that feel like they go to the center of the earth and have millions of threads per inch? Minimize threads per inch and bolt length. On practically any joint, no more than six threads are needed for maximum holding force.[13-3] Even better, implement quarter-turn fasteners and/or clamps wherever possible.

Anti-Seize Compound

Bolts get stuck, especially when metals are dissimilar or there are sharp tempera-ture fluctuations. If such possibilities exist, use anti-seize compound. Several years ago, I worked at a plant where the changeovers took hours. Many times, a culprit was that bolts would get stuck and extraordinary measures would have to be taken to remove them. Even though there was an experienced old hand who repeatedly recommended that anti-seize compound be used to prevent this, the other employees continued with business as usual. Some people simply refuse to listen.

Penetrating Oil

Sometimes, bolts get stuck despite the best efforts at prevention. When this hap-pens, it isn't always practical to apply heat. In addition, extra force may not work as there can be problems with rounding off bolt heads or stripping out recesses. While I have had mixed results with the use of penetrating oils like WD-40, they are better than nothing and some oils are significantly better than others. Based on testing, Liquid Wrench performs best across a wide variety of cases.[13-4] In addition, Sea Foam works well.[13-5]

Metrinch

When I was working on a car several years ago, I was at my wit's end when a bolt that I was trying to loosen wouldn't budge. Of course, the fastener head was rel-atively soft and excessive force would round it off. In addition, the spaces were tight and I couldn't easily get other types of tools in the space. It seemed hope-less until Metrinch tools entered the picture. Metrinches are specially designed sockets that absolutely grab bolt heads and will not round off the head under any circumstance. Since using them, my existing socket sets have collected dust. In fact, I am still irritated that I ever had to use the conventional kind. Look for these online and especially at sites like eBay.

Torx-Head Fasteners

In many cases, a fastener head is configured so that a screwdriver must be used to remove it. Unfortunately, Phillips head recesses are very common. In case you haven't noticed, they are extremely prone to stripping out. The bottom line is that the Phillips head is garbage. Fortunately, the Torx head does for recessed heads what Metrich does for hex-heads. With a Torx recess, the ease of fastener installation and removal is orders of magnitude greater than a Phillips head. If there are Phillips heads on equipment, banish them from the premises and replace them immediately with Torx. Future generations will thank you.

SUMMARY

At companies with lengthy changeovers, a multitude of negative effects will sty-mie any lean initiative. To minimize setup time, the QL techniques are similar to SMED, but harmonized to the QL framework. Basically, it's the same procedure one would perform when improving any process:

- Develop a PPD of the changeover process with the affected machine be-ing the product.
- Each step is only recorded if it occurs during a production run for a new manufactured article.
- Prioritize investigation of delays, conversions, or non-conversions ac-cording to how much time is accounted for by each source.

In addition to these basic steps, there are a couple of variations when it's time to apply the PPD:

- *Efficiency phase*—first, prioritize decreasing the real time involved with a setup.
- *Shifting phase*—after efficiency has been maximized, focus on minimiz-ing the setup time relative to the production run. In other words, this would involve shifting changeover tasks from occurring during produc-tion (online) to taking place at a different time and/or location (offline). While this does nothing to improve the speed of the tasks, it does elimi-nate setup times from an *online* standpoint.

Taken together, the QL phases take the same actions as SMED, but determining what to do is easier. As a final point, a QL goal for changeover should be reducing the time so that setups have no influence on business decisions. If this is followed, the benefits of lean will be realized without crossing the point of diminishing returns.

CHAPTER 14

QUANTUM LEAN MAINTENANCE (QLM)

Total productive maintenance (TPM) is a well-regarded and useful approach to maximizing equipment effectiveness. However, TPM is a resource-focused lean tool, and it can conflict with a Quantum Lean (QL) system unless the program is harnessed to serve the product. By diffracting TPM through a QL lens, the benefits of a maintenance program can be elevated while minimizing the drawbacks. However, doing this requires familiarity with the TPM program.

TPM BACKGROUND[14-1]

TPM consists of the following elements:

- *Autonomous maintenance*—as a first line of defense, operators are enlisted to monitor equipment conditions so that potential issues can be detected early and bigger problems are prevented. In addition, operators handle simple maintenance tasks so technician time can be freed up for jobs that require higher skill levels.
- *Early equipment management*—proactively specifying and/or designing equipment so it is more reliable, more durable, and/or easier to repair.
- *Focused improvement*—continuous improvement for TPM.
- *Quality maintenance: Quality@Source for TPM*—targets quality issues with improvement projects focused on removing root causes of defects.
- *Planned maintenance*—another word for predictive, preventative, scheduled, and/or any maintenance that is not triggered by an actual machine problem or breakdown.
- *Training and education*—training for TPM.
- *Health, safety, environment (HSE)*.
- *TPM in administration*.

Taken together, these elements constitute a comprehensive approach that weaves every phase of a company's operations into maintenance. However, when it is part of a larger lean undertaking, does it need to? Taken further, does the structure of this program best serve QL ends? The next section explores these questions.

QL AND TPM

Since most of TPM's pillars are implied or already covered by other lean tools, it could be argued that much of this program involves needless duplication. For example, if a lean tool such as visual techniques was handled the same way, it might look like this:

- Visual techniques
- Visual techniques—shop floor
- Visual techniques—office
- Visual techniques training
- Visual health, safety, and environmental
- Visual techniques—continuous improvement

However, it's not defined in this way. In fact, apart from TPM, no other lean tool is characterized this way either. A fair question is, "Why?"

While there's no window into the soul of the man who formulated TPM, his background was in maintenance—and the probable goal was to optimize this function. Therefore, it was fitting that he created a comprehensive system that addresses maintenance holistically. While this strategy makes sense from a maintenance-centric view, it breaks down in a QL framework. Instead of a situation where the product is the end and tools are a means, TPM can become an end in itself. In other words, the servant becomes a master. Since QL only has one boss, the challenge is harnessing TPM's power so that its actions revolve around the product's priorities. In that spirit, here is what maintenance with a QL twist would look like:

- *Maintain equipment function*—in QL, maintenance's first priority should be assuring that the product gets what it needs. In turn, this means that keeping processes capable is the first order of business. Specifically, the ability to produce parts at specified rates and quality levels should take priority. An example would be lubricating and cleaning moving surfaces on machine tools so that their ability to hold tolerances is maintained.
- *Minimize repair time*—since reducing equipment failure is often time consuming, minimizing repair times offers many facilities a better

near-term impact. To this end, the following tools can be used to accelerate repairs:

- *Andon*—andon reduces the time to signal breakdowns to support staff. In addition to increasing responsiveness, repair times are improved by apprising staff of the nature of the problem and its relevant location.
- *5S*—5S reduces repair time by organizing parts, information, and tools.
- *Inventory*—keeping an adequate supply of spare parts so that delays due to part outages are minimized.
- *Hiring practices*—although maintenance requires specialized knowledge, companies frequently hire personnel who are not equal to this task. Simply put, hiring competent technicians is indispensable for minimizing repair time.
- *Training*—while any field is subject to change, keeping technicians current reinforces good hiring decisions and prevents turnover. In turn, the reduced turnover minimizes the risk of hiring incompetent personnel.

• *Minimize equipment failure*—while QL assigns prevention a lower priority than streamlining repairs, this point carries a caveat. If prevention has a greater near-term impact on product delivery than optimizing repair time, prevention should carry the higher priority. With that being said, TPM elements that play a role in minimizing machine breakdowns include:

- *Planned maintenance*—while planned maintenance includes tasks that extend equipment life, initial emphasis should be on specifying actions that increase uptime.
- *Autonomous maintenance*—although autonomous maintenance is a separate line item in TPM, it's really just a subset of planned maintenance and should be thought of this way. Like planned maintenance, initial efforts should emphasize decreasing downtime.

Although maintenance should involve more than keeping a line running, the three-legged stool of functional equipment, rapid repair, and minimal breakdowns best serves QL's primary mission. Prioritizing anything else is detrimental to efficient operations. However, once this trinity is in motion, other objectives may enter the picture:

- *Extend equipment life*—the financial impact from extending equipment life is pretty significant. Elements of TPM that advance this include:
  - *Planned maintenance*—like assuring reliability, the routine tasks that extend equipment life should be a part of planned maintenance.
  - *Early equipment management*—proactively specifying and/or designing equipment so it is easier to work on, more reliable, and/or more durable. This would carry a higher priority in QL, but the rewards from this effort tend to be longer-term.
- *Improve maintenance efficiency*—pursuing improved maintenance efficiency risks undermining higher priority objectives should be approached with caution. However, if maintenance can be performed with less outlay and still serve the product, go for it.

As a capper, an ideal maintenance program should also include:

- *Feedback mechanisms*—any viable program should gauge:
  - *Effectiveness*—how well does the maintenance program perform with respect to the product? As they are generally indifferent to a product's time-in-system, many maintenance metrics undermine this goal.
  - *Fidelity*—how closely is the program followed? This question must be answered in order to distinguish whether the results are because of or in spite of the maintenance program:
    - *Program followed and results are bad*—probably means that the program needs to be revised.
    - *Program ignored and results are bad*—inconclusive, but means that the program needs to be followed before definitive conclusions can be drawn.
    - *Program ignored and results are good*—probably means that there are some highly competent people who are keeping things running. At the least, rethink the program and why it is being ignored.
    - *Program followed and results are good*—at the least, this means that the maintenance program is on an acceptable track.

From a QL perspective, the remainder of TPM is already addressed by other lean tools or otherwise provided for in any functional organization:

- *Focused improvement*—focused improvement is continuous improvement by another name. In the interest of minimizing duplication, no company that comprehensively pursues continuous improvement needs to embed this within maintenance.

- *Quality maintenance: Quality@Source for TPM*—like focused improvement being another word for continuous improvement, quality maintenance is Quality@Source by another name. Like continuous improvement, it is unnecessary to embed Quality@Source within maintenance.
- *Training and education*—training concerns every department and is in no way unique to maintenance.
- *HSE*—being integral to every lean tool, safety isn't unique to any particular one. Why single it out in maintenance?
- *TPM in administration*—regardless of the setting, maintenance is maintenance. There is no need to delineate it by department.

All in all, QL includes all of the TPM provisions, but is configured for product-centricity and to reflect that maintenance is part of a larger picture. Where the elements aren't explicitly called out, they are outsourced to other lean tools or company departments. Nevertheless, they are available when the need occurs.

QLM

While the approach to maintenance that was just described has the ingredients of TPM, there are key differences. It's like water and ice; although both are comprised of H_2O, no one would say the two are identical. Therefore, it makes sense to characterize the QL version under a new moniker. Since it is used to serve QL ends, it's called QLM. Again, for all intents and purposes, QLM can be thought of as TPM that's been tweaked to prioritize the needs of the product. To recap, the key elements of this approach include:

- Maintain equipment function
- Minimize repair time
- Minimize equipment failure
- Extend equipment life
- Improve maintenance efficiency
- Implement relevant feedback

Together, all of these elements represent the ultimate in QLM. If doing all of them is beyond the near-term capabilities of a company, the first three should be prioritized because they are maintenance's bottom line. The rest are useful, but shouldn't be pursued at the expense of the primary objectives.

With program definition out of the way, the task ahead is putting it all into play. To round out a QLM program, there are issues to address in human resources and computerized maintenance management that can make or break your results.

PERSONNEL

No matter how thoroughly a program is specified, it's all for naught without qualified personnel. To emphasize this point, consider two scenarios:

- Company A has excellent technicians, but no formalized maintenance program.
- Company B has mediocre technicians, but a formal maintenance program that is specified to the nines and followed to the letter.

If both plants have otherwise identical conditions, which one will run better? Anyone who's lived in the real world knows the answer is Company A. While it's ideal to get the best of both worlds with a great system and people, the upshot is that the first order of business for any successful maintenance program should be developing a sound approach to attracting and retaining competent personnel. If this flank isn't covered, QLM will end up being a worthless piece of paper. While finding and retaining good employees is always challenging, what follows are some little ideas that will make a big difference in this undertaking.

Specifying Requirements

In an ideal process, an applicant will be surveyed to determine his aptitude, skill, and attitude. Among a variety of reasons for bad fits, the inability to accurately evaluate talent stands out. Incorporating the following ideas will improve the chances of a great hire:

- *Relevant requirements*—when canvassing for talent, carefully determine where to cast your net. As good technicians aren't a-dime-a-dozen, the requirements that are imposed on a prospect should fit the need as closely as possible. Anything beyond this runs the risk of disqualifying what might be a good hand. As one example, some interviewers look for employees who can *fit in*. Although it's nice when you can get it, it's better to have a cantankerous guy who can fix equipment than a smooth talker who can't tell a nut from a bolt.
- *Skills versus credentials*—on technical job requirements, many businesses obsess over credentials. The problem is that sheepskins don't mean much without context. In many cases, it only indicates that the applicant is good at taking written tests. When practical application enters the

picture, things can start to break down. However, screening an applicant for both skill and credentials offers insights into a multitude of abilities:

- ▫ Reconciling theory and practice.
- ▫ Fulfilling duties.
- ▫ The capacity to handle paperwork.
- ▫ Perseverance—the ability to stick with the certification process suggests this.

While this principle can manifest itself in a myriad of ways, don't lose the key point. By gauging applicants on more than one dimension, a richer and more accurate picture of their capabilities emerges. In turn, the chances of a good fit increase substantially.

In addition to these principles, consider incorporating the following provisions when screening maintenance prospects:

- *Basic skills test*—at a minimum, verify that applicants can demonstrate facility with tools and the ability to select the correct ones. An advantage to such a basic test is that it is a quick and inexpensive way to screen out candidates who are abjectly unqualified.
- *Advanced skills*—if basic trials are passed, verify that the prospect can demonstrate the ability to perform some of the repairs that they would be expected to perform. For example, when hiring an electrician, have him set up measurements on various circuits (unpowered, of course) like he might find in your shop. If he can't do this, what are the odds he/she is a good fit?
- *Troubleshooting ability*—if a candidate has the right skills, consider him/her. If he/she also demonstrates the ability to diagnose a problem in a logical and systematic way (i.e., troubleshooting), hire him/her immediately. While skills are essential, troubleshooting ability is that rare quality that elevates a technician to the next level. On average, this person will arrive at the right answer in the quickest and least expensive way. Troubleshooting tests are available online.

Beyond the bottom-line skills requirements, add as few criteria as possible. By properly screening candidates for actual abilities, you should be able to improve or preserve the quality of the maintenance workforce.

PLANNED MAINTENANCE

A maintenance program enumerates tasks, defines them, and specifies affected equipment and personnel. In addition, maintenance intervals, documentation, procedures, tools, supplies, and retained records need to be determined. It's simple, but implies a lot of work—I repeat, *a lot* of work.

The bottom line is that choosing your battles will be critical if you are just beginning a formal program. In the desire to be comprehensive, it is tempting to add every single job and machine to the program. However, it's very easy to end up with a bunch of incompletely specified tasks that are only partially deployed. To avoid this fate, there are some issues to think about when beginning a program.

Start Small

As previously stated, planned maintenance (computerized maintenance management [CMM] especially) can be very data-intensive and require a great deal of investigation. To keep things manageable, start with a few high-priority activities. Once the specification and implementation of these jobs are successful, proceed with a few more. It's probably better to have one task done right than several done poorly.

Prioritize according to the following order:

- Tasks that maintain equipment function
- Tasks that will decrease breakdowns
  - *Bottleneck*—incorporate tasks that benefit the bottleneck first. This helps maximize plant capacity.
  - *Risk profile*—a machine that can shut down production should have higher priority than one that won't.
  - *Expected downtime*—the longer the potential downtime, the higher the priority should be.
- Tasks that extend equipment life

SIDEBAR—MAINTENANCE AND UPTIME DON'T ALWAYS GO HAND IN HAND

A stubborn, widespread, and dismaying misconception is that all maintenance improves uptime. The reality is that different tasks have different benefits. Some extend life, others increase reliability, and a few do both. While increased durability and decreased downtime are great, it is important to keep these distinctions in mind. In the case of production, the priority should be improving reliability. Although important, extending equipment life should

Continued

---

be the second objective. To illustrate the point, consider some typical car maintenance tasks:

A. Oil change
B. Transmission fluid change
C. Inspect belts
D. Inspect tires
E. Change air filter
F. Change spark plugs
G. Inspect windshield wiper blades
H. Maintain brakes

Of the actions from the preceding list, *C*, *D*, *G*, and *H* predominantly concern uptime. By contrast, *A*, *B*, *E*, and *F* primarily affect durability. In other words, the former tasks will be prioritized in a QL setting and the latter would be elevated if long life were the main objective. Where the product is concerned, maximizing uptime and minimizing delay should be the top concerns. Since setting up a maintenance program requires significant effort, keeping this point in mind is critical for assuring the quickest path to a QL operation.

Rethink Job Tickets

Although it's not a part of planned maintenance, conventional wisdom suggests that job tickets should be issued for repairs so that a history of breakdowns can be compiled. As the thinking goes, uptime, parts usage, and other associated information about equipment reliability can be gleaned. From there, improvement can become more data-driven. Although this idea tends to be a triumph of hope over experience, some companies will require such information to be recorded and kept.

If such data must be gathered, leverage office 5S techniques (see Chapter 11 for more information) to make recordkeeping less painful and improve the odds of accurate data collection. For example, forms that incorporate checkboxes and are preprinted to the maximum extent will simplify and accelerate data entry. These tickets can be distributed to maintenance personnel or production supervision ahead of time and then used as breakdowns occur. Advantages from this include:

- Easier and quicker recordkeeping.
- Repair jobs are more likely to be recorded.
- Accurately recorded downtime—since production supervisors love having explanations for production shortfalls, involving them in this process improves the chances that downtime will be recorded.

- Easier parts tracking—if a company has a parts crib, using unique iden-
tifications on each job ticket allows a rapid assignment of parts issued to
a particular repair. By extension, tracking is easier.
- Removing technicians from the process—if a CMM requires job tickets,
one can be issued after a completed form is turned in and technicians
don't have to be involved in computerized data entry.

With a well-defined structure, highly-qualified personnel can take their performance to the next level. Of course, a question that might follow is, "How can
you know whether all of this work amounts to anything?" In the next sections,
metrics to answer this question are explored.

OVERALL EQUIPMENT EFFECTIVENESS (OEE)[14-2, 14-3]

Most programs like to keep score and maintenance is no exception. A frequently
used metric is called OEE. While this measurement has a lot of utility, it can be
easily misused due to its resource-centricity. Nevertheless, if it's evaluated with
product-centricity in mind, it is highly beneficial. In particular, OEE consists of
the following formula:

$$OEE = Q \times P \times A$$

where:

- Q: quality = (total qty of good product)/(total qty of product made) =
% yield
- P: performance = (actual speed)/(specified speed)
- A: availability = (up time)/(scheduled time)

This measure can be applied to one piece of equipment or to an entire facility.
The following is an example of how OEE may be applied.

Simple Example: Machine Level

A machine is scheduled to operate over a 10-hour shift with two 15-minute
breaks and a 30-minute lunch period. Over this shift, the machine was down
for 30 minutes. With a capacity to process 100 units per hour, the machine

produced 700 pieces over the shift. Furthermore, out of the 700 units made, 7 were scrapped.

- Q: quality = (total qty of good product)/(total qty of product made) = $(700 - 7)/700 = 693/700 = 99\%$
- A: availability = (up time)/(scheduled time) = $(10 \text{ h} - 15 \text{ m} - 15 \text{ m} - 30 \text{ m} - 30 \text{ m})/(10 \text{ h} - 15 \text{ m} - 15 \text{ m} - 30 \text{ m}) = 8.5 \text{ h}/9 \text{ h} = 94\%$
- P: performance = (actual speed)/(designed speed) = (actual qty produced over uptime)/(ideal qty produced over uptime) = $700/850 = 82\%$

$$\text{OEE} = Q \times P \times A = 99\% \times 82\% \times 94\% = 77\%$$

In principle, OEE is simple enough. In practice, it can get more complicated. However, the good news is that returning to OEE's essentials will go a long way in making matters a lot simpler.

OEE DATA COLLECTION

"Never sacrifice truth on the altar of accuracy."

Weldon Steel

"Nobody should try to use data unless he has collected data."

W. Edwards Deming

"Whenever there is fear, you will get wrong figures."

W. Edwards Deming

Despite the fact that OEE can be a good measure of program effectiveness, the way it is generally explained has downsides:

- Calculating OEE at the facility level can be complicated.
- The way OEE is explained tends to lock people into one way of collecting data.

As an example of how bad it can get, consider this OEE data collection sheet that is frequently used in industry (see Figures 14.1 and 14.2).

OEE Observation Form

Equipment ID and Description:

Location in Facility:

Observer:

Date:

Start From	End To	Run Time	Idling and Minor Stoppages				Breakdowns		Setup & Adj.	Startup	Reduced Speed	Defects & Rework	Comments
			Jam	Tool	Material	Other	Belt						
Totals													

Figure 14.1 Overall equipment effectiveness form (blank)

OEE Observation Form

Equipment ID and Description: Vertical Turret Lathe   **Date**: 1/24/24

Location in Facility: Machine Shop   **Observer**: John Doe

Start From	End To	Run Time	Idling and Minor Stoppages				Breakdowns	Setup & Adj.	Startup	Reduced Speed	Defects & Rework	Comments
			Jam	Tool	Material	Other	Belt					
6:00 am	6:10 am											Toolbox meeting
6:10 am	8:00 am							110				
8:00 am	11:00 am	180										
11:00 am	11:05 am			5								
11:05 am	Noon	55										Lunch
Noon	12:30 pm						120					
12:30 pm	1:10 pm	40										
1:10 pm	3:10 pm								110			
3:10 pm	4:00 pm	50										
Totals		325		5			120	110	110			

Figure 14.2 Overall equipment effectiveness form (filled out)

Example—Filling Out an OEE Chart

Drilling down on the example OEE form, consider some of what is involved in filling it out:

- *Breakdowns*—every time a machine is down, an operator must document the nature of the breakdown, the time it started, and the time it ended. Frequently, details surrounding the breakdown need to be provided in the comments field. If such occurrences are frequent enough, this could become a major distraction.
- *Reduced speed*—if equipment slows down, this form requires recording the time the event began and the time it ended. In all likelihood, this also means that the nominal and reduced rate needs to be documented in the comments field. A big problem is that an employee will have to estimate the compromised rate. Often, there won't be a clear-cut way to do this. If there is, it might not be easy. Ultimately, the prospect of an accurate number isn't good.
- *Setup*—since setups are often infrequent and lengthy at many companies, this is probably the easiest data to collect. If a changeover takes two hours and occurs every other day, it's reasonable to ask an employee to spend two or three minutes to record the times.
- *Idling and minor stoppages*—in contrast to setup, asking operators to fill out the times associated with idling and minor stoppages is probably excessive. As one example, quick adjustments to compensate for misfeeds are common. Put another way, spending minutes to document a stoppage that takes seconds is questionable.

In addition to distracting the workforce from its primary mission (which is . . . ?), there is a whole host of problems with approaching data collection this way:

- *Cost*—although QL is about the product, consider the potential cost of this data collection in terms of resource time (see Figure 14.3).

	Avg Frequency	Avg # Per Hour	Avg Time To Document	Minutes Per Hour
Breakdowns	1x / 10 hours	0.10	1	0.10
Setups	1x / 4 hours	0.25	1	0.25
Minor Stoppage	5x / 1 hour	5.00	1	5.00
Reduced Speed	1x / 3 hours	0.33	1	0.33
Total				5.68

Figure 14.3   OEE data collection time

Even with a minimal amount of time required to fill out an OEE form per incident, the collective time per hour amounts to almost 10% of an operator's time that could be given to the job.

- *Accuracy*—considering the potential inconvenience associated with collecting OEE data, don't be too surprised if the resulting information is inaccurate. Many shop-floor employees are outdoorsy types who consider paperwork useless, boring, or even intimidating. Over time, this can manifest itself in the following ways:

  - Timeliness—often, people procrastinate on tasks that they do not enjoy. When the form is eventually filled out, details inevitably get lost.

  - Missing information—a further casualty from waiting to record information is that there will be events that are not captured at all.

  - Accuracy—even if the information is gathered in real time, don't bet that it's accurate. It will probably be estimated, and that may not be good enough to arrive at valid conclusions.

  - Management expectation—in addition to problems on the floor, there can be a tendency to sugarcoat information before it gets kicked upstairs. After all, with measurement comes accountability. If a metric like OEE gets adopted, chances are fair that expectations will soon follow. When this happens, supervision understands that they need to hit the number regardless of whether the underlying process really does.

Ultimately, approaching data collection the way that was just described is subject to pitfalls. With the level of attention required, it may be unrealistic to expect good information. In the defense of those who use traditional approaches to data collection, the example OEE form was created by experts—and regular people tend to defer to professionals. However, if all of the costs were counted in the beginning, their approach would probably be different. What follows is one alternative way to think about gathering OEE data.

Data Collection—An Alternative Approach

When thinking about data collection, considering a metric at an elemental level is a good place to start. Put another way, what is OEE really about? Distilling it into its essence, OEE can be thought of as:

OEE = (what actually happened)/(what should ideally happen)

Thinking of OEE along this line is liberating and it allows a corresponding increase in flexibility. In other words, if one of the OEE factors infrequently occurs or is otherwise insignificant, why not disregard it? For example, in a setting where a machine either works at full speed or it doesn't work at all, speed reduction isn't relevant and should be ignored.

Example: Alternative Method

A machine is scheduled to operate over a 10-hour shift with two 15-minute breaks and a 30-minute lunch period. Over this shift, the machine was down for 30 minutes. With a capacity to process 100 units per hour, the machine produced 700 pieces over the shift. Furthermore, out of the 700 units made, 7 were scrapped.

OEE = (what was actually produced)/(what should ideally be produced)

Over 9 hours of scheduled work at 100 units per hour, 900 units should be made. As 693 good units were produced, this translates into an OEE score as follows:

$$OEE = (693)/(900) = 77\%$$

Wasn't that easy?

Summary

OEE is a powerful metric for measuring maintenance effectiveness. However, even with streamlined and accurate data collection, a remaining weakness of OEE is that it could show a perfect score of 100% while the product's time-in-system remains high. And where's the victory in that? To supplement this metric, a measurement called overall product effectiveness (OPE) exists to address this shortcoming.

OPE

While OEE has its merits, OPE is another way to account for all aspects of productivity. In typical lean thinking, a perfect value stream is one that flows and where all activities are exclusively value-added. While QL's theoretical goal is zero time-in-system, the OPE metric borrows from conventional lean principles. By comparing a product's actual time-in-system to its sum of standard conversion times, a company can have an idea of where an implementation stands. Although it shouldn't be the ultimate objective, a product path solely comprised of conversion times would still represent exceptional performance. With this in mind, OPE is defined as follows:

$$OPE = I/A$$

where:

- I: ideal time-in-system for conversion tasks = (total of standard conversion times + ([job quantity − 1] × takt time))
- A: actual time-in-system

Points to Clarify

- *Job quantity*—in job shops, it is easier to track an entire order than it is to follow one piece. Consequently, OPE allows for this by including the term that corrects I for job quantity:

  (Job quantity − 1) × takt time

  Ideally speaking, this term must be used for orders that include more than one piece. Since a job shouldn't ship until an entire order is ready to go, there is an inherent batching involved at the end of fulfillment. This is true even if one-piece flow is used everywhere else in a facility. Since this batching is built-in to even the most ideal situations, the time required for one batch is included in the calculation.

- If a piece is being tracked that isn't tied to a job, consider the order quantity to be 1. In such cases, the term that corrects for job quantity ends up being zero and OPE's numerator reduces to just the sum of conversion times.

With OPE, it's only possible to have a good score if the time-in-system is low compared to conversion times. It also requires machines that are functional and running at normal operating speeds. In other words, it is a metric that is consistent with good flow and resource utilization.

OPE Example

A product has several conversion operations that total four hours. Based on the date/time stamps for an order of 101, the time that the job stayed on the shop floor was 100 hours. In addition, the takt time is 15 minutes or .25 hours. Solving for OPE:

- Total of standard conversion times = 4 hours
- Job quantity = 101

- Takt time = .25 hours
- A = actual time-in-system = 100 hours
- I: ideal time-in-system for conversion tasks = (total of standard conversion times + ([job quantity − 1] × takt time)) = (4 hours + ([101 − 1] × .25 hours)) = (4 hours + ([100] × .25 hours)) = (4 hours + 25 hours)) = 29 hours

$$\text{OPE} = \text{I/A} = 29 \text{ hours}/100 \text{ hours} = 29\%$$

Despite the fact that a time-in-system of 100 hours wouldn't seem impressive at first glance, knowing that 29% of this example's time is due to conversion and the fact that the job quantity is 100 pieces puts a different spin on it. When typical companies can only trace 5% of fulfillment time to conversion tasks, it turns out that this example actually represents decent achievement.

In addition to offering a relative perspective on performance, an edge from collecting OPE is that operators are free to do their work without the distraction of data collection. Like any measurement, there will come a point where considerable headway has been achieved and the next order of business is looking at resource utilization. While OEE addresses this, it offers an incomplete picture since equipment only represents one facet of a company's resource base. To expand on the idea that drives OEE, a measurement called overall resource effectiveness (ORE) can be employed.

ORE

As a supplement to OEE, ORE is a good measure that can work for man or machine and is defined very similarly to OEE:

$$\text{ORE} = Q \times P \times A$$

where:

- Q: quality = (total qty of good product)/(total qty of product made) = % yield
- P: performance = (total of ideal cycle time × qty produced)/(total of utilized times)
- A: availability = (total of utilized time)/(time allotted)

Whether evaluating man or machine, this formula works. However, make sure that OPE isn't compromised when maximizing ORE. While time-in-system is the ultimate measure, it's hard to lose when tracking OEE, OPE, ORE if the product's time-in-system is kept front and center.

SUMMARY

Ultimately, great maintenance is simple, but it's not easy. The elements of QLM are:

- *Maintaining equipment function*—like QL, maintenance's first priority should be assuring that the product gets what it needs. In turn, this means that keeping processes capable is the first order of business. Specifically, the ability to produce parts at the specified rate and quality is maintenance's first order of business.
- *Minimize repair time*—regardless of equipment condition, the next priority should be minimizing the time it takes to fix production breakdowns. In the near term, maintenance's biggest impact on timely deliveries can be made by minimizing the time it takes to repair equipment. While preventing breakdowns is preferable, achieving significant reductions in failure rates can require a great deal of time and investment.
- *Minimize equipment failure*—while prevention may carry a lower priority than streamlining corrective action, this point carries a caveat. If working on prevention has a greater near-term impact on product delivery than optimizing repair time does, make prevention a higher priority.
- *Extend equipment life*—the financial impact from extending equipment life can be significant.
- *Improve maintenance efficiency*—since pursuing this objective can easily undermine higher-priority objectives, tread carefully. However, if maintenance can be performed with less outlay and still serve the product, feel free to go full speed ahead.
- *Feedback mechanisms*—any viable program should gauge:
  - *Effectiveness*—how well does the program perform with respect to the product? This point is critical. At best, maintenance metrics are typically indifferent to a product's time-in-system. At worst, they actually undermine this goal.
  - *Fidelity*—how closely is the program followed? This question must be answered to distinguish whether the results are because of or in spite of the maintenance program.

In addition, addressing the following will take something that looks great on paper and make it fly under real conditions:

- *Human resources*—no matter how well a program is specified, it's all for naught without qualified maintenance personnel. In addition, hire machine operators that don't abuse equipment.

- *Equipment*—if you have competent technicians and allow them a major say in equipment acquisitions, reliable and functional equipment will come as sure as night follows day.
- *Environment*—in addition to hiring people who can take care of equipment, controlling workplace temperature and cleanliness will have major benefits on equipment life and long-term function.
- *Tender-loving care*—in addition to providing a sheltered environment, try to run equipment under less-than-maximum loads. Doing so carries disproportionate benefits.

With a lot of lean principles, sound business practice, and a little common sense, the prospects for QLM are quite promising.

CHAPTER 15

VISUAL/AUDIBLE/TACTILE WORKPLACE

"The more you say, the less you say."

Frank Chimero

"When it comes to communication, less is more. Period."

Steve Tobak

"You say it best when you say nothing at all."

Paul Overstreet and Don Schlitz

Visual workplace is an approach to improve communication using simple visual techniques. Beyond 5S (workplace organization) and andon, this tool involves deploying different means to raise visibility of workplace issues including:

- *Huddle boards*—a tool for visualizing work and workflow. Huddle boards are often whiteboards that include cards or sticky notes to show status, progress, and issues related to a project (see Figure 15.1).

Figure 15.1 Huddle board

- *One-point lessons (OPLs)*—a tool used to educate operators to improve operations. The main point of learning is written in one or two sentences accompanied by photos (see Figure 15.2).
- *Key performance indicator (KPI) boards*—boards that display progress against KPIs to help track and reach objectives (see Figure 15.3).
- *Kanban/task boards*—see Figure 15.4.

As the thinking goes, signaling of this kind improves information flow and raises awareness of problems in the workplace. Furthermore, isn't anything that increases awareness desirable? Maybe. But then, maybe not.

One-Point Lesson

Location :	Area :	Line :	OPL#	IM02
Home	Kitchen	N/A	Rev#	0
			Date	2/22/22

Theme : Best Practices

Objective : Food & Energy Conservation and Safety

Prepared by : Mom

Aproved by : Mom

Type:
- ☑ Safety
- ☑ Basic Knowledge
- ☐ Improvement Cases
- ☐ Trouble Cases

Close the refrigerator door once you retrieve the food/beverage you need. The door should be closed anytime you are not using the refrigerator. Food can spoil and energy is wasted if this is not done!

Figure 15.2 OPL

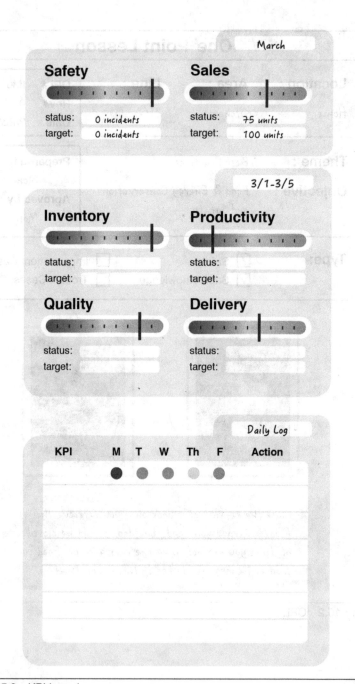

Figure 15.3 KPI board

Figure 15.4   Kanban/task board (image by Gerd Altmann, https://pixabay.com/)

VISUAL WORKPLACE—PITFALLS

Frequently, in the desire to keep everyone apprised about everything, problems can come up:

- *Style over substance*—with visual workplace, form can take precedence over function. In other words, appearances may be emphasized at the expense of anything useful happening. This phenomenon manifests itself in bells and whistles that may gratify some parties, but that do nothing for the product. One example you might find is a plant with OPLs that elaborate on topics that everyone already knows. I have seen OPLs on washing hands, keeping shoelaces tied, and the need to keep items in designated spots. What are the odds that employees aren't aware that shoelaces need to be tied, hands need to be washed, or that stuff needs to be put away?
- *Information overload*—a desire to expand communication can end up drowning the recipient in a sea of data. Even if useful information exists amidst all this content, the trivial many can drown out the vital few.
- *Inconvenience*—boards don't update themselves. Frequently, shop-floor workers are assigned to collect and disseminate these data. By the same token, this activity takes time away from the product.

- *Lack of utility*—aside from 5S, kanban, and andon, my experience with visual workplace is that most of the tools aren't useful to the shop floor. Instead of being an aid to operations, it could be argued that these tools are both unhelpful and high maintenance.
- *Apathy*—if the information conveyed is useful, will anyone look at it? My sources say no.

Despite the exercise in negativity in the previous list, visual tools actually have something to offer. The trick lies in knowing when to use them and, more important, when not to.

VISUAL WORKPLACE—WHEN

Problems with visual workplace can frequently be traced to organizations that start with a lean tool as a solution and then search for problems to which it may be applied. By contrast, Quantum Lean (QL) starts with the product and uses a product path diagram (PPD) to determine what is keeping the product from getting what it needs. If visual methods will eliminate the identified barriers, they may be useful. If such tools won't help, QL looks elsewhere. Put another way, creating a visual workplace should end up with the product being served better, faster, and cheaper.

Example—PPD and Visual Methods

In a plant that fabricates sheet metal parts, an example PPD was shown earlier in this book and revealed the following delays (see Figure 15.5).

Two delays that can be arguably traced to a lack of timely information are:

- *Wait for program*—the need for a program was not properly communicated and caused a delay in initiating the cutting process.
- *Wait for forklift*—in the example, the cutting table operator communicates to the forklift operator in the middle of another job. In addition to a resource being busy, there could be other situations where a forklift is in a distant location and a delay is caused from waiting for the forklift to travel to pick up materials.

Although the problems are associated with a lack of communication, it may or may not mean that visual techniques are the best way to address them. In many situations, implementing alternative material handling methods may be a better idea for addressing forklift-related delays. In addition, the production planning stage is possibly a better target for ensuring that a program reaches the cutting

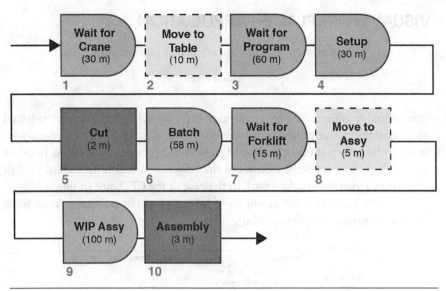

Figure 15.5 PPD: fabrication

table at the right time. However, there will be times that visual methods are the best answer and the PPD will be a first indication that this is the case.

Beyond the idea that visual methods are considered when delays can be traced to unclear, incomplete, or incorrect information, additional questions should be answered in this sequence before going any farther with visual tools:

- Do the tools have a realistic chance of influencing the issue? If the answer is no, do something else.
- Is visual workplace the best way to address this problem? If another approach will probably work better, table the visual approach.

As a case in point, an OPL for keeping shoelaces tied fails the QL test on every level. Nowhere on a PPD will it ever show delays being traced to employees failing to keep shoelaces tied. Furthermore, the idea that employees will fly right once an OPL is issued is preposterous.

A huddle board could be considered a borderline case. Although they are often window dressing to give the impression that things are being done, huddle boards might help a company under the right conditions. I haven't seen it personally, but then again, I haven't visited every facility in the world either! If a huddle board can genuinely help employees solve shop-floor problems, consider it. When in doubt, ask the people who will have to use them and respect their answer if they tell you no.

VISUAL WORKPLACE—APPLICATION

"Great shop-floor control is worth a million words."

Weldon Steele

Once visual techniques are selected, priority for applying them should be based on proximity to the product and the time frame involved. The person who receives the information should be as close to the product as possible. In other words, shop-floor workers who serve the product in real time should benefit most from a visual workplace tool. In the case of the CEO, not so much.

To clarify, here are some examples of how appropriate common visual tools are in a QL system (see Figure 15.6).

	Example	Proximity	Timeframe	Priority
Andon Board	Speed up response to machine breakdowns	Yes	Yes	High
Shadow Board	Reduce retrieval time for shop floor tools	Yes	Yes	High
5S	On maintenance tools to speed up repair time on shop floor	Yes	Yes	High
KPI Board		No	No	Zero

Figure 15.6   Visual tools and QL

Once visual techniques have passed these hurdles, additional points to consider include:

- *Determining the minimal information to convey*—anything beyond the bare bones of what the product needs has a good chance of being a hindrance
- *Specifying effective means of communication*
- *Disseminating information conveniently*—it is desirable to make information gathering and dissemination as convenient as possible and leave the task to people who don't work on the shop floor
- *Providing information at the lowest cost and with the least effort*

Tools

You may have gathered that many visual techniques don't make the grade with QL. A question that might follow is, "What does?" The simple answer is that whatever provides the most efficient way to communicate in a timely, accurate, and understandable manner.

With the exceptions of concepts like kanban, QL shies away from recommending a standardized approach. As there are so many ways to visually communicate, it is unlikely that a few standardized methods like task boards could adequately address even a fraction of the possibilities. With that being said, here are some guidelines for visualizing an organization:

- *Minimize the need for communication*—minimizing the amount of information that needs to be conveyed goes a long way toward improving communication. The improved focus that comes from decreased complexity allows employees to execute without distraction. Some ideas include:
  - Properly implementing QL indirectly minimizes the need for explicit information. For example, eliminating work-in-process inventory (WIP) eliminates the need for instructions on handling.
  - To the greatest extent possible, communications should ultimately be about benefiting the product. For example, companies can impose 5S to such dizzying levels that employees are left bewildered and resentful. Keeping a product-based focus will minimize the worker's load.
  - The thinner the rule book, the better. Minimize rules to only what's absolutely necessary and simplify from there.
- *Leverage shop-floor control as a communication medium*—the way a company manages flow speaks volumes about workplace status. Implementing a scheduling system like drum-buffer-rope and coupling it with first-come, first-served inherently communicates job priority to the shop floor without saying a word.
- *Don't shy away from computers*—many lean techniques were developed when computers were gigantic, expensive, and inferior to today's pocket calculators. It would stand to reason that companies like Toyota used cards and other manual methods to control production at that time. It was all that was available. Even though computers are now ubiquitous and cheap, many still deploy sticky notes, cards, and other non-electronic methods to convey information. While manual techniques are sometimes more effective, these cases are becoming fewer by the minute. For the most part, judiciously using computers will be better, faster, and cheaper.
- *Engage every sense possible*—although the assumption is that everyone is visual first, some people's auditory sense is their strength, where others might be tactile. With disabilities, some may be missing at least one

sensory function. In other words, why not engage as many senses as possible? With smartphones, this is possible.

General Method

While there can't be a cut-and-dried procedure for identifying when visual techniques should be used, here are some instances where visual workplace might help:

- *Scrap and rework*—if scrap or rework is consistently occurring at a specific task, this tool may be helpful if operators are getting information and/or feedback that is inadequate or untimely. For example, some general approaches are listed in Figure 15.7.

Example	Proximity	Timeframe	Rating
Key features are highlighted or in specified locations on blueprints/specification sheets. Operator can explicitly know their requirements without hunting around the document.	Operator that serves product	Proactive	Good
Automatic measurement of critical features that alert the operator when machine adjustments must be made.	Yes	Yes	Better
Automatic measurement of critical features that make adjustments and alert the operator when machine adjustments have been made.	Yes	Yes	Best

Figure 15.7   Scrap: visual feedback

- *Inventory outages*—orders that are communicated too slowly or inaccurately can make good candidates for visual communication. In addition, visuality may come in handy if breaches in reorder points are difficult to detect. On the shop floor, cues can be used to indicate the need for supplies or materials. Examples of some approaches are detailed in the deep-dive chapter on kanban.
- *Breakdowns and slowdowns*—visual communication may decrease the time it takes to respond to a breakdown and to further decrease time to repair.
- *Misplaced tools and inventory*—time spent looking for tools and materials typically represents a rich target for visual approaches. Methods to deal with this are detailed in the chapter on 5S.

- *Failure to follow priority*—whether it's done with shop floor control or visual methods, priority must be explicitly communicated in a way that everyone understands it. Otherwise, there will be chaos and orders will get out late.
- *Waiting delays*—in instances where the product is waiting for material handling or quality control, could better signaling decrease the response time?

While there will always be more targets for visual techniques, the enumerated situations represent good candidates where one should entertain using such methods.

SUMMARY

Visual workplace is a powerful option for improving communication and business performance. However, the key to fully reaping the benefits lies in honoring QL principles. While many companies start with solutions like huddle boards or OPLs and look for problems to apply them to, strictly utilizing these techniques based on product requirements will result in a much better fit. In addition, following QL principles will help an organization minimize unnecessary expenditures on tools that look good, but offer little substance.

CHAPTER **16**

STANDARD WORK

As delays and non-conversions disappear, there comes a point where conversions show up on Quantum Lean's (QL) radar. To minimize the latter sources of time, standard work is often used. In addition to reducing labor costs, substantial benefits can accrue when variation reduction is done at the same time. In many cases, this lean tool can even reduce the delays that still exist. Like quick changeover, the product path diagram (PPD) is the key tool used to achieve efficient and consistent work.

STANDARD METHODS—TASK TIME

To minimize task times, a PPD is the starting point. Like an atom that consists of subatomic components, conversion steps can generally be subdivided into conversions, delays, and non-conversions. And in the same manner that an operation gets streamlined, individual jobs can be improved. Although conversions should account for the lion's share of time, the priority of attack should go where the majority of time lies. If conversions get reduced so much that non-conversion steps occupy a majority of time, non-conversion should be prioritized.

Example—Peanut Butter and Jelly (PB&J) Sandwich

This analysis involves making a PB&J sandwich in a kitchen with ingredients located as shown in the following diagram (see Figure 16.1).

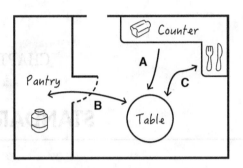

Figure 16.1   Kitchen layout: Phase 1

If the person making the PB&J isn't particularly organized, they proceed in the order indicated on the ensuing list. For the sake of brevity, a few immaterial details are skipped in this description:

A. Obtain the bread from the kitchen counter and take it to the table.
B. Gather jars of peanut butter and jelly from the pantry and take them to the table.
C. Get two knives from the utensil drawer, a plate from the kitchen cabinet, and take them to the table.
D. Place two slices of bread on the plate, open the peanut butter jar, and spread peanut butter on one slice of bread.
E. Open the jelly jar and spread jelly on the other slice of bread.
F. Assemble the two slices of bread into one sandwich.
G. Return ingredients to their original spots and place dirty knives in the kitchen sink.

While this job is considered conversion overall, delays and non-conversions are interspersed throughout this process. The PPD for this procedure looks like Figure 16.2.

As a PPD refresher, the product starts as the ingredients. Once they coalesce into the sandwich, the sandwich takes over as the product.

- As nothing is happening to the product during the actions of *retrieve knife* and *put back peanut butter, jelly, bread, and knife*, these are considered delays.
- Since bread is stored on the kitchen counter and peanut butter and jelly are kept in the pantry, their retrieval is performed in separate steps. As a result, they are captured on separate symbols. In addition, since the product is being moved, the time is non-conversion.

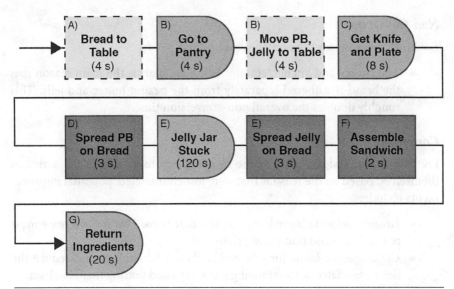

Figure 16.2   PPD: PB&J sandwich (before)

- Because the product is being attended to and these actions are not primarily movement, handling, rework, or scrap, spreading peanut butter and jelly along with putting the sandwich together are conversions.

Based on the PPD for this task, the break down for times is:

- *Conversion*: 8 s—5%
- *Non-conversion*: 8 s—5%
- *Delay*: 152 s—90%

Funny enough, a majority of this conversion process is actually delay. According to priority, the order of investigation should be delays, then non-conversions, then conversions.

Example—PB&J Sandwich: Analysis

Looking at reasons for the delays, it would appear that:

- The reason for the majority of time associated with retrieving the knives is due to their location across the room from the bread.
- The delay in opening the jar of jelly is due to the lid being stuck.
- The time it takes putting things up is mostly due to storage locations being far from each other.

Non-Conversion

Looking at reasons for the non-conversion time:

- The pantry and kitchen counter being far apart is the main reason that the bread is gathered separately from the peanut butter and jelly. This roughly doubles the overall non-conversion time.

Conversion

Looking at conversions, most of the time appears to be due to the activities themselves. Based on the reasons that were just enumerated, potential improvements include:

- *Layout*—relocate ingredients to minimize trips. This will decrease most of the delays and non-conversions.
- *Use a squeeze bottle for jelly rather than a jar*—this would reduce the delay associated with removing stuck caps and putting them back on. In addition, it might speed up the time it takes to spread jelly.
- *Evaluate the knife and the technique used*—determine if spreading time can be sped up.

Example—PB&J Sandwich: Improvements

If the improvements could be implemented according to Figure 16.3:

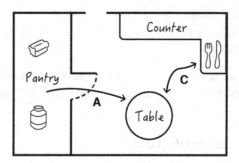

Figure 16.3   Kitchen layout: Phase 2

The new PPD would look like Figure 16.4.

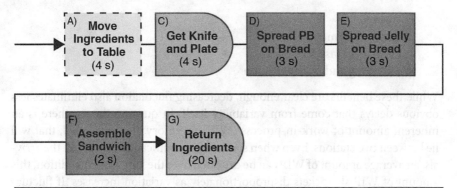

Figure 16.4 PPD: PB&J sandwich (after)

From these improvements, the new components of process time are:

- *Conversion*: 8 s—25%
- *Non-conversion*: 4 s—13%
- *Delay*: 20 s—62%

For future efforts, the new order of attack would be delay, conversion, and then non-conversion.

Minimizing Time (Conclusion)

Ultimately, a PPD can be applied repeatedly to improve jobs and progressively decrease the time involved. To build on this effort, variation reduction techniques can be used to improve job consistency.

STANDARD METHODS—VARIATION REDUCTION

> *"The slower but consistent tortoise causes less waste and is more desirable than the speedy hare that races ahead and then stops occasionally to doze."*
>
> Taiichi Ohno

Unfortunately, standardized work often reduces itself into a fixation with minimizing labor hours. While the benefit from this is obvious, the potential from variation reduction is frequently overlooked. In fact, the gains from reducing a job's fluctuations can outweigh the advantages of shortening a job's average time. With the improved quality brought on by consistency, there are a whole host of delays and non-conversion times that may be avoided as well:

- Rework
- Impound time
- Follow-up inspections
- Handling and transportation

While these benefits are clear enough, decreasing fluctuation also eliminates less obvious delays that come from variability itself. In queuing theory, there is an inherent amount of work-in-process (WIP) inventory, however small, that will lie between two stations. Even when servicing is significantly faster than the arrivals, an average amount of WIP can be expected over the long run. In addition, this amount of WIP skyrockets disproportionately as variation increases. If fluctuations are kept below a threshold, this issue can remain negligible. However, once a critical point is exceeded, WIP increases exponentially. Consider the simple case of product arriving to a single workstation with a single server.

Once the standard deviation (a measure of variation) of a task's cycle time exceeds three-tenths of its average, the waiting time begins to skyrocket. By the time a cycle time's standard deviation equals half of its average, the waiting time at a station grows to 600% of the average cycle time! In other words, 86% of a product's time at that workstation can be chalked up to delay. And this is under ideal conditions where there are no other delays associated with material handling, downtime, or material shortages. As the following graph indicates, the situation gets substantially worse from there (see Figure 16.5).

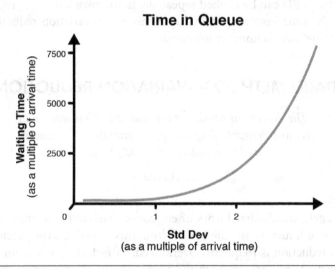

Figure 16.5   Queue time versus variation graph

Taken to even greater extremes, a cycle time's standard deviation at three times the average would create a queue time that is over 790,000% of the average cycle time. A 600% variation increase results in a waiting time increase of over 13,000%! Although you aren't likely to encounter such worst-case scenarios, the point is made.

By contrast, maintaining a consistent process time will go a long way toward preventing WIP and delay. The best way to do this is analyzing variation systematically and applying standard methods to tasks with excessive variance.

ANALYZING VARIATION

The first step to addressing variation is finding out where it comes from. In many cases, the fundamental sources of job variation can be broken down as:

- *Operator-to-operator variation*—if John, Paul, George, and Ringo are working on the same job, their differences in method, pace, tools, and skills will lead to variations in time and quality.
- *Within-operator variation*—while some people are more consistent than others, everyone experiences fluctuating performance.
- *Part-to-part variation*—a task's difficulty can vary greatly due to differences in the products and materials they work with. As one example, shifts in hole sizes and locations can make a significant difference in how easily two pieces assemble. In turn, this affects process time and quality.

Breaking down variation by its source helps prioritize where to focus and allows progress to be tracked. In addition, proper analysis can prevent working on the wrong issue. For example, a first glance might suggest that operators need retraining when their times are wildly inconsistent. However, what are the odds that all of the operators are inconsistent? Probably low. When something like this happens, chances are higher that production inputs, like inconsistent parts, may be the culprit. If this were the case, focusing on employee performance would have limited effect until something is done about standardizing working conditions.

In addition to increasing the magnitude and pace of improvement, measuring variation by source is a good way to validate whether efforts to improve consistency are effective. If they are, averages and ranges for task times should be trending down and across the board.

Measuring Process Time Variation

Whether the analysis is basic or sophisticated, time study data should be collected in such a way that it's possible for the major sources of variation to be identified. Statistical techniques called *analysis of variance* (ANOVA) are frequently used to do this. Although this approach offers the greatest degree of insight, simpler methods are effective and can be used by anyone. The following chart shows one way to collect times that will work in many cases (see Figure 16.6).

Operator	Task	Description	Part I Trials			Part II Trials			Part III Trials		
			1	2	3	1	2	3	1	2	3
John	1										
	2										
	3										
Paul	1										
	2										
	3										
George	1										
	2										
	3										
Ringo	1										
	2										
	3										

Figure 16.6   Standard work data collection example

In the task entries, the major steps on the PPD would be entered. So that variability can be estimated, several samples should be taken. Once each element is timed, the results are placed in the appropriate entry that corresponds to the operator/task/sample combination. Data that are gathered this way allow for analysis and improvement without complicated formulas.

Analyzing Process Time Variation

Although minimizing variation from any source is never a bad thing, being able to prioritize target areas for minimization will bring about quicker impact. The nature and magnitude of the results indicate what should be worked on and in what order:

- *First: inconsistent performance across the board*—look for tasks where the vast majority of operators are experiencing excessive variation. If there are cases where variation is high across the board, it makes sense to take a first look at upstream conditions like part or material consistency. Also, investigating equipment dependability may be in order.

- *Second: inconsistent performance in pockets*—among the tasks that weren't identified during the first step, look for excessive variation among just a few of the operators. Where some operators are uniform on one task when others aren't, compare and contrast the approach of a consistent operator with another who isn't. This comparison may point the way to methods revision that all employees can benefit from.
- *Third: inconsistent average among operators*—for the tasks that weren't identified in the first and second steps, calculate the absolute difference between the average task time for the fastest and slowest operators. Where the difference in average time is high, compare and contrast the approaches between the fastest and slowest operators. Like the previous scenario, this analysis may point the way to methods revisions that may help others.

If multiple candidates for improvement are available, start with the greatest magnitudes. For the first step, go for the highest range. For the second, prioritize to the difference between the biggest and smallest range. In the third case, prioritize to the difference between the biggest and smallest task time average. To shed some additional light on this subject, let's return to the PB&J sandwich example to variance reduction.

Example—PB&J Sandwich

For making PB&J sandwiches, suppose that time studies were conducted with the following results (see Figures 16.7 and 16.8).

From these figures, the following targets should be considered in the following order:

- *First: inconsistent performance across the board*—for *Task 6: Return ingredients*, the variation in time is excessive for both John and Paul even though they are consistent when performing other tasks. Start by taking a look at the production conditions for *Return ingredients*.
- *Second: inconsistent performance in pockets*—for the remaining tasks (i.e., Tasks 1–5) being inconsistent from person to person, *Task 2: Retrieve knife and plate* is a case in point where John's variation is substantially higher than Paul's. From there, an additional candidate for investigation might be *Task 5: Assemble sandwich*. Although John takes longer on average, he is twice as consistent as Paul is when performing this task. There may be something John is doing that Paul can benefit from imitating.

Operator	Task	Description	Trials					Average	Range
			1	2	3	4	5		
John	1	Move ingredients to table	3	3	4	2	4	3.2	2
	2	Retrieve knife and plate	6	6	7	8	11	7.6	5
	3	Spread peanut butter	3	4	3	3	3	3.2	1
	4	Spread jelly	2	3	3	3	3	2.8	1
	5	Assemble sandwich	2	3	2	2	2	2.2	1
	6	Return ingredients	12	14	12	12	9	11.8	5
Paul	1	Move ingredients to table	2	2	4	2	4	2.8	2
	2	Retrieve knife and plate	9	7	9	7	9	8.2	2
	3	Spread peanut butter	3	3	4	3	3	3.2	1
	4	Spread jelly	3	4	3	3	4	3.4	1
	5	Assemble sandwich	2	1	2	1	3	1.8	2
	6	Return ingredients	8	13	15	4	9	9.8	11

Figure 16.7 Standard work data collection (PB&J)

		Average [John/Paul]	Range [John/Paul]
1	Move ingredients to table	1.14	1.0
2	Retrieve knife and plate	0.93	2.5
3	Spread peanut butter	1.00	1.0
4	Spread jelly	0.82	1.0
5	Assemble sandwich	1.22	0.5
6	Return ingredients	1.20	0.45

Figure 16.8 Ratios of John's and Paul's Results

- *Third: inconsistent magnitude*—for the tasks that remain from the previous steps (i.e., Tasks 1, 3, and 4), there are a couple of tasks where there is a difference in averages. Since the greatest disparity is with *Task 4: Spread jelly*, this is a good candidate to look at first. From there, *Task 1: Move ingredients* might be investigated.

Although statistical approaches offer greater potential for analyzing variation, the approach just detailed can be done by almost anyone. While simple methods like these are highly preferable to doing nothing, learning more advanced techniques will help expand and improve efforts to reduce variation. For those who want to explore statistical methods, the statistical skills you will want to acquire are detailed in the chapter on Quality@Source. In addition, good books on this subject are referenced in the bibliography.

As candidates for improvement are identified, there are some rules of thumb and guidelines you can reference when trying to bring greater consistency to the work.

GUIDELINES—VARIANCE REDUCTION

Significant variation on tasks can be vexing. If identical methods are used, delays are minimized, and the employee is able-bodied, the inconsistencies that remain often boil down to the fact that some people are slower than others. If the pace is due to meticulousness, that's one thing. However, if an operator is neither fast nor detail-oriented, there's not much of an upside. Addressing this is primarily a people issue as opposed to a technical one.

Short-Term Measures

In the near term, there are some ways to deal with differences in pace, including:

- *Use jigs, fixtures, and/or automation to the greatest extent possible*—shifting efforts from man to machine minimizes the time that is held hostage by a slow person.
- *Incentives*—team-based incentives encourage individual performance in two ways:
  - When faster people perceive that someone is sandbagging, peer pressure is typically applied for the slower person to step up. Although some employees may end up feeling like they've been unfairly singled out, people on the floor typically have a good handle on who is and who is not putting in full effort.
  - When a person's pace is perceived as beyond their control, faster people often don't mind picking up the slack. For example, physical disability, age, thoroughness, or even a slow person who is clearly trying can elicit a sympathetic response.
- *Adjust job duties*—in an assembly-line environment, accounting for different paces when balancing the line can help. Preferably, allow extra idle time for quicker operators. In other words, reward desirable behavior.

- *Move up/move down*—give employees pre-assigned tasks to help the processes immediately after and before them according to the following priority:
  - If a station is idle due to the successor station being occupied, help this station complete its tasks.
  - If a predecessor is starving a station for a unit, help the predecessor complete its tasks.

There is more information about this technique in Chapter 17.

Long-Term Measures

While it takes all kinds of people to make an operation work, hiring innately fast people has its edge. Some ways to screen for this include:

- *Walk the production floor*—have a prospective employee walk the production floor with an interviewer who moves at a good clip. Can the prospect easily keep up?
- *Assembly trial*—have the prospect put simple assemblies together. In addition to speed, does the applicant demonstrate dexterity, efficient motion, and steady pace?
- *Sandbagging versus slow*—when evaluating pace, there are markers for why a person may lag:
  - *Sandbagging*—in case the term is unfamiliar, sandbagging is deliberately working below capability. A prominent marker for this is intentional pauses that are inappropriately timed. Also, the rate of motion will vary from average to slow.
  - *Innate slowness*—in addition to a glacial clip, innate slowness is indicated by excess motion, flourishes, and repetitious movements. Even when the pace is decent, poorly thought-out technique is often present. For example, this might manifest as several trips to get materials due to absentmindedness. Where faster people will simply hand an object to someone without fanfare, a person on a slower burn might fold it, pat it, or otherwise handle it excessively before sending it on.
  - *Lack of skill*—if the previously mentioned markers are absent, a person may simply lack the knowledge and/or dexterity to efficiently complete a job.

At the end of the day, a disability must be worked with to the maximum extent possible and optimizing jobs will go a long way toward accommodating physical challenges. For the nondisabled, lack of skill is the easiest to address with training and repetition. Dealing with innate slowness is more difficult, but not impossible. At the same time, a slower pace might work if the product quality is impeccable. Avoid sandbaggers as their mindset is detrimental to workplace culture and is contagious. While such attitude issues can sometimes be corrected, the percentages suggest otherwise.

SUMMARY

Optimizing and standardizing job methods entail:

- *Job analysis using a PPD*—breaking down jobs into delays, conversion, and non-conversion components
- *Minimizing task times*—specifying optimal methods to minimize delay, non-conversion, and conversion times
- *Variance reduction*—analyzing and minimizing inconsistencies in time

Taken together, a company can benefit from reducing the time a product spends in fulfillment, reducing labor costs, and improving workplace conditions. Although standardizing jobs requires significant effort, the carrot of improved product consistency, reduced delays, and quicker process times is pretty attractive. At the same time, the use of QL methods will allow a focus that maximizes benefits while minimizing the burdens.

CHAPTER 17

WORK BALANCING

"Many hands make light work."

John Heywood—English writer

"Too many cooks spoil the broth."

Famous Proverb

Although Quantum Lean's (QL) first priority is the product, there comes a point where resources come into focus. As a part of minimizing fulfillment time, increasing labor and equipment utilization eventually take their place as the next step in elevating efficiency. One good way to do this is by adopting an assembly line or cellular production. On top of further reducing costs, these approaches help morale by ensuring that everyone carries his load. Sometimes, it can even create more production capacity. Like anything worthwhile, balancing workloads entails significant effort. To cut things down to size, a structured approach makes for efficient and effective work balancing.

WORK BALANCING ELEMENTS

The fundamental components of work balancing include:

- *Defining tasks*—for those inexperienced in time studies, the first impulse might be to start by stop-watching people. Not so fast! To make sense of collected times, precise task definition is initially necessary to ensure:
    - *The ability to distribute work evenly*—distributing work requires jobs being broken down into smaller elements. Doing this increases the possible combinations of tasks and allows more options to even out the load. If studies are performed before this

happens, the resulting elements may be too large to balance out assignments.

▫ *Streamlined data collection*—once tasks and elements have been enumerated, this information can be leveraged to prepopulate data collection sheets (or apps) and streamline data gathering.

▫ *Multitasking*—although most people perceive manufacturing to be a split-second affair, cycle times in the hours are common. Consequently, time studies can drag. As an alternative, collecting times for several tasks simultaneously will greatly accelerate work measurement. However, doing this first requires that tasks be defined.

▫ *Future improvements*—without detailed job definitions, systematic method improvement isn't possible. Since this is an integral part of any lean program, careful task analysis has to occur at some point. To realize all the benefits, this might as well happen sooner rather than later.

- *Estimating times*—although many perceive this process to be some efficiency expert following employees around with a stopwatch, there are alternative methods to fit a wide array of circumstances.
- *Allocating tasks*—many production situations involve several steps and elaborate precedence relationships. In such cases, allocating work is cumbersome, but line-balancing techniques can lighten the load.
- *Validation*—no matter how thorough the preparation is, reality can depart from the plan. In the case of a work balance, validation is a necessary three-fold verification that:
  ▫ Work distribution is equitable
  ▫ Product quality is maintained
  ▫ The product's time-in-system doesn't increase
- *Refinement*—when theory and reality are at odds, judicious adjustments will mitigate the bad effects and highlight the best candidates for method improvement.

In all, these defined steps comprise a comprehensive and sound strategy for achieving optimal work balance. Although there is upfront work, the gains will far outweigh the costs. To aid in this endeavor, techniques exist to streamline the effort and improve the results.

DEFINING TASKS

Task definition involves four key phases:

- *Determine level of detail*—the extent to which jobs are broken down should be based on the production rate. For a takt time of a few hours, subdividing tasks to the second is overkill. Conversely, this resolution is appropriate when cycle times are less than a minute. Keeping in mind that any individual task needs to be at least as fast as the production rate, aiming for elements that take no longer than 10% of the takt time should allow for the flexibility to distribute work. Because of precedence relationships, safety, and other practical considerations, this may not always be possible, but it remains a good target.
- *Enumerate steps*—list the major conversion steps in product fulfillment. For non-conversion tasks, add them to the list if they are assigned to the employees on the production line. If they are the responsibility of support functions, leave them out. While work balancing shouldn't be performed in an environment where significant delays remain, leave minor delays out of the scope.
- *Break down steps*—break down the enumerated steps into finer tasks until they are at the desired level of detail or they can't be subdivided any further. For beginners, it may not always be clear how far to go. As there are situations that can't be categorized by cut-and-dried rules, defining tasks can sometimes be this way. In addition to common sense, factors that may be considered when breaking down steps include:
  - *Continuous motion*—if a task requires continuous motion, refrain from breaking it down any further. For example, applying a bead of caulk to a seam or drilling a hole should be uninterrupted.
  - *Safety*—although the goal should be to make a job completely fail-safe, there may be times where this is not possible. For example, during the installation of structural supports or the movement of heavy objects, keeping this job in one person's hands may be essential for safety. In such cases, avoid subdividing the task. Even if robust protocols could be developed to prevent accidents, increased chance of injury is unacceptable.
  - *Quality*—do not split a task if it could impair quality. For example, on a machine tool, performing all possible machining operations on one setup helps maintain precision. While it's technically possible to break up machining operations across multiple machines, only do so if the quality will remain acceptable and the production rate requires it.
- *Determine precedence relationships*—each task needs to have its immediate predecessors (or successors) defined. For example, to fill a glass of

water, a glass must be obtained first. From there, it can be filled. In this case, an immediate predecessor to *fill a glass of water* is *obtain glass*. As the work dictates, tasks can have several predecessors or none at all.

◻ As a key point, notice that the word *immediate* comes before the word *predecessor*. When listing a predecessor for a particular task, any jobs that come before the predecessor itself don't need to be included. Taking the water glass example further, the only predecessor that would need to be listed for *drink water* would be *fill glass with water*. While *obtain glass* is a predecessor for *fill glass with water*, there is no need to list *obtain glass* as a predecessor to *drink water*.

• *Use a flowchart*—although precedence relationships can be recorded in tabular form, entering tasks and predecessors in flowchart form is easier to visualize and verify, as is shown in the following chart example (see Figure 17.1).

Figure 17.1 Precedence chart

• *Use a Visio flowchart*—using a flowcharting package like Visio will make compilation and revision much easier. For line balancing, there are ways to utilize Visio's features to automate this undertaking.

Once tasks have been defined, most of the drudgery is out of the way. Although subsequent phases remain, what was done in task definition will enhance the speed and efficiency of those stages.

ESTIMATING TASK TIMES

Once tasks are defined, the next measure is estimating the times. While many assume that a stopwatch will be involved, there are many other methods available:

- *Stopwatch*—with task definitions, stopwatch studies are relatively straight-forward. In the interest of efficiency, a rule of thumb is that task times must be relatively quick for this method to be timely. When the individual times are less than one minute, stopwatches are absolutely recommended because sampling sufficiency is almost always achieved rapidly. Between one and 15 minutes, it's a toss-up depending on how consistent the times are. Beyond this, work sampling is probably in order.

- *Work sampling*[17-1]—from marketing studies to elections, sampling is a useful way to draw conclusions with limited data. As one category in this genre, work sampling may be used to estimate cycle times by observing jobs at randomly selected moments. In particular, work sampling can enable quicker results with less effort when the tasks take more than 15 minutes. The important point is that such a technique enables several jobs to be studied within the same time window. In turn, this allows for efficient and accurate data collection. Despite these advantages, there are two potential pitfalls to look out for. One is that workplace relations can skew the results. If there is little trust between employees and management, employees will strive to look like they are doing whatever they think management wants them to do. To clarify, if they think that the boss wants them to be busy all the time, they will do everything possible to make it look this way. On the other hand, if intentions are perceived as honest and communication is good, people tend to open up and a more accurate estimate of times can be made. Another potential problem is that people who perform these studies may undermine accuracy by making observations based on convenience rather than at randomly scheduled times. For situations that fit work sampling, this technique utilizes observations of work activity over an extended period. For statistical accuracy, the samples must be taken at random times and the period must be representative of the work mix. However, as most of these studies are geared toward estimating the percentages of time devoted to different tasks, determining task times requires a twist on the way it's generally done. To convert a percentage into times, there needs to be a way to relate the product's time to the task percentages. One way this can be done is illustrated in the following example:

▫ Example—work sampling: an assembly enters a workstation and tasks *A, B, C, D* are performed on this unit. To estimate the task times using work sampling methods, the station will be observed at random times to determine how much of the time is spent on each task. Based on this survey, the proportion of time spent on the tasks (with *Other—Product not at Station* meaning that the operator is idle due to product not being at their station and *Other—Product at Station* meaning the product is at the station but no conversion tasks are being performed on it) is shown in Figure 17.2.

Task	%
A	35
B	27
C	12
D	12
Other Product @ Station	10
Other Product **not** @ Station	4

Figure 17.2 Task proportions

Given that the data are in percentages rather than being time-denominated, the information wouldn't appear to be very useful. However, if the time that units spent at the station is tracked, the estimate for task time can be calculated as follows:

(Average time product spends at station) ×
(% operator time on task)/(% of time product is at station)

Specifically, if a product spends an average of 10 minutes at a station, task *A* takes 3.65 minutes on average:

10 minutes × (35%)/(96%) = 3.65 minutes

• *Predetermined motion time systems (PMTS)*[17-2]—PMTS are techniques that circumvent stopwatches and estimate cycle times by breaking work down into basic elements and assigning times to each one. By looking up each element type in a reference source, time estimates can be obtained. In addition to lacking the subjectivity that can accompany conventional methods, the focus of PMTS on work content serves as a natural gateway to method improvement. Although there are several systems of this kind, a prominent example is Maynard Operation Sequence Technique (MOST) with different versions available depending on the type of work being studied. When a predetermined time standard like MOST is selected, the company that sells this package can recommend the version that best fits an operation.

Since organizations can face a wide variety of circumstances, any or all of these methods may be deployed as necessary to match operational conditions. Once times have been estimated, the next order of business is figuring out an efficient way to distribute work so that the product is served and employees are given a fair shake.

LINE BALANCING—ALLOCATING WORK[17-3]

For an assembly line, line balancing is the allocation of tasks among stations so their workload comes as close as possible to matching the demand rate. The most commonly used line-balancing methods include:

- *Largest-candidate rule (LCR)*—the LCR arranges work elements in a descending order based on task times and precedence relationships and assigns the tasks to workstations accordingly.
- *Kilbridge and Wester column method*—this approach assigns tasks based on their position in the precedence diagram. This technique avoids the main disadvantage associated with the LCR method, where lengthy tasks are front-loaded during task assignments.
- *Ranked positional weight (RPW) method*—this method was introduced in the 1960s and uses a calculated parameter for each task that reflects time and position on the precedence diagram. In turn, this number is used to allocate work. While it is a little more complicated than the LCR, RPW tends toward more evenly distributed work.
- *Reverse critical path (RCP) method*—this technique is a QL variation on the RPW method. Using critical path management principles, identical results to RPW are achieved, but executing and programming this method are much simpler.

With the exception of the RCP method, references for the aforementioned procedures can be found in the bibliography. Although none of these methods generate perfectly even work distributions, they give good results that can save a great deal of time in the creation of optimized line balances. Since these methods' lineages trace back to a time when computers were unavailable, they can be performed manually. However, since many situations entail a staggering number of potential combinations, a software assist may come in handy. As one option, Microsoft's Office and Visio can be programmed to automate this undertaking. On top of making the chore faster and easier, the software can be customized to a company's needs. At the same time, there are off-the-shelf packages that are specifically developed for line balancing.

In an environment of fluctuating demand, the ability to automatically generate line balances offers companies the prospect of rapidly responding to changing market conditions while maintaining high labor efficiency and minimal work-in-process inventory (WIP). Furthering lowering costs, the overhead needed to plan production is minimized as well. Once a line balance has been determined and deployed, validation follows so that adjustments, corrections, and improvements can be made.

VALIDATION

Regardless of how thorough the due diligence may be, there are always potential complications including:

- *Product variations*—there may be times that a product's variations require an operator to expend more time than would normally be required. For example, if there were cosmetic problems or variations in materials, time may have to be spent rectifying the situation.
- *People variations*—people don't keep the same work pace at all times. Even if a job is specified so that every employee is capable of keeping pace, there will be a range in output rates, however small. In addition, one person's results can fluctuate significantly within the same day.
- *Environmental variations*—processes like coating can be sensitive to environmental factors. Although it's always desirable to tightly control ambient conditions, this is not always feasible in the short run.
- *Process drift*—processes sometimes change without everyone's knowledge.

In addition to assuring that quality is maintained and a product's time on the floor doesn't increase, the validity of time estimates can be checked. By using work sampling, clues can be generated regarding where times need to be reexamined.

Example—Validating

On a production line with John, Paul, and George manning different stations, each operator's idle time could be monitored (see Figure 17.3).

Station	%
George	3
John	12
Paul	15

Figure 17.3   Time validation

From these results, George's station is significantly busier, suggesting that an examination of his workload may be in order. Without getting into too much detail up front, this information can be valuable in narrowing down where correction might be in order. Taken further, it can also help prioritize the tasks that should be improved.

REFINEMENT

Due to variations, the reality on the floor will depart from even the best estimates. In addition, a combination of outlier personnel or misguided policies can compound this. For example, there are employees who can far outpace mere mortals. In such cases, these overachievers can be left idle much of the time. Too much of this can diminish other employee's morale. On the other hand, if policy compels outliers to always stay busy, the WIP can skyrocket. While this conundrum is a catch-22 in a resource-obsessed framework, product-centricity offers an out.

Returning to a situation where John, Paul, and George work at different production stations, a principle called *look ahead—look behind* can be applied. To keep the employee's and product's idle time under control, a specific plan is needed for employees to help each other. In the example of John, Paul. and George, the arrangement might work as shown in Figure 17.4.

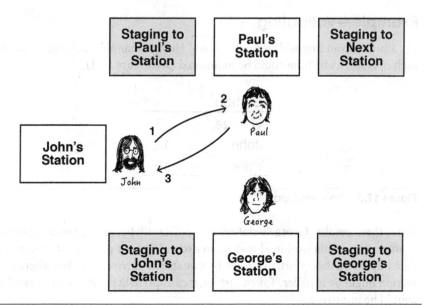

Figure 17.4 Look ahead

Look Ahead

Looking at Figure 17.4:

1. If John finishes a subassembly and Paul's staging area is full, John moves to Paul's station.
2. John helps until Paul's staging area can be freed up. Once this happens, John moves his subassembly to Paul's staging area
3. From there, John goes back to his station to work on a new unit.

Look Behind

Looking at Figure 17.5:

1. If John is ready to work on a new unit but waiting on material from George, John moves to George's station.
2. John helps George until a unit is completed and moved to John's station.
3. John returns to his station to work on the unit that was completed at George's station.

To keep WIP under control, *look ahead* should only apply to a station immediately following an operator's station. Similarly, *look behind* should only apply to a station immediately preceding an operator's station. In other words:

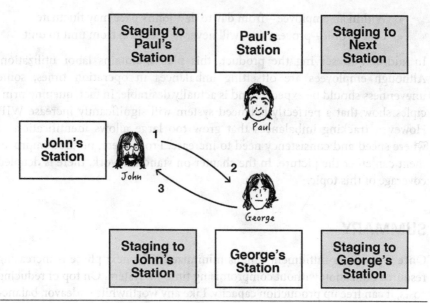

Figure 17.5 Look behind

- If Paul is helping his subsequent station as part of *look ahead*, John should not attempt to help Paul nor any station that follows Paul's.
- If George is helping his preceding station as part of *look behind*, John should not attempt to help George nor any station that precedes George's.

As a refinement to *look ahead—look behind*, a case can be made to restrict John's help to an enumerated set of tasks. There are several reasons this is a good idea:

- *Morale*—requiring operators to be continually busy is a disincentive to efficient work. If there is no prospect of rest no matter how hard one toils, efforts will wane. By limiting what is required to a well-defined set of tasks, an operator can still work their way into free time.
- *Quality*—limiting the number of additional tasks an operator has to perform simplifies training and improves the odds of high-quality work.
- *Accountability*—where tasks are limited to an enumerated list, accountability is easier to enforce.

Implementing this type of plan prevents WIP accumulation and ensures smooth product flow due to operators helping each other to offset natural variations such as:

- Employee to employee—on average, John's pace may be different from Paul's

- Within an employee—from day to day, John's pace may fluctuate
- Unit to unit—process time will never be identical from unit to unit

In addition to serving the product, this plan maintains labor utilization. Although employees are offsetting imbalances in operation times, some unevenness should be expected and is actually desirable. In fact, queuing principles show that a perfectly balanced system will significantly increase WIP. However, tracking imbalances that grow too large allows identification of where speed and consistency need to increase. From there, method improvement can enter the picture. In the chapter on standard work, there is detailed coverage of this topic.

SUMMARY

Once a product's fulfillment time is minimized, QL's next phase is increasing resource utilization without compromising time-in-system. On top of reducing costs, it can free up production capacity. Like any worthwhile endeavor, balancing workloads is involved. To cut this undertaking down to size, there are steps that will make work balancing as efficient and effective as possible:

- Define tasks—enumerate the steps involved in a product's fulfillment, subdivide each step so work can be distributed, and determine precedence relationships.
- Estimate task times.
- Allocate tasks—apply line-balancing techniques to distribute work efficiently while meeting required production rates.
- Validation—validation is a three-fold verification that:
    □ Work distribution is fair.
    □ Product quality is maintained or improved.
    □ The product's time-in-system doesn't increase.
- Refinement—correct, offset, and adjust to production imbalances.

Together, work balancing caps off a complete package to ensure that resources are utilized while the product is served. Although shortcuts may be tempting, a comprehensive attack is necessary for the best possible results.

SIDEBAR—ADAPTING LINE BALANCING
FOR CELLULAR MANUFACTURING

As opposed to a typical assembly line with a straight configuration, work cells are laid out in a U-shaped arrangement. Compared to the assembly line, a cell design offers more options for sharing tasks. To illustrate, if the cell in the figure was arranged in single file, it would be virtually impossible for one employee to perform both operations 1 and 8 (see Figure 17.6).

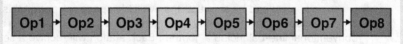

Figure 17.6   Straight line diagram

Conversely, the U-shaped arrangement allows an employee to perform more than one operation (see Figure 17.7).

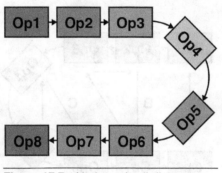

Figure 17.7   U-shaped cell diagram

As good as they are, conventional line-balancing techniques break down for cellular manufacturing configurations. If a cell is relatively simple, allocating tasks can be done manually. However, if there is complexity, distributing work this way can be unwieldy. In this case, a workaround so line balancing can be used would consist of:

- Determining the target takt times.
- Identifying common factors among those production levels. If the takt times are six, nine, and 12 minutes, three minutes is a common factor. If six, 12, and 18 minutes are possibilities, the common factors are two, three, and six minutes.

Continued

- Prioritize one of the common factors identified to be the amount of time assigned to each station. This will make it easier to ramp production up or down. For example, if each cell's stations were specified for 45 minutes of work, it would be difficult to redistribute tasks if the takt time shifted to 60 minutes. Conversely, if the stations were designed for 15 minutes of work, it would be much easier.
  - If possible, try to use the lowest common factor since it will allow the greatest flexibility for work distribution.
  - At the same time, keep in mind the minimum number of stations (total work/station time) that will be required for the time factor you select and be sure that the available space will permit this.
- With the station time as the takt time, generate a line balance using a conventional line-balancing algorithm. Each station will receive a set allocation of tasks.
- Based on tooling and equipment limitations, adjust the allocations to the stations.
- Arrange the stations/assignments in a *U-shaped* configuration.
- Working visually from the cell layout, assign work to operators so that:
  - Operator's travel paths don't overlap. This will prevent employees from accidentally colliding (see Figures 17.8 and 17.9).

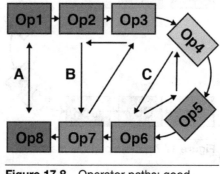

Figure 17.8   Operator paths: good

Continued

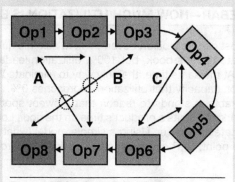

Figure 17.9   Operator paths: bad

- Work is as evenly distributed as possible.
- Takt time is satisfied.

While this approach can be applied to simple cases, it will be most useful for complicated situations. Although adjustments are likely, following this approach will generate starting solutions that can be rapidly refined into a good answer.

SIDEBAR—HOW MUCH UTILIZATION IS BEST?

In business, most people wouldn't even think to ask this question. The point has been repeated in this book, but 100% utilization leads to skyrocketing WIP inventory. At the same time, the only way to eliminate WIP is to have so much production capacity that utilization approaches 0%. Since either scenario is undesirable, it stands to reason that a sweet spot exists that puts resources to work and limits a product's time on the floor. Looking to queuing theory will indicate an answer. Using a simple model (what is called *M/M/1*) to illustrate the point, WIP can be charted against resource utilization (see Figure 17.10).

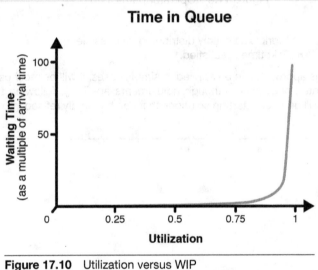

Figure 17.10   Utilization versus WIP

Looking at the chart, an inflection point can be observed where WIP skyrockets once utilization exceeds 90%. With the complications that come from variation, QL aims for a lower utilization of 80% to 85% to err on the side of serving the product. Consider yourself advised.

SIDEBAR—WHICH TIME STUDY METHOD?

Despite rules of thumb working most of the time, knowing underlying principles comes in handy when situations don't allow for cookie-cutter answers. The basis for the guidelines for selecting time-study methods is a formula for determining sample size (see Figure 17.11) where:

$$\left(\frac{3 \cdot s}{\% \cdot \mu} \right)^2 = n$$

Figure 17.11   Sample formula

- n = sample size;
- % = margin of error;
- s = standard deviation of cycle time; and
- m = average cycle time.

For those unfamiliar with statistics, 3s is an indication of cycle-time variation. For example, consider an operation that requires 60 seconds, give or take 10 seconds. In this case, as 6s approximates a cycle time's entire range of 20 seconds, 3s represents half of that and would roughly equal 10 seconds. Put another way, 3s would represent half of a cycle-time's range. Keeping in mind that a reasonably consistent job should vary by no more than (+/–) 15% of their average cycle time, the following values can be entered into the formula for sample size:

- Set 3s = 15% × m
- Allow a 10% margin of error

Based on these inputs, the formula for sample size reduces to a formula that estimates the number of samples that need to be taken (see Figure 17.12).

$$\left(\frac{0.15}{\%} \right)^2 = n$$

Figure 17.12   Modified sample-size formula

Continued

To determine the minimum amount of time that might be spent with time studies, multiply the required sample size by the average cycle time. If the result is greater than the budgeted time, work sampling or predetermined time systems need to be considered. For an allowable error of 10% of average and a budgeted time of 30 minutes, the cutoff point for cycle time would be 14 minutes. Beyond this time, work sampling should be strongly considered.

CHAPTER 18

CELLULAR PRODUCTION

Of all the concepts that get missed about lean production, cellular flow is one subject where the point sails past quite a few. The most prominent ideas that are lost include the following.

IT'S ABOUT THE PRODUCT

Despite all of the benefits that come from radically reduced lead times, decreased floor space, and minimized non-conversion work, many managers miss this and fixate on cells as a way of forcing employees to multitask. While this latter effect can be a side benefit of properly devised cells, starting with a goal of trimmed payrolls has a way of resulting in an arrangement that fails to realize a cell's biggest advantages.

For example, an employee who attends to one machine might get reassigned to attend to two machines at the same time. Since this may even involve processing two different products at the same time, some will still call this a cell even though it is no such thing. At the same time, little to no thought will be given to decreasing a product's time-in-system. Making matters worse, there will often be indifference to production delays that may come from the operator's attention being divided.

By contrast, product-centricity will achieve the benefits in lead time and its associated cost reductions. By the same token, true cellular flow will allow operators to share tasks and utilize labor more fully. All it takes is being fixated on the product rather than the resource!

CELLS ARE SEQUENTIAL

Even for companies that understand cellular flow's possibilities, a common blind spot is the lack of awareness that cellular flow is sequential flow. For example, consider a situation that involves doubling the production rate. Instead of subdividing jobs so that the resulting tasks take half the time, a company might decide to duplicate stations instead. A fair question would be whether this should matter since the production rate will be the same. An even fairer answer is that it absolutely does for the following reasons:

- *Space*—with duplicate stations, two identical subassemblies can come out at the same time. Extra space must be allotted for this possibility.
- *Tooling*—sequential flow minimizes cost because tools can be divvied out among stations. Duplicate stations mean duplicate tools.
- *Variation*—no two stations' outputs can be identical, and variation begets quality and productivity problems.
- *Training*—as opposed to sequential flow, duplicate stations require an operator to learn more tasks, which means more training and a slower learning curve.

To drive the point home, consider bucket brigades for firefighting like you might see in a cartoon or western. When a pump is unavailable, a line will form between the water source and the fire. From there, the person by the water fills a bucket and passes it to the next guy. When someone in the line gets a bucket, he passes it to the next person until the last person gets the bucket and pours water on the fire. Going forward, everyone keeps repeating the actions until the fire is extinguished. As an alternative, we could have all of these people filling a bucket of water at the same time, running to the fire, and pouring water on it. On average, the same amount of water reaches the fire. However, if everyone fills his own bucket, water will come in spurts. In the meantime, the fire has the potential to grow out of control. By contrast, bucket brigades provide a constant flow for better results. Also, everyone's effort is minimized. A cell is based on the very same idea. To make a long story short, avoid duplication and subdivide tasks among unique stations to the maximum extent possible.

CHAPTER 19

QUALITY@SOURCE

*"Politics is the art of looking for trouble; finding it everywhere,
diagnosing it incorrectly, and misapplying the wrong remedies."*

Ernest Benn

Although the previous quote singles out government conduct for criticism, it could be argued that any organization is capable of similar behavior—even businesses. Since there are many ways to misapply the wrong remedies, there are several reasons why a company might misdiagnose a problem:

- *Politics*—when agendas are about anything but business, it's safe to say that real problems won't be addressed.
- *Information*—even if motivations are pure, key knowledge may be missing.
- *Problem-solving ability*—if knowledge is good, a lack of systematic problem-solving ability can be a deal-breaker.
- *Resources*—if intrigue is eliminated, information is available, and problem-solving abilities are good, a lack of resources may derail a solution.
- *Type I error*—even if all other elements are perfect, the possibility remains that an ineffective solution may be mistaken for an effective one. This problem is common due to the fact that people often confuse luck for actual improvement.

Among these causes, type I error comes to the fore when Quality@Source comes up. Although it's rarely put this way, this lean tool ultimately revolves around understanding and avoiding type I error. To expand on this idea, some background in Quality@Source is helpful.

QUALITY@SOURCE BASICS

Beyond mistake-proofing tasks and making quality everyone's job, Quality@ Source is ultimately about achieving a level of process control where monitoring can move from outputs (i.e., inspection) to inputs (men, material, machines, method, environment, information) without any negative effect on the product. Doing this builds quality into a process, achieves consistency, and minimizes the need for inspection. The key foundations for monitoring are:

- Understanding a process so that outcomes can be accurately predicted. If this is not possible, control will not be achieved. Conversely, mastering cause and effect allows the establishment of controlled conditions that can be monitored. Where this can be done, it ensures quality better than after-the-fact inspections.
- Typical methods involve measuring the results of a process and correlating them against their production inputs. The goal is understanding what settings must be maintained to create consistent product.
- Once the required process inputs are understood, employees are empowered, equipped, and trained to monitor the process.
- Once controlled conditions are established, Quality@Source methods can be used to further improve process consistency and quality.

QUALITY@SOURCE AND STATISTICS

While some may be skeptical, doing Quality@Source correctly often requires statistics. To illustrate why this is so, consider a continuous improvement team that is working to decrease the level of impurities in a hypothetical process. Before revisions were made, samples were drawn showing a process average of 176.6 parts-per-million (ppm). The individual results can be seen in Figure 19.1.

191
161
199
184
148

Average 176.6

Figure 19.1   Process pre-treatment

After making process modifications, more samples were taken. This time, the process average showed 156.3 ppm. The individual readings can be seen in Figure 19.2.

127

185

120

193

148

Average 154.6

Figure 19.2   Process post-treatment

Based on the numbers, was anything accomplished? Many would say yes. While a decrease of over 11% might seem significant, the team's efforts actually had no effect statistically speaking. Analysis performed on this data will show that the difference between the samples was probably due to chance. Since the underlying process impurity level fluctuates between 80 and 240, this significant variation made a wide range of sample results possible. Because of this disparity, what appeared to be an improvement was only due to the fact that these samples can vary greatly. On another day, the results might have shown that the process impurity level increased by 11%. Without the perspective that statistics offers, a company could easily adopt *solutions* only to have problems continue. And this is exactly what happens in many organizations.

To negotiate the type I minefield, the concept of *statistical significance* was developed. The idea is to use statistics to determine whether the results from an experiment are due to chance. As the term *statistical significance* implies, statistical knowledge is necessary. While the efforts needed to learn this subject may not be pleasant, using statistics will streamline efforts and ensure the validity of changes and process settings. Otherwise, identifying effective solutions is reduced to making judgment calls. While coverage of statistical tools is beyond the scope of this book, providing a roadmap to gain the ability to properly apply them isn't.

SIDEBAR—TAMPERING AT GENERAL MOTORS

In the 1980s, the United States auto industry was under considerable pressure from foreign competition. At the time, the Japanese were producing higher quality cars at a lower cost. To address this, General Motors (GM) embarked on a crash automation program to rectify these disparities. Since GM had not addressed more fundamental problems, this considerable investment (to the tune of 90 billion dollars) backfired spectacularly. Among a series of follies that included robots colliding with each other and labor-saving devices that increased man-hours, one that stands out was a misguided attempt to improve quality.

At a transmission plant, a part was processed on a computer numerical control (CNC) machining center. Once finished, the part was gauged on a coordinate measuring machine (CMM). Based on how much the measurement departed from the nominal dimensions, the CNC was adjusted to make sure that the next part would be perfect. Ironically, by making these corrections, GM was making the variation far worse. Instead of tightening the process spread, the fluctuations skyrocketed. When the company shut off the CMM, the output from the CNC machine tightened up on its own. GM made the type I error of erroneously concluding that any measured deviation was due to the process having changed, when the reality was that most of the spread was simply due to the natural process variation. If you think an education in statistics is expensive, try ignorance!

STATISTICS—CORE KNOWLEDGE

Although statistics is a subject that is deep enough to require a PhD, the good news is that it doesn't take anything so drastic to be an effective practitioner. The challenge is to funnel the multitude of possibilities into a body of knowledge that a single person can grasp. The trick is:

- Knowing what you don't know
- Once you know what you don't know, knowing where to look for more information
- Once information is available, having the ability to properly select a technique to address a problem

Although looking something up might seem simple enough, it's not as straightforward as it might first appear. In fact, it can take a long time to become proficient with these skills. The upshot is that even trained people misdiagnose problems and misapply the wrong remedies. You will too. With the recommendations in the following text, the goal is to keep these mistakes to a minimum.

This prescribed body of knowledge is about quality rather than quantity. Instead of the ability to recite facts and figures, the object is to understand how to properly use the tools and look up the details as necessary.

Although there is more than one way to get somewhere, an ideal path to core knowledge will probably require formal coursework. The reason is that accountability is extremely helpful in providing the discipline necessary to internalize unfamiliar subjects. Although you should select an approach to learning that works well for you, most people grasp the material better if they have to perform in a classroom setting. With that being said, the following are excellent subjects to study on the path to core knowledge.

Basic Statistics

If you aren't familiar with basic statistics, a first semester college-level course on this topic will help. While insight doesn't typically come with this offering, it's an introduction to key terms and concepts including:

- *Standard deviation*—a measure of variation.
- *Histograms*—a graph that shows the spread of a population. For example, the range of results for a process parameter might have a spread similar to Figure 19.3.

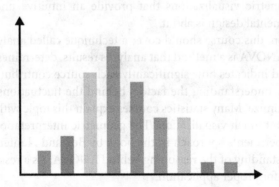

Figure 19.3 Histogram

- *Statistical distribution*—for a population, a statistical distribution shows a range of possible values and how frequently they occur. A population can consist of people, parts, or anything that can be sampled. By matching a population to a distribution and using its corresponding properties, predictions can be made.

- *Type I error*—concluding that something has happened when it hasn't really occurred. For example, a jury returning a verdict of guilty when the accused is innocent.
- *Type II errors*—concluding that something has not happened when it really has. For example, a jury returning a verdict of *not guilty* when a defendant is guilty.
- *Statistical significance*—when a change is made (e.g., modifying a method, incorporating new tools), saying it has a statistically significant effect means that there is a high degree of confidence that the difference in outcomes isn't due to chance.

At this point, there is no need to study these terms too closely. The intent is to preview some of the ideas that you will be exposed to with this course. By learning the vocabulary of statistics, a foundation will be paved to understand this subject at a deeper level.

Design of Experiments

As a marker for a good course in experimental design, look for one that uses the book *Statistics for Experimenters* by Box and Hunter. In my opinion, this tome clearly explains the subject. In addition to numerical explanations, the authors provide geometric visualizations that provide an intuitive understanding of what experimental design is about.

In addition, this course should cover a technique called analysis of variance (ANOVA). ANOVA is a method that analyzes results, determines the sources of variation, and indicates how significantly each source contributes to the range of results. By understanding the factors behind the fluctuations, they become easier to minimize. Many statistics courses explain this topic with a lot of calculations and not much visualization. The geometric interpretation found in the design of experiments approach in the book by Box and Hunter offers a much better understanding of the reasoning behind ANOVA. As a result, this lays the groundwork for proper application.

I can only speak for myself, but experimental design changed the way I look at things. I highly recommend taking a good course in this subject. Not only will it provide insight into statistics, but potentially affect your outlook.

Linear Regression

Though optional, understanding linear regression will reinforce concepts learned in the design of experiments approach. In this topic, creating predictive models is covered. Besides modeling techniques, the most significant concept introduced is what is called an *R-squared* value. This measure indicates how valid a model is. The closer it comes to the number one, the better the model.

Statistical Process Control (SPC)

SPC is absolutely brilliant. Being all about preventing type I error, SPC is a technique to monitor processes and use statistical rules to make corrections only when a process has changed in a statistically significant way. This prevents overcompensating a process and making matters worse.

Although the framework is powerful, SPC has real-world difficulties due to:

- SPC's proper application requires a process that's in a state of statistical control, which is pretty rare. In other words, doing SPC correctly is frequently infeasible.
- Many processes require that multiple factors/dimensions/parameters be monitored. The more that have to be tracked, the greater the likelihood that a process will need to be shut down and adjusted. Taken far enough, a process will need to be shut down more often than not.
- There are multiple rules for determining whether a process is out of statistical control. Getting people to properly follow these cumbersome guidelines is difficult.
- A rule of thumb is that at least 30 samples of a production run must be taken before there are adequate data to start monitoring. Unfortunately, many shops don't have production runs of over 30 pieces.

Summary—Core Knowledge

Although there is more to statistics than what has been outlined, a grounding in *basic statistics*, *design of experiments*, and *linear regression* paves a way forward. While SPC is often impractical, understanding its principles will boost your grasp of statistics. With this core knowledge, there is an excellent chance of developing into a highly effective statistical practitioner. Of course, this takes time and ongoing application.

APPLYING STATISTICS

Although statistics can be applied in a wide array of settings, this section is intended to suggest candidates where it is most likely to be helpful. Statistical tools are frequently applied in the following areas:

- Improving process time or quality
  - Validating effectiveness of changes

- Improving measurement precision
- Reducing process spread (time or quality)
- Moving process monitoring from checking outputs to verifying inputs
- Validating processes
  - Determining input ranges that ensure a process can produce consistent output
  - Process capability; establishing the tolerances that a process can reliably hold
- Monitoring processes
  - In particular, a technique called cumulative sum control chart (CUSUM) can be useful

The statistical tools that are recommended for core knowledge can help with the previously mentioned tasks in numerous ways.

Design of Experiments

For complex processes, the relationship between inputs and outputs is often unclear. When there is a desire to optimize settings in these situations, design of experiments is a good option. Although many processes can benefit, prominent cases where this technique can help include casting and molding.

ANOVA

Systematically analyzing variation with ANOVA techniques allows an understanding of the sources of variation and how significant they are. In turn, it facilitates and accelerates process improvements. At the same time, an understanding of type I error makes it possible to validate when variance reductions are effective. Equally nice, it can also establish when efforts have been for naught.

Process Monitoring

For all the prior pessimism about SPC, CUSUM can help avoid some of the problems found with standard SPC. This method was developed to detect small shifts in process averages. In particular, a key strength of CUSUM is that it can be used in small-run CNC machine shops to detect dimensional variations as tooling inserts wear down and other process inputs change. With proper application, this technique allows operators to adjust their machines proactively and with high accuracy. In addition, this can greatly improve process capability. The key ingredients to make CUSUM work are:

- *Computing capability*—this method involves calculations that are best left to a computer
- *Repeatable and reproducible measurement techniques*—if measurements are inaccurate, the corresponding adjustments will compromise dimensional integrity
- *Knowledge of CUSUM*
- *Trained operators*

Shainin Techniques

For problem solving, statistical techniques can be painstakingly slow. To speed up the process, an industry practitioner named Dorian Shainin developed a set of methods that are now known as Shainin Techniques.

What makes these tools so powerful is that they leverage statistical insights to maximize simplicity, minimize computation, and get results more quickly than would otherwise be possible. As an example of what they can offer, NASA's use of this toolset was instrumental in achieving a perfect track record for the Apollo lunar module in the 1960s.

A downside of Shainin Techniques is that they are carefully guarded and having access to that information often requires attending fee-based courses. However, there is a good book on the subject that is referenced in this book's bibliography.

SUMMARY

Beyond mistake-proofing tasks and making quality everyone's job, Quality@Source is about achieving a level of process control where monitoring can move from outputs (i.e., inspection) to inputs (men, material, machines, method, environment, information) with no negative effect on the product. In addition, these methods can be used to further improve process consistency and quality on an ongoing basis.

To implement Quality@Source most effectively, statistics are often necessary. Although vast knowledge of this subject isn't needed, it's critical to know the essentials so that a company is capable of selecting the proper methods and applying them correctly. While comprehensive coverage of statistics is beyond the scope of this book, guidance was given on techniques to investigate, where to apply them, and where to find more information.

Regardless of how Quality@Source is approached, it's important to remember that mistakes and miscalculations will be made. With follow-up and improvement in this endeavor, the results should continually get better. Applying yourself is key.

This book has free material available for download from the
Web Added Value™ resource center at *www.jrosspub.com*

CHAPTER 20

LEAN IMPLEMENTATIONS—
IMPROVING THE ODDS

"In the beginning was The Plan.
And then came the assumptions.
And the assumptions were without form.
And the plan was without substance.
And darkness came upon the face of the workers.
And they spoke amongst themselves saying:
'It is a crock, and it stinketh mightily.'
And the workers went unto their Supervisors and said,
'It is a pail of dung, and none may abide the odor therefore.'
And the Supervisors went unto their Managers saying,
'It is a container of excrement, and it is very strong,
such that none may abide by it.'
And the Managers went unto their Directors saying,
'It is a vessel for fertilizer, and none can abide by its strength.'
And the Directors spoke amongst themselves, saying to one another,
'It contains that which aids plant growth, and is very strong.'
And the Directors went unto the Vice Presidents saying,
'It promotes growth, and it is very powerful.'
And the Vice Presidents went unto the President saying unto him,
'This new plan will actively promote the growth and vigor
of the company, with very powerful effects.'
And the President looked upon the Plan and saw that it was good.
And the Plan became Policy.
This is how sh*t happens."

Unknown

Ask a practitioner about the success rate of lean initiatives (other than theirs) and you might be surprised at how low it can go. Depending on the source, failure rates as high as 95% have been claimed. However, it shouldn't be too surprising as implementations have obstacles that can stymie the most seasoned professionals. Although there are no guarantees, this deep dive offers suggestions to improve the odds. Since a lean endeavor has technical and people-related facets, the approach that follows begins with technical points and concludes by addressing the human element. Generally, an implementation should include or address the following:

- *Problem definition*—although an effective project has several angles, it rests on problem definition. After all, the real issues can't be addressed if they are not properly identified. When the wrong target is chosen, effective solutions will elude even the most sophisticated techniques. By contrast, a sound analysis up front dramatically increases the odds of success even when trailing-edge methods are used.
- *Planning*—by anticipating stumbling blocks, problems can be bypassed. At the same time, it is rare that a project is entirely free of complications. However, preparation allows a team to be more responsive should issues come up.
- *Follow-up*—no matter how sound a plan may be, human fallibility means it will not be perfect. Ignoring the mistakes can derail the entire undertaking. To catch and address problems in a timely way, proactive follow-up is a must.

Once these foundations are laid, deft navigation of company politics is imperative. On the soft side of implementations, the following issues deserve serious consideration:

- *Persuasion*—although compulsion is sometimes necessary, persuading a workforce to embrace a program will result in a more thorough and sustainable implementation.
- *Motivation*—getting people to agree on an idea is often easy; it is getting them to act that can be daunting. Motivation bridges the gap between belief and practice.

While the soft side of business must be handled throughout an implementation, technical soundness will lay the best possible groundwork for maneuvering within a company's culture.

PROBLEM DEFINITION

> *"We cannot solve our problems with the same thinking we used when we created them."*
>
> Albert Einstein

While problem definition is the foundation for proper analysis, it can be argued that valid assumptions are essential in order to accurately define a problem. Taken further, many lean implementations start with flawed suppositions. Even when they aren't explicitly acknowledged, the financial and resource-based obsessions that accompany many lean projects will sometimes pit customers against companies, company against product, and employers against employees. Since sustainable results aren't possible without everyone coming out ahead, these contradictions practically guarantee long-term failure. By contrast, Quantum Lean's (QL's) product-centricity provides a framework that accommodates the fact that customers, companies, and employees ultimately share the same interests. Although there will be company specifics that must be addressed, maintaining a QL framework and realistic expectations for the workforce will help ensure that problems are defined accurately and that planning is sound.

PLANNING

> *"Planning is everything."*
>
> Dwight Eisenhower

> *"Even the best team, without a sound plan, can't score."*
>
> Woody Hayes

Even with sound assumptions and follow-up, issues will arise. To deal with or even prevent them, it pays to anticipate these issues. Although it is primarily considered a problem-solving tool, fishbone (a.k.a. Ishikawa, cause-effect) diagrams are useful for planning because they provide a structured approach to brainstorming and anticipating potential problems. For the unfamiliar, these diagrams were popularized in the 1960s by a quality guru named Kaoru Ishikawa. The diagram consists of what looks like a fish head, spine, and ribs (see Figure 20.1).

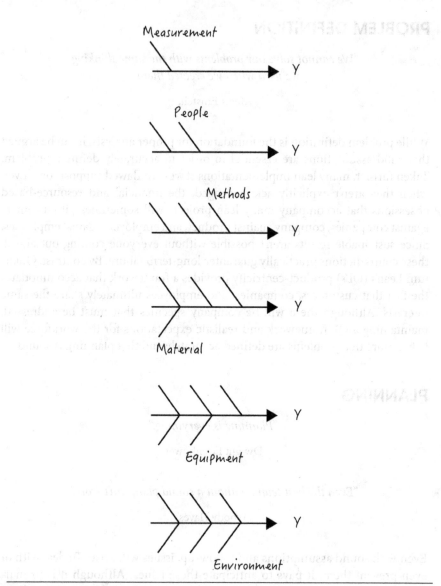

Figure 20.1   Fishbone diagram—blank

The problem is shown as the fish's head with ribs branching off the backbone representing six categories for potential causes. For defects, some possible culprits might fall under the following categories:

- Method
  - Are the methods properly specified?
  - Are the methods being followed?
  - Are the methods understood?
- Machine (equipment)
  - Is the proper machine used?
  - Is the equipment operating as specified?
- Man (people)
  - Are authorized people on the job?
  - Do they have adequate knowledge?
- Materials
  - Is the right material specified?
  - Is the right material in use?
  - Is the material being used within specification?
- Measurement
  - Are the valid features being measured?
  - Are the measurements being properly performed?
  - Are the measurement devices accurate?
- Milieu (Mother Nature, environment)
  - Does the workplace encourage sending bad product forward?
  - Are temperature and humidity consistent with manufacturing good product?

The diagram is used to facilitate brainstorming, record potential issues, and comprehensively document sub-causes and factors. Each issue should be located on the diagram under the most appropriate category.[20-1]

Fishbone for Lean Initiative

If a fishbone diagram can aid in planning, it can also help anticipate issues in a lean implementation. The following figure shows a fishbone with some common problems that might occur during a lean project (see Figure 20.2).

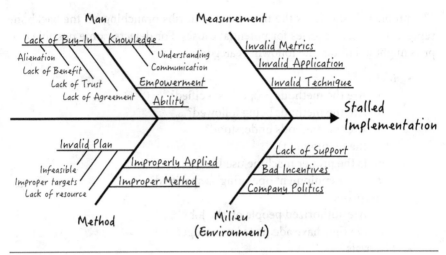

Figure 20.2   Lean fishbone diagram

The problem is defined as a stalled implementation and the potential causes in this diagram are elaborated in the following paragraphs. Typically, while faulty machines and materials are a barrier to lean outcomes, these categories are rarely the root cause of a delayed project. However, culprits related to man, method, milieu (environment), and measurement are generally abundant.

Man

This particular *rib* points out issues dealing with the human factor (see Figure 20.3).

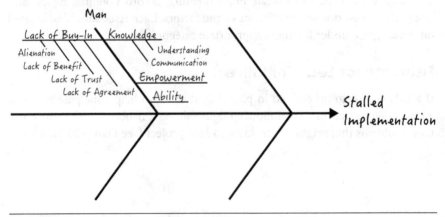

Figure 20.3   Lean fishbone diagram (man)

Lack of Buy-In

There are many potential reasons for a lack of buy-in.

- *Alienation*—are employees exasperated? For an example of a disgruntled workforce, consider this true story: a company required outdoorsy employees to attend a classroom-based course. The attendees were required to complete a homework assignment on their own time, and the course content had no relevance to their jobs. Worst of all, the employees weren't even compensated. Needless to say, this is a less-than-perfect way to sell a plan.
- *Lack of benefit*—is the plan in the employees' interest? Does it:
  - Make the job easier?
  - Improve job security?
  - Increase compensation?
  - Avoid penalties?
- *Lack of trust*—is management trusted and trustworthy?
- *Lack of agreement*—does the workforce think that the plan and objectives make sense?

Knowledge

Do employees understand what they need to do and how to do it? For example, if hands-on employees are asked to do clerical tasks, they may be unclear regarding what they are supposed to do or how you want it done. The same might be true if a clerical worker is asked to perform hands-on work. To this point, consider:

- *Communication*—has the plan been thoroughly communicated early, often, and in multiple ways?
- *Understanding*—just communicating to employees isn't enough. Has understanding/perception of the plan been *verified*?

Empowerment

Does an employee's authority match his/her responsibility?

Ability

Does an employee have the training and ability to do what he/she is asked?

Measurement

Invalid measurements can negatively affect production. Consider the following points (see Figure 20.4).

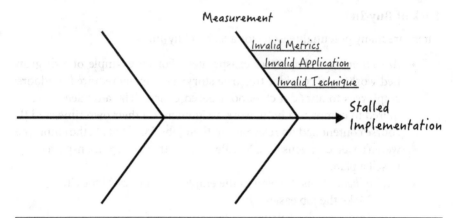

Figure 20.4   Lean fishbone diagram (measurement)

Invalid Metrics

Are the right measurements being tracked? In particular, legacy metrics have a way of undermining lean goals. The following is a true story: a general manager (GM) at a fabrication plant doubled production, halved the lead time, maintained level staffing, and increased morale. Not taking this news lying down, the company president confronted the GM with the question, "Where's the beef?" To make a long story short, this disconnect was traceable to upper management's fixation on man-hours as the key metric. While the improvements had radically decreased the product's time-in-system, the man-hours hadn't been reduced yet. Since management's key performance indicator hadn't improved but everything else was clearly better, the president was probably experiencing cognitive dissonance.

Invalid Application

Are results unduly influenced by management's wishes or otherwise skewed? Are measurement techniques applied properly and consistently?

Invalid Technique

Are measurement techniques properly specified?

Milieu (Environment)

The work environment has a definite effect on production. Examine the following topics (see Figure 20.5).

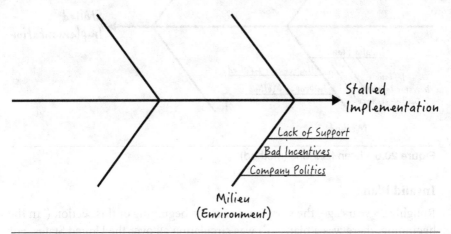

Figure 20.5 Lean fishbone diagram (milieu)

Company Politics

Do company politics unduly influence decisions?

Bad Incentives

Does the company compensation structure undermine lean?

Lack of Support

Does management properly support the lean initiative? Is the plan a priority for management?

Method

The plan chosen and the method in which it is applied will have a big influence on the outcome. Consider the issues in the following diagram (see Figure 20.6).

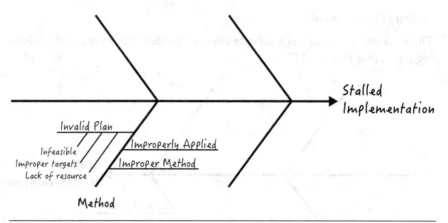

Figure 20.6   Lean fishbone (method)

Invalid Plan

Roughly 25 years ago, the story quoted at the beginning of this section ("In the beginning, there was a plan . . .") was circulating all over the United States. For those who weren't around at the time, it was popular from coast to coast. In fact, this tale was decidedly viral before the concept of virality came into existence. The overwhelming reception strongly suggested that plans without form or substance were prevalent. Fortunately, there are common and foreseeable reasons for this.

- *Infeasible*—action items can fall victim to *technical infeasibility*. The following is a true story: management demanded that a team achieve on-time delivery despite the fact that necessary parts were routinely unavailable until after the jobs themselves were due. Employees with the audacity to protest were hectored to stop making excuses and to think *outside the box*.
- *Improper targets*—common problems include prioritizing areas where the impacts will be low, nonexistent, or counterproductive. It is vital that the proper issues are targeted.
- *Lack of resource*—proper resources are essential. Does the plan allot enough time, manpower, and money to this priority?

Improper Method

Is something other than QL being used? The proper method can make all the difference.

Improperly Applied Method

Are QL methods being applied properly? Conventional lean ideas can be so ingrained in people's thinking that they may default to conventional lean without realizing it.

While the possibilities are practically unlimited, the problems documented on the fishbone diagram are very common in lean implementations. Although roadblocks will remain, foreseeing issues will allow for time to formulate workarounds and make the best of less-than-ideal situations. In some cases, the issues can be forestalled. In others, complications have to be managed as they come up. At the same time, problems will always be present. Despite the fact that perfection is out of reach, follow-up provides a way to get close.

FOLLOW-UP

"The best laid plans of mice and men often go awry."

Robert Burns—*To a Mouse*

"There is no such thing as one trip to the hardware store."

Weldon Steele

Based on the authors' observations, even under near-ideal circumstances, most attempts to implement lean have only about a 60% chance of success on the first try. The 40% chance of failure is due to the following:

- Even the brightest and most well-trained people have limited knowledge and capacities.
- Information is often incomplete and/or inaccurate.
- In the absence of the two aforementioned limitations, problems would still occur due to unpredictable circumstances that may arise.

Further compounding the failure rate is that lean implementations frequently downplay complications. In addition, the prospects for correction are remote once a project is declared complete. Over time, problems will accumulate and compound. In such a situation, a company had better get it right the first time. However, with a 60% success rate as the best-case scenario, that is unlikely.

The saving grace is that there's always a do-over. Even better is that follow-ups work a lot like compound interest, which converts a modest nest egg into a fortune over time. Similarly, do-overs eventually transform slim odds into a sure thing. The following table includes columns that showcase that the odds of first-time success for a genius, regular Joe, and a less-than-gifted person are 60%, 51%, and 30%, respectively. Each row shows the number of trials and each entry shows the likelihood of failure for each person after the corresponding number of tries (see Figure 20.7).

Odds of Success	Genius	Regular Joe	Less Than Gifted
Trial #	60%	51%	30%
1	60	51	30
2	84	76	51
3	93.6	88.2	65.7
4	97.4	94.24	75.6
5	98.9	97.2	83.2
6	99.6	98.6	88.2
7	99.8	99.3	91.8
8	99.3	99.7	94.2
9	99.9	99.8	95.9
10	99.9	99.2	97.2
11	100	99.9	98
12	100	99.9	98.6
13	100	100	99
14	100	100	99.3
15	100	100	99.5
16	100	100	99.7
17	100	100	99.8
18	100	100	99.8

Figure 20.7   Odds of success

In the genius scenario, it takes five follow-ups to raise the odds of success to 99%. What may be unexpected is that it only takes one additional try for an average Joe to reach the same point. Even more surprisingly, a lesser talent who gets it wrong 70% of the time has a sky-high chance of success after 12 attempts! In other words, persistence practically guarantees results. These numbers are compelling and common sense shared by uncommonly successful people backs them up:

"Persistence and determination alone are omnipotent."

President Calvin Coolidge

"Genius is one percent inspiration, ninety-nine percent perspiration."

Thomas Edison

"Success is stumbling from failure to failure with no loss of enthusiasm."

Prime Minister Winston Churchill

The bottom line is to make peace with the fact that great implementations will probably require at least five runs before exceptional results should be expected. In other words, be prepared to follow through with follow-up.

During much of this process, many of the problems encountered will probably be employee related. Since deft handling of people offers the glue that can hold all of the elements together, what follows are some guidelines to bolster this side of the equation.

THE SOFT SIDE

"The soft side of the business is the hard side."

Unknown

Despite all that has been written about management, examples of great leadership are rare. In all fairness, this subject is challenging and silver bullets are elusive. At the same time, many management shortcomings are traceable to misconceptions that were debunked a long time ago. However, the good news is that common-sense ideas that are validated by research can rectify some of these missteps. Drawing on principles of persuasion and motivation will help build consensus.

THE POWER OF PERSUASION

*"Not brute force but only persuasion and faith
are the kings of this world."*

Thomas Carlyle

Before delving into what persuasion is, it is important to know what it isn't. In particular, it is not the presentation of facts followed by an audience carefully deliberating the pros and cons. Although there is a widespread perception that this is the way influence works, this is a misperception. While many like to think that people are rational and will make up their minds once they are presented with the facts, the reality is that most people make up their minds long before facts enter the picture. Once a decision is made, information is selectively gathered to justify the conclusions. Regardless of intelligence or beliefs, this is the way most people are wired. Although facts have their place, the field of persuasion isn't one of them.

Instead of being a meticulous presentation of data, persuasion is a two-part problem of convincing others to believe in the messenger and forging a consensus that mostly accommodates preconceived notions. While this may sound cynical, this is only a practical concession to human nature. Ironically, any approach that emphasizes reason is ignoring scientific findings. How rational is that?

Although many acknowledge persuasion's potential, there is a tendency to resort to coercion since it seems so much easier. Although it's initially quicker to demand that people do what you want them to, an up-front investment in persuasion has a way of transforming the never-ending push of compulsion into the pull of people volunteering to help.

Although there is always a prospect that force becomes necessary, authority has its limits. As authority approaches absolute levels, the effort that must be expended to achieve it rises significantly (see Figure 20.8).

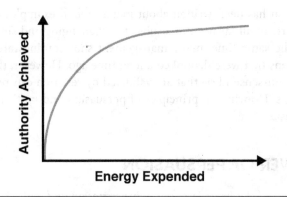

Figure 20.8   Effort versus authority

At some point, any benefit that might be gained from increased authority is far outweighed by the corresponding effort necessary to maintain it. In addition, people who act from fear only give the minimum; get agreement and they might move heaven and earth to help you. This inflection point can come sooner than many expect (see Figure 20.9).

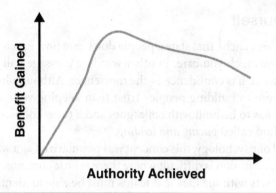

Figure 20.9   Authority versus benefit

In addition to persuasion's power and sustainability, there are other reasons to keep force as a last resort.

Authority Is Self-Defeating

Since every action triggers an equal and opposite reaction, defiance and sabotage are natural responses to arbitrary rule. In addition, the fact that an increase of force will only escalate resistance is one reason that additional investments in authority bring diminishing returns. Over the long run, persuasion is often achievable with significantly lower effort. As a bonus, it is self-reinforcing because every convert has the potential to proselytize others.

Authority Is Available to Few

Another reason persuasion should be the first resort is that most people don't have authority. Considering that the Pareto Principle would suggest that 80% of power resides with 20% of the population, the fact is that the vast majority of people come up short in this department.

Although influence is not easy, its inherent advantages of efficiency and staying power make it a strong alternative to more conventional techniques. For those who are interested in this approach, there are general principles to bolster such efforts.

PERSUASION PRINCIPLES

Even though influence is nuanced and challenging to achieve, its fundamentals are easy to understand.

Selling Yourself

There is a famous cliché that states: people don't care how much you know until they know how much you care. In other words, a message will sell a lot better when an audience has confidence in the messenger. Although honesty is essential, there's more to building people's trust than keeping your word. On some level, rapport has to be built with colleagues and a time-honored way to do this is with a method called *pacing and leading*.[20-2, 20-3]

In the field of psychology, this concept was popularized as a way to bond with others. Since persuasion is difficult where there is little common ground, pacing and leading starts with the idea that teams must be able to identify with leaders before they are willing to follow them. The process of establishing a connection is called *pacing*. Once a mutual understanding is established, influence becomes possible. While success can never be guaranteed, pacing significantly improves the odds. In addition to emphasizing points of genuine agreement and common background, actively attempting to learn about and understand others' situations are critical. For example, working on the shop floor and actively engaging with co-workers will go a long way to establishing trust. Since common ground can always be enhanced, some additional factors to consider when selling yourself include:

- *Ask for help*—one of the quickest ways to forge a bond is to ask for someone's help. And surprisingly, it's the person providing the assistance that gets the most from it. From the Florence Nightingale Effect to the affection we feel for babies, it is well-established that the act of helping others engenders positive feelings toward the person who receives assistance. However, be careful to ask for assistance sparingly and only when you are clearly unable to handle matters yourself. In addition, make your request as convenient as possible for the helper.
- *Concede the argument*—since it is often impossible to win an argument, concede the point. At the very least, table it. If this is done the right way, it is amazing how fast people can let their guard down and become receptive to new information. For example, if someone says that lean won't work in their environment, the most effective and appropriate reply is, "You're probably right." At the very least, this response is honest because little is possible in an environment where someone is dead set against an idea. Second, acknowledging objections makes people much more receptive to other ideas and allows for genuine communication.
- *Emphasize the positive*—as a variation on conceding the argument, phrase questions as if the status quo is perfect. For example, a question

like, "How high is the scrap rate?" is better asked in the following manner: "Is the scrap rate pretty close to zero?" If the situation is far from ideal, the likelihood of this being acknowledged is much higher if the question is asked in the latter way.

- *Competence*—skill is the universal language that dissolves barriers. Everyone respects it. If you can help someone solve a problem with your skills, it can't help but bolster your credibility.

Although techniques like *mirroring* are often suggested to build rapport, it may come off as superficial or insincere, and it is critical to build a connection by being genuine. In other words, don't try to force common ground where none exists. Examples of this could be mimicking another person's style if it does not align with your own, or adopting any approach that doesn't reflect who you authentically are. In such cases, others will probably see through the facade. Other than con artists, few have the ability to fool others for any length of time.

Ultimately, there is a lot of latitude possible when applying these points. The main goal should be to stay genuine. Even with a lackluster personality, staying respectful, honest, and comfortable in your own skin tends to work. And once trust is built, it becomes possible to influence.

Selling Ideas

Once credibility is established, there's a good chance that you can convince people to take a particular position. While an idea should be sound, human nature will make any associated persuasion less than straightforward. Instead of attempting to change that reality, working with it can advance objectives farther in less time.

- *No persuasion may be the best persuasion*—while the highest impact actions should come first in a perfect world, the effort necessary to convince someone to take specific actions might be a daunting task. Due to the difficulty that can come with gaining buy-in, it might make sense to minimize the risks and start with ideas that have widespread acceptance. After all, if someone is already convinced, persuasion can't get a lot easier. While this will vary with the work environment, there are different lean tools that a company might consider adopting. The following list contains lean tools and their estimated impacts. With 1 representing the best case to 5 representing the worst, the mix of projects might be characterized as shown in the chart (see Figure 20.10).

Tool	Impact
DBR	1
Cellular	1
5S	2
Product-Based Layout	2
One-Piece Flow	2
Kanban	3
TPM	4
Standardized Work	4
Quality @ Source	4
Andon	5
Work Balancing	5

Figure 20.10   Priority by impact

If impact were the sole consideration, drum-buffer-rope (DBR) or cells would be done first. However, at many companies, DBR can be an extremely tough sell to management that is obsessed with resource utilization. Similarly, cells typically lower machine utilization and entail the expense of moving equipment around. If a practitioner is exceptionally persuasive, prioritizing according to impact will make sense. However, when salesmanship is in short supply, starting with something that will face less pushback may be in order. Because nothing can happen without management support, a far different picture emerges if the lean tools are prioritized by management buy-in (see Figure 20.11).

Tool	Management
5S	1
Kanban	1
Standardized Work	1
Work Balancing	1
TPM	2
One-Piece Flow	3
Quality @ Source	3
Andon	3
DBR	5
Cellular	5
Product-Based Layout	5

Figure 20.11   Priority by persuasion

In this instance, tools like 5S and standard work take precedence. Although these are subpar candidates for impact, a practitioner has to know his/her limitations and get as much impact as possible given his/her persuasiveness. Depending on the situation, factors like effort and workforce buy-in can also be considered when setting priority. Since half a loaf beats none, this idea is offered as a compromise rather than the best way to do things. As persuasive ability grows, the priorities can more closely align with QL.

- *Behavior creates attitudes*[2-4]—although many try to change behaviors by shaping attitudes, research has demonstrated that this belief has cause and effect reversed. In other words, behavior is what changes attitudes. Implicitly, maximizing buy-in means that lean efforts should emphasize actions that reinforce lean beliefs. For example, making sure that employees maintain 5S will eventually cause skeptics to believe in 5S. Although the numbers will vary, an average of 66 days of consistent application is required for behavior to become internalized into an attitude. While exerting some authority is implied with this strategy, the effectiveness of this approach can't be ignored.

Although the task of selling ideas can be challenging, gaining followers is not the finish line. From that point, keeping converts in the fold is the next challenge. With all the obstacles and pitfalls on a new journey, finding motivation will make or break whether people can stay on the path.

MOTIVATION

"Coaches who can outline plays on a black board are a dime a dozen. The ones who win get inside their player's heads and motivate them."

Woody Hayes

"It is difficult to get a man to understand something, when his salary depends on his not understanding it."

Upton Sinclair

> *"It must be considered that there is nothing more difficult to carry out nor more doubtful of success nor more dangerous to handle than to initiate a new order of things; for the reformer has enemies in all those who profit by the old order, and only lukewarm defenders in all those who would profit by the new order."*

Niccolo Machiavelli—*The Prince*

Once someone agrees to a principle, motivation is necessary to bridge the gap between theory and reality. For example, multitudes begin fitness programs but can't sustain them. The difference lies in motivation. Although the objectives of QL are entirely consistent with an organization's long-term interests, there can be incompatibilities with an individual's real or perceived interests. Two issues need to be considered in order to have a chance of motivating those involved:

- *Hidden and not-so-hidden agendas*—it is possible for someone to believe in an idea, but to also lack interest due to current incentives.
- *Energy*—since improvement involves effort and re-effort due to mis-steps, significant energy is necessary to offset this.

Unless a way is found to address or work around these points, the barriers may prove too great.

Agendas

The following are some reasons that hidden agendas may exist:

- *Frame*—some ideas are clearly counterproductive from an operational standpoint, but rational in a different framework. One example is that some corporations prioritize selling shares over selling a product. Consider the push toward vendor-managed inventory. Although it often increases material costs, the ability to shift inventory from a company to a supplier improves the return on equity and may increase a company's attractiveness in the stock market. In other words, what is questionable from a QL standpoint makes sense in another frame.
- *Job security*—one small reason change is resisted is that it tends to make people less proficient at their current job. For example, when a new version of software is released, users have to adjust to the revisions. Someone who was well-versed in the old package suddenly becomes a lot less adept. Often, operational changes work the same way. When personnel possess unique and useful knowledge, a de facto priesthood forms and job security (perceived or real) accrues with it.

- *Skimming*—don't rule out unethical motivations. If someone is cashing in on inefficiency, it's reasonable to expect a complete lack of interest in its elimination.

SIDEBAR—MOTIVATION

At a hypothetical die cast plant that is in no way based on a true story, cosmetic requirements on castings were so demanding that scrap rates of 20% were routine. When a part was rejected, it was sent back to the furnace for re-melt. Since accounting allowed for an overly generous amount of metal loss on re-melt, the likelihood of exceeding the budget on materials was negligible. However, considerable expense was incurred in energy, handling, and lost productivity.

Simultaneously, an engineer (who was in no way one of the authors) applied design of experiments techniques to determine if any settings could be revised to improve yield. As it turned out, a set of process parameters were found that cut the scrap rate in half. Surprisingly, the plant manager took no interest in these findings, assigned the engineer to a new project, and business as usual was resumed.

Why?

Hint: the plant manager exclusively handled metal purchases and conducted this business in great secrecy.

Answer: due to the generous amount of metal loss that was budgeted by accounting, a substantial amount of metal loss occurred on paper. In reality, this loss wasn't taking place. For example, the books might have shown 1,000 pounds of loss when only 10 pounds were truly lost. The plant manager was skimming this 990 pounds of excess aluminum and getting kickbacks from the supplier. For every 100 pounds of scrap that this die cast plant generated, a 1% metal-loss allowance yielded one pound of aluminum. Since die cast plants typically process a lot of material, this was a lucrative arrangement. No wonder the plant manager wasn't interested in reducing scrap!

In addition to agendas that are hidden, there are others that lie in plain sight:

- *Home office*—standard business practices encourage counterproductive ideas like resource obsession. As intelligent as some managers are, some believe in seriously counterproductive ideas. And those who don't still have to accommodate others who do.
- *Incentive*—if there is any incentive plan, the odds are that the reward structure will not be aligned with QL. In fact, the chances are good that the incentives will be diametrically opposed to product-centricity.

In any of these cases, it's possible that a person can entirely agree with QL, but is unable to support it for completely rational reasons. Identifying and adjusting to these motivations will improve the odds of a successful outcome.

Energy

If agreement is forged and interests are aligned, a lot of work remains. Frequently, this requires that participants expend significant mental energy. One of the best ways to sustain this energy is to understand what the workforce's currency is. From there, trade in it. By denominating QL in terms that employees value (management and rank-and-file alike), it increases the chance that the desire for an outcome will exceed the difficulties involved.

Maslow's Hierarchy of Needs[20-5, 20-6]

Although there is a belief that only extrinsic rewards motivate people, this isn't entirely true. In advanced industrial societies, this notion is often false. Back in the 1940s, a psychologist named Abraham Maslow formulated what was called a *hierarchy of needs* (see Figure 20.12).

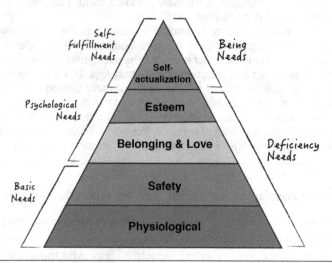

Figure 20.12   Maslow's hierarchy of needs

In this theory, the idea was that needs that are lower in the hierarchy must be addressed before higher-level issues can be attended to. For example, an ample supply of air must be available before one can think about the meaning of life. If employees are chronically behind financially, dangling payoffs in self-actualization will probably go nowhere. Conversely, when potential gains are congruent with aspirations, real motivation becomes possible. One point to keep in mind is that self-actualization is the only motivation that isn't self-limiting. In other words, as any of the lesser needs are increasingly met, the motivation that comes from satisfying them decreases (see Figure 20.13).

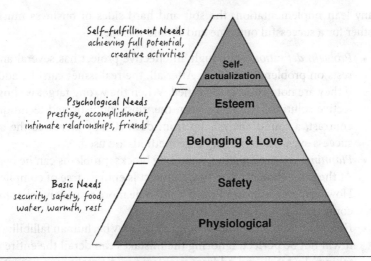

Figure 20.13 Maslow's hierarchy of needs 2

The following chart lists appropriate incentives for a given level of *need* that a workforce displays (see Figure 20.14).

Level	Appropriate Motivators
Self Actualization	Career Development
Esteem	Accomplishment, Recognition
Belonging	Team Building
Safety	Financial, Incentive Plan, Job Security
Physiological	Safety Program

Figure 20.14 Reward chart

As a caution, Maslow's theory is a guide and not an absolute. In other words, someone can be motivated by a higher level of needs even though the lower ones aren't completely met. However, to a large extent, the hierarchy remains valid and provides a good model to guide your approach. Also, in practice, some people stop at the esteem level of the hierarchy and go no further. Incentivizing this type of person requires invalidating the status quo to create a setting where they have to reestablish self-esteem.

SUMMARY

In any lean implementation, the soft and hard sides of business must come together for a successful outcome and should include:

- *Problem definition*—although an effective project has several angles, it rests on problem definition. After all, the real issues can't be addressed if they are not properly identified. When the wrong target is chosen, effective solutions will elude even the most sophisticated techniques. By contrast, a sound analysis up front dramatically increases the odds of success even when trailing-edge methods are used.
- *Planning*—by anticipating stumbling blocks, problems can be bypassed. At the same time, it's rare that a project is entirely free of complications. However, preparation allows a team to be more responsive should issues come up.
- *Follow-up*—no matter how sound a plan may be, human fallibility means it will not be perfect. Ignoring the mistakes can derail the entire undertaking. To catch and address problems in a timely way, proactive follow-up is a must.

Once these foundations are laid, deft navigation of company politics is imperative. On the soft side of implementations, the following issues merit serious consideration:

- *Persuasion*—although compulsion is sometimes necessary, persuading a workforce to embrace a program will result in a more thorough and sustainable implementation.
- *Motivation*—getting people to agree on an idea is often easy; it is getting them to act that can be daunting. Motivation bridges the gap between belief and practice.

Once these foundations are established, deft navigation of company politics is needed to further increase the odds of success. On the soft side of implementations, proper consideration should be given to the following few key issues. Although implementation can be challenging, applying sound ideas up front will make for the best possible start. From there, it's critical to learn from experience, reexamine your assumptions, and make adjustments. With sound assumptions, planning, follow-up, persuasion, and motivation, it's possible to make the most of QL techniques and get great results for owners, employees, and customers.

CHAPTER 21

POTEMKIN LEAN[21-1]

"All that glitters is not gold."

William Shakespeare—*The Merchant of Venice*

In the 1700s, Russia annexed the Crimean Peninsula and appointed Grigory Potemkin as its new governor. One of the tasks assigned to the new overlord was rebuilding the region. After a few years, a government delegation announced an upcoming visit for an update. As reality wasn't going to come close to what the officials wanted to see, Potemkin came clean and resigned his position to save everyone the time and trouble of a disappointing visit.

Just kidding! Of course, anyone who's worked in the real world knows *that* didn't happen. Instead, Potemkin bridged the gap between dreams and reality by setting up portable villages along the delegation's tour path. Before the dignitaries arrived, a phony settlement would be erected, accompanied by actors portraying peasants. After the visit, the structures would be disassembled and reassembled farther down the route, where they were fashioned to look like a different community. Although historians disagree about this story's details, the term *Potemkin Village* has come to mean any kind of setup devised to deceive others into thinking that a situation is better than it really is. And when lean comes up, Potemkin Villages definitely come to mind.

POTEMKIN LEAN IN THE WORKPLACE

In a lot of workplaces, all kinds of tools are deployed with the nominal goal of improvement. However, many of these *aids* are just glorified versions of the infamous status report. Instead of helping, they're actually a distraction from productive efforts. At the same time, they are sometimes used to paint a pretty picture that is at odds with a gritty reality. The following sections include a few cases in point.

Huddle Boards

Boards to show status, progress, and issues related to a project. Although it's supposed to help with visualizing workflow, huddle boards are so useful that employees typically ignore them until visitors come. At that point, everything will be updated and brought up to presentation quality. Upon the dignitary's departure, a normal return to activities (or lack thereof) occurs (see Figure 21.1).

Figure 21.1   Huddle board

One-Point Lessons (OPLs)

A one-point lesson is a work instruction that consists of one or two sentences along with explanatory diagrams. Generally, they are kept to two or fewer pages. Visitors to plants will often see them plastered everywhere, even in bathrooms. The idea is to convey information in digestible quantities so employees can internalize the lesson, improve work quality, and sustain continuous improvement. What is overlooked is that anything simple enough to summarize in two sentences probably doesn't need to be documented and is almost certain to be common knowledge. The best case is that OPLs will remind employees to do what they should already be doing (see Figure 21.2).

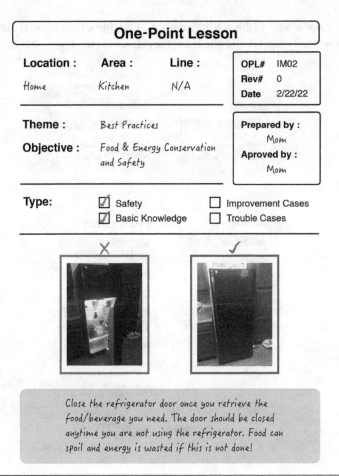

Figure 21.2 One-point lesson

Key Performance Indicator (KPI) Boards

There is a famous saying that what gets measured gets done. Taking this to heart, companies adopt what are called KPIs to elevate the business. And if measuring makes things happen, it stands to reason that gauging a lot of things should cause a whole lot of things to take place. Consequently, goals and objectives are often adopted for multiple levels, departments, and individuals. To monitor all of these numbers, boards that display progress against KPIs are used. Instead of being an aid to daily work, they are primarily used to convey status to managers and visitors. Even worse, updating and maintaining these boards takes attention away from the product. Instead of being a servant, these boards have a way of becoming masters. Outside of occasional shows, these boards typically receive the attention they deserve (see Figure 21.3).

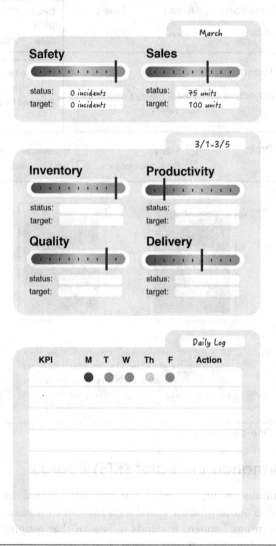

Figure 21.3   KPI board

Kanban/Task Boards

Although kanban is simple in concept, a kanban board can really complicate things. This tool is generally a white or magnetic board used to display work status. For example, there might be columns labeled *backlog, in progress,* and *complete.* Sticky notes or magnets that represent the different projects are placed under these column headings to indicate what stage a project is in. In theory, this is a simple way to track work and avoid dropped balls. However, a spreadsheet does the same job in a way that is better, faster, and cheaper. On a KPI board, post-its and magnets have to be written on, modified, and rearranged continuously. On top of this, a board lacks a search function, the capability to manipulate data, and the ability to share information remotely. Nevertheless, if the object is maintaining appearances, a KPI board has a visual impact that a spreadsheet doesn't. So, a board it will be (see Figure 21.4).

Figure 21.4 Kanban/task board (Image by Gerd Altmann, https://pixabay.com/)

These are just a few prominent examples of lean best-in-show. To feed this Potemkin beast, employees frequently have to gather data that doesn't exist to answer questions that shouldn't be asked, and to provide managers inaccurate and irrelevant information they will never act on. And the fact that managers never act on it may be the best news of all.

Of course, if tools like the ones mentioned serve the product and improve flow, then absolutely employ them. The point is not to bury lean tools, but avoid being mesmerized by them. If a company can avoid confusing style with substance, it will also avoid wasting resources, exasperating employees, and squandering time.

Of course, there will always be people who want to maintain appearances, and this has to be kept in mind. However, the challenge is attacking priorities in the right order. If substance is front and center, the aesthetics that follow can be shockingly good!

ANOTHER WAY

One of the refreshing aspects of Quantum Lean (QL) is the way it demolishes frequently held beliefs about what constitutes good business. Where one school of thought pits the interests of the customer and provider against each other, the QL framework brings them back into alignment where they should have been all along. Similarly, many inaccurately think that style and substance must come into conflict. However, both goals can be met with proper prioritization.

Specifically, serving the product first allows a company to elevate performance while achieving a first-class image. The reason this works is that there are few ways to serve the product but many ways to look attractive. Starting with appearances runs a high risk of dead ending when other goals come into play. By contrast, locking down the proper objective leaves a lot of paths for achieving cosmetics. As long as the finishing touches don't detract from the previous work, the best of both worlds is possible. The following sections describe a few examples.

SIDEBAR—CADILLAC XLR

A notable case of elevating style over substance occurred at General Motor's Cadillac division. Among a wide variety of bells and whistles, this company's Cadillac XLR vehicle prominently featured the Northstar engine. Widely regarded as the most sophisticated motor in company history, this powerplant possessed the most current technological features. With Cadillac's target market consisting of consumers wanting the latest and greatest features, the marketing considerations from incorporating such a leading-edge product might have blinded this automaker to a superior alternative that was readily available.

On the same production line that produced the Cadillac XLR, General Motors manufactured the Chevrolet Corvette. However, instead of the Northstar, the Corvette used the LS motor. Compared to the Northstar, the LS was actually a far superior engine in terms of power, reliability, or economy. In other words, Cadillac probably allowed the glamour of the Northstar to overpower more substantive considerations. Had Cadillac opted for the superior motor, the XLR would have performed better and been much less expensive to produce.

5S

Using the product path diagram (PPD) to tell you when 5S is needed ensures that 5S takes care of the prime goal of serving the product. For example, if a delay is related to the fact that employees have to spend time retrieving tools to do a job, implementing something like shadow boards would probably be the response. Based on what the PPD is showing, the shadow board may be all that's needed. However, with shine, standardize, and sustain, workplace organization can go well beyond this. A common question is, "How far should I take 5S?" At a minimum, 5S should be applied to the extent that it benefits, and does not detract from, the product. For example, there are elements that sound good, have little to do with the product's needs, but probably won't detract from serving the product. Such measures are compatible with QL:

- *Polished/painted floors*—most of the time, polished or painted floors are primarily for the sake of appearance; although sometimes they are helpful.
- *Shadow boards for cleaning supplies*—although these boards are useful for expediting cleanup, there is little explicit effect on deliverables.
- *Signs identifying work areas*—while it's nice to have signs to acquaint newcomers with the workplace, they probably don't help the product.

By contrast, the following approaches may have either positive or negative impacts:

- *Standardization*—if standardization makes 5S efforts better, faster, or cheaper, then proceed full speed ahead. On the other hand, if different areas of a plant have different needs, what's good for one department might be detrimental to another. In that case, standardization would actually impair performance.
- *5S audits*—follow-up is important, and how it is done is even more critical. Commonly, companies commit numerous man-hours to audit 5S compliance. If the purpose is to monitor and improve the 5S program, that's one thing; however, if it harasses employees, that's another. At the end of the day, it's impossible to police a company into being lean.

In addition, here are some 5S provisions that are counterproductive:

- *Extending 5S into personal effects*—some companies will specify minutiae like beverage placement, where employees can hang their coats, and prohibiting family photos.
- *Overspecification*—beyond personal effects, locations are often designated for every conceivable object in a workspace. If the item doesn't

affect a deliverable's flow, overspecification only adds to the issues that require employee attention. This practice takes attention away from more urgent tasks, not to mention annoys people. In addition, a permanent piece of equipment that is inherently findable doesn't need its location marked off.

Drum-Buffer-Rope (DBR)

Like 5S, using PPD to indicate that DBR is needed ensures that DBR takes care of QL's prime goal. As DBR minimizes work in process, this will reduce clutter and create a clean canvas. In fact, the canvas can be so blank that the temptation to fill it may overwhelm actual need. In the interest of simplifying shop-floor control, tools that could be considered, but should be unnecessary include:

- *First-in, first-out (FIFO) lanes*—FIFO lanes are buffers placed in front of bottleneck processes. As opposed to other kinds of buffers, jobs are lined up so they are processed on a *first-come, first-served* basis. In an environment where priority isn't subject to change, this could be a good and simple way to ensure proper shop-floor control. Conversely, a dynamic situation where priorities will frequently shift would render such a provision useless or it could create additional handling.
- *Heijunka box*—Heijunka is a concept where uneven demand is grouped together for a time interval and averaged out so that production can be scheduled at a constant rate. At the same time, the goal is also to produce a daily product mix that comes as close as possible to reflecting demand. A Heijunka box is used to schedule a shop and maintain a level and smooth production flow. A typical example might consist of pigeonholes with the horizontal rows representing each product and vertical columns representing a time interval (e.g., hours, days, shifts). Although QL and the DBR philosophies are largely at odds with the Heijunka concept, such a tool could come in handy (see Figure 21.5). However, if it were useful, why not use a spreadsheet and print out the schedule for production?

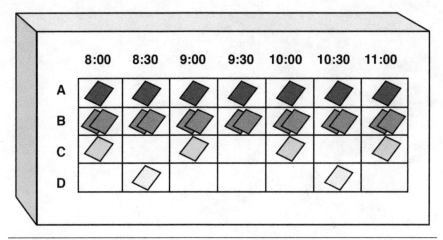

Figure 21.5   Heijunka box

SUMMARY

To create the veneer of a lean system, many businesses deploy lean tools without considering whether they are really necessary. What follows are wasted efforts, disgruntled employees, and wasted money on tools that do not serve the product. However, starting with need allows a company to elevate performance and also achieve a first-class image. The reason this works is that there are few paths to serve to the product, but numerous ways to maintain appearances. Beginning implementations with a goal of deploying tools runs an elevated risk of undermining proper priorities. By contrast, ensuring that the product is served allows many possibilities for cosmetic touches. As long as these finishing touches don't detract from the previous work, the best of both worlds is possible. The bottom line is that adhering to the QL principle of prioritizing the product will streamline production while eliminating costs associated with unnecessary bells and whistles. At the same time, a foundation for an attractive workplace will be laid.

APPENDIX A

INVENTORY PRIMER

As a springboard into the Quantum Lean (QL) approach to inventory control, a refresher on fundamentals may be useful for those with a limited background. Although the principles detailed in this section are not explicitly tied to QL, they will underscore practically any effort to implement a lean system. In other words, a familiarity with these basic ideas is warranted for those who want to adopt QL.

INVENTORY—FUNDAMENTAL ELEMENTS

Regardless of business philosophy, a comprehensive materials management system includes:

- *Objectives*—to know how a system is doing, performance should be gauged. Before there is an ability to track, objectives must first be established.
- *Scope*—an understanding and definition for what is kept in inventory and when and where it is done.
- *Inventory parameters*—a consistent approach to setting system parameters so that fulfillment is achieved.
- *Procedure*—specification of the who, what, when, where, and how of materials management.
- *Inventory checks*—periodic checks to verify inventory quantity, condition, and location.
- *Designated locations*—explicit and uniquely identified storage locations.
- *Tracking*—monitoring of the system and its performance.

Objectives

An ideal inventory control system can be summarized by the following statement:

> *"Having the right material in the right place at the right time in the right sequence and at the right quantity and quality."*

Taken a step further, a perfect system would mean that all of these requirements are met without keeping any inventory. While such a goal is too lofty for the real world, organizations can still reach excellence by setting proper objectives. Some frequently used metrics to this end include:

- *Inventory turns* (*also called stock turn or inventory turnover*)—the cost-of-goods-sold (COGS) divided by the average inventory level. This ratio is used to indicate the number of times inventory is sold or consumed over a given time.
- *Accuracy*—for a business to have any ability to plan effectively, inventory counts must be accurate.
- *Fulfillment*—after higher priority jobs receive their part allocations, fulfillment is all necessary materials being available when an order is received. To clarify, a filled space on a shelf is not fulfillment. To phrase it another way, an order is fulfilled only if all of its required materials are available in sufficient quantity when they are needed.
  - To expand on this idea, an outage is when product is unavailable after an order is received and this order cannot be fulfilled after material is allocated to all the higher priority jobs. In the QL framework, an empty space on a shelf is not an outage in and of itself. Before such an event occurs, a need for the part must first exist.
- *Man-hours committed to inventory management*—the time and effort involved in checking inventory counts, maintaining stock, and updating systems is significant. Some companies may want to balance these costs against other objectives like accuracy.

Once goals are set, devising and refining a system to achieve them is the next order of business.

Scope

Determining when and where to keep inventory is a critical decision. If the necessary items aren't stocked, frequent outages will result in late deliveries and problems with customer satisfaction. On the other hand, maintaining unnecessary inventory significantly increases operating costs. Although an unpredictable future means that miscalculations will occur, there are good guidelines to help determine when and where inventory should be kept. Before delving into these guidelines, familiarity with the three categories of inventory is essential:

- *Raw inventory*—raw material consists of items that are acquired for incorporation into finished product and have not yet been released to production.
- *Work-in-process (WIP) inventory (aka semi-finished items)*—WIP is product that is partially processed, but not ready for sale. Typically, WIP is found on a production floor during the manufacturing process.
- *Finished goods inventory (FGI)*—FGI is product that has been processed by the company and is ready for shipment.

A few examples are listed in the following sections to clarify the differences among these classifications. At a mine, iron ore is finished product, but becomes raw material when it reaches a steel mill. An engine is finished product at an engine plant and raw product when it reaches an automotive assembly plant. For additional clarification, an engine would be considered WIP if it were located at an integrated plant that includes engine production and car assembly (see Figure A.1).

	Raw	WIP	Finished
Iron Ore	Steel Mill		Mine
Steel Round Stock	Fastener Manufacturer		Steel Mill
Nuts and Bolts	Automotive Plant		Fastener Manufacturer
Engine	Automotive Assembly Plant	Automotive Plant (Integrated)	Engine Plant
Car	Automotive Dealer		Automotive Assembly Plant

Figure A.1 Inventory type

For each category of inventory, there are conditions where keeping stock is in a business's interest. Understanding these guidelines is critical to cost-effective inventory management.

Generally speaking, inventory should be kept when its absence threatens a company's ability to deliver an order within the lead time that customers need. Specifically, there are useful rules of thumb for when product should be inventoried.

Raw Inventory

Maintain a supply when:

- Vendor delivery windows are too long to fulfill customer turnaround requirements without keeping materials on hand.
  - For example, if a customer's required delivery is two weeks and a vendor requires at least a month to deliver parts, material needs to be stocked.
- Supplier quality or delivery is inconsistent and necessitates that stock be maintained to cushion against supply chain disruptions.
  - Even if a vendor's average lead time is quick enough to fulfill on-time delivery, their turnarounds may fluctuate such that it becomes a *hand-to-mouth* arrangement and cannot be relied on.

WIP Inventory

WIP should be considered when:

- A product's time on the shop floor exceeds customer lead-time requirements. For example, a product requires one week on the shop floor, but a customer's lead time is three days.
- Production is too inconsistent to meet on-time deliveries.
- Level loading is being used. Level loading is a technique that is used to smooth out fulfillment and meet demand when there is a mismatch in production rates among processes (see Figure A.2). Doing this allows an organization to maintain production without additional capital investment. For example, consider a process with an average production rate that equals the average demand rate, but in which the peak pace is slower than the maximum demand rate:
  - The market consumes product at 30 units per day. Machine 1 produces 10 units per shift over three shifts while subsequent machines produce 30 units during one shift. One way to meet demand is by allowing WIP to build up between Machine 1 and the next step in production.

    In many cases, this arrangement is desirable since it doesn't require investment in additional equipment.

buffer smooths production

Figure A.2 Level loading

FGI

FGI is called for when:

- Lead times are longer than customer requirements.
  - Customer needs units within three days and the lead time is far longer.
- Production rates are insufficient to meet peak demand.
  - Plant produces 10 units/day. While sales average 10 units/day, peak daily demand is 30 units.

At a minimum, the bottom line is to keep inventory when it's needed to ensure on-time performance. Once the what, when, and where of inventory is determined, the next task is figuring out how much material to keep so that production stays supplied.

Inventory Parameters

When supplies run low, a robust approach to trigger purchases is necessary to prevent outages. This involves determining the following:

- *Reorder point (ROP)*—ROP is a stock level that triggers reorder. If a purchase order should be initiated when the inventory count falls below 1,000, the ROP is 1,000.
- *Reorder quantity (ROQ)*—the specified quantity to order when an ROP is reached. For instance, if a quantity of 500 needs to be acquired when the ROP is arrived at, the ROQ is 500.
- *Safety stock (SS)*—a supply of material kept in the case that demand overwhelms specified ROPs and ROQs.
- *Min/max*—minimum and maximum stocking levels.
- *Lead time*—the time required for an order to be delivered. Put another way, the time from order initiation to delivery.

The following chart shows how this system would behave under the ideal situation of constant demand and constant lead time (see Figure A.3).

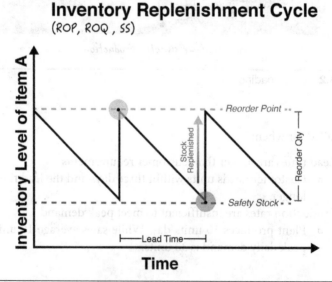

Figure A.3   Ideal reorder system

Once an ROP is reached, a purchase order would be sent to a vendor to replenish the supply. During the time required for the shipment to be delivered, a business will have the necessary stock to keep the operation going. By the time the delivery arrives, the supply has dwindled. At this point, the replenishment increases the inventory level back up to the ROP. From here, the cycle repeats.

Reality will depart from this, but the ideal situation provides a start. There are many methods for handling uncertainty in lead time and usage; a few of those methods are covered in the chapter on QL inventory control. Once a replenishment system is specified, measures must be taken to ensure that inventory levels are accurately tracked. Without this, even carefully formulated plans will go awry.

Inventory Count

Most are familiar with the idea of comprehensive inventory counts. While many are also aware of cycle counting, it's important to review this approach as it should be used in a QL system.

ABC Analysis

Cycle counting's linchpin is a method of prioritizing inventory counts by focusing on the items that have an outsized influence on company performance. Typically, the criteria are financial. In other words, the more expensive an item is, the more it will be checked.

Cycle Counting

As opposed to counting every stock keeping unit (SKU) once per year, cycle counting schedules inventory checks throughout the year and offers the following advantages over annual inventories:

- *Less disruptive*—due to the need to check every inventory item, annual physical inventories are labor intensive, time consuming, and disruptive. Since fewer SKUs are involved in an individual cycle count, this method requires fewer people, less time, and creates less disruption.
- *More accurate*—all things being equal, cycle counting is more accurate than annual checks.
- *More timely*—by updating counts more frequently, information is timelier.

Regardless of the method employed, efficient counts need every SKU to have an address so that materials can be accessed conveniently.

Designated Storage Locations

Designated storage locations make rapid retrieval and efficient inventory checks possible. The following should be factored in when specifying locations:

- *Unique identification for each spot*—this prevents confusion on the ground and in the computer.
- *Limited number of items per location*—limiting the number of items per location is intended to expedite inventory checks. Too many SKUs in one area can cause excess searching. While one SKU per location is ideal, this may not always be practical. At the least, try to size locations so that they hold a limited number of items. Even better, size locations so they are modular with smaller storage units like bins and drawers. In turn, these subsidiary units can have unique identifiers.
- *Minimize backtracking*—ideally, location IDs should be specified so that check sheets can be sorted to allow counts to occur with minimal backtracking. However, many aspects of a business (like naming conventions) are grandfathered in and wholesale revisions may be impractical. In such cases, providing an additional sort column in a spreadsheet will achieve the same outcome while honoring existing arrangements:
    - *Location sort column example*—at a hypothetical company, a cycle count is most convenient when it's performed in the following order:
        - Warehouse 4
        - Production area
        - Warehouse 1
    - However, sorting by location name would yield this less-than-ideal sequence:
        - Production area
        - Warehouse 1
        - Warehouse 4
    - A sort column in a spreadsheet allows the checklist to be arranged so that an employee can start at one end of a facility and check all of the parts on the list without backtracking (see Figure A.4). Setting this field as text will allow maximum sort flexibility, but keep in mind that alphabetical entries arrange differently from numeric ones. In the alphabetical case, 1,000 will precede 2, whereas the number 1,000 comes after 2. Also, provide enough digits in the sort key so that it can easily accommodate the number of storage locations you expect in the foreseeable future. Specifically, an alphanumeric code like the

Part ID	Location	Sort
1234 - Nut	Warehouse 1 - Row 1 - Rack A - Level 2	CC0067
2345 - Bolt	Warehouse 4 - Row 4 - Rack Z - Level 1	AA0001
3456 - Screw	Production Area - Station 1- Shelf A - Level 3	BB0004

Figure A.4   Inventory sequence

one in the table shown (e.g., CC0067) allows for 6,760,000 spots (26 possible letters × 26 possible letters × 10 possible digits × 10 possible digits × 10 possible digits × 10 possible digits = 6,760,000 possibilities). As a final note, there is nothing significant about the letters or numbers chosen. It's only to illustrate a point.

Tracking

In addition to tracking how an inventory management system performs against objectives, it is also wise to periodically review system validity. Some of the issues to consider during such an evaluation might include:

- *Suitability of objectives*—are the right objectives being monitored?
- *Scope*—are the right items being kept in storage? Are there any parts that need to be added that aren't presently in the system? Do any SKUs need to be discontinued?
- *Reorder system*—is there a significant number of outages traceable to improperly specified ROPs and ROQs?
- *Overall system effectiveness at preventing outages*—since there is more to properly timed orders than inventory parameters, the following can also be checked:
  - Are purchase orders issued in a timely manner?
  - Are purchase orders accurate and complete?
  - Are system data (lead time, usage, etc.) accurate?
- *Inventory count accuracy*
- *Fidelity of parts to storage locations*—is there a place for every part, and is every part in its place?
- *Efficacy*—is there efficacy in identifying and dispositioning suspect material?
- *Adherence to protocols*—is the system being followed?
- *Review frequency*—is the system being reviewed enough?

SIDEBAR—WHAT'S AN OUTAGE?

Although outage and fulfillment are simple ideas, defining them so they are captured consistently is another matter. For example, would the following be considered outages?

- For an order with a four-week lead time, what if a company was out of bolts that can be acquired in a day and the delivery was not affected?
- When order 1234 was received, all of the materials needed to process this order were available in adequate quantity. However, emergency order ABCD arrived a few days later and the materials that were originally allocated to 1234 were redirected to ABCD. As a result, 1234 doesn't have enough material.
- Instead of emergency orders robbing 1234, suppose that one of the parts for 1234 turned out to have quality problems that rendered it unusable. In addition, this caused 1234 to be shorted.
- A customer places an order and specifies that he does not want delivery until a much later date. Although the necessary parts were not available at the time of order, the materials could be easily acquired in the interim and not delay fulfillment.

In cases like these, it would be easy to make exceptions and allow for extenuations. While it may be more technically accurate, it will probably be an administrative nightmare. At the same time, such concessions might obscure failings in the system's performance. Establishing a consistent and simple approach to outage definition will help for two reasons:

- Allowing too many exceptions increases the likelihood of measurements being gamed.
- It is much easier to track outages with clear-cut rules. Although there may be mitigating factors, accommodating these will probably require significant deliberation and time.

For instance, defining an outage as strictly being *determined at the time an order is placed* will yield consistency. For example:

- For an order with a four-week lead time, what if a company was out of bolts that can be acquired in a day and the delivery was not affected?
  - *Answer*: It's an outage. The shortage appeared at the time of the order.
- When order 1234 was received, all of the materials needed to process this order were available in adequate quantity. However, emergency order ABCD arrived a few days later and the materials that were originally allocated to 1234 were redirected to ABCD. Is this an outage?
  - *Answer*: It's an outage for ABCD, but not for 1234. Although the materials were robbed from 1234, no shortage occurred when the order for 1234 was placed. The outage only appeared when the order was placed for ABCD.

Continued

- Instead of emergency orders robbing 1234, suppose that one of the parts for 1234 turned out to have quality problems that rendered it unusable. In addition, this caused 1234 to be shorted. Is this an outage?
  - *Answer*: It's not an outage. The shortage didn't occur at the time the order was placed.
- A customer places an order and specifies that he does not want delivery until a much later date. Although the parts were not available at the time of order, the materials could be easily acquired in the interim and not delay fulfillment.
  - *Answer*: It's an outage. The shortage occurred at the time the order was placed.

As shown, one consistently applied definition can prevent a lot of ifs, ands, or buts. Of course, the correct approach for different companies will vary. However, if a company does not have an easy and consistent technique, their methods should probably be reassessed; otherwise, a company will have no idea of its true performance.

SUMMARY

A comprehensive materials management system includes:

- *Objectives*—to know how a system is doing, performance should be gauged. Before there is an ability to track, objectives must first be established.
- *Scope*—an understanding and definition for what is kept in inventory and when and where it is done.
- *Inventory parameters*—a consistent approach to setting system parameters so that fulfillment is achieved.
- *Procedure*—specification of the who, what, when, where, and how of materials management.
- *Inventory checks*—periodic checks to verify inventory quantity, condition, and location.
- *Designated locations*—explicit and uniquely identified storage locations.
- *Tracking*—monitoring of the system and its performance.

With a grounding in inventory basics, a foundation now exists to implement QL inventory principles.

GLOSSARY

ABC analysis—ABC analysis is a prioritization technique that divides an inventory into three categories that allow differing levels of scrutiny.

Abraham Maslow—Psychologist who devised Maslow's Hierarchy of Needs.

Andon—Approach to notify support personnel of production problems like breakdowns, parts outages, and quality issues.

Bill of material (BOM)—Defines the parts that comprise a product and the quantity of pieces per finished unit.

BOM—Bill of material.

Bottleneck—By having the lowest production rate, the resource that sets the capacity for an operation.

Capacity constraint resource—By having the lowest production rate, the resource that sets the capacity for an operation. Also known as a bottleneck.

Cargo cult lean—Implementations that have the trappings of a lean system, but lack in the substance or results. Term is derived from cargo cults that developed in the South Pacific, where followers imitated Western behaviors in the hopes that the modern conveniences that they associated with Western societies would materialize.

Cause-effect diagram—A visualization tool that provides a structured approach to brainstorming and categorizing potential causes of problems. These are also known as Fishbone and Ishikawa diagrams.

Changeover—Preparation of equipment so that it can switch from processing a particular product in order to produce another. Also known as setup.

CMM—Computerized maintenance management.

CNC—Computer numerical control.

COGS—Cost-of-goods-sold.

Conversion—Activity that requires a man or machine's time and effects progress toward fulfilling a product's finished form.

Cost-of-goods-sold (COGS)—The direct costs of producing the goods sold by a company. This calculation includes the cost of the materials and labor directly used to create the goods and excludes indirect costs like distribution.

CUSUM—A sequential analysis technique used in statistical process control (SPC).

Cycle time—The time that a product spends in the process of fulfillment including all delays, non-conversion activities, and conversion activities. Also known as time-in-system.

Decoupling point (conventional definition)—A position in the material pipeline where the product flow changes from *push* to *pull*.

Decoupling point (Quantum Lean definition)—Point where product is delinked from one fulfillment schedule and enters a different fulfillment schedule.

Delay—Activity that occupies time but does not require a man or machine's attention.

Deming, W. Edwards—Noted American management philosopher who developed and implemented quality management systems that were widely adopted by Japanese companies.

Drum-buffer-rope—Scheduling tool that paces work to bottlenecks.

Effectiveness—How well something is done.

Efficiency—The amount of result compared to the amount of effort.

FGI—Finished goods inventory.

FIFO—First-in, first-out—A term used in inventory management to indicate that the first products to arrive in storage will be the first items pulled from storage.

FIFO lane—A method to regulate the sequence and quantity of work between processes.

Finished goods inventory (FGI)—Product that has been processed by the company, ready for distribution, and is sitting in storage waiting to be shipped or sold.

Fishbone diagram—A visualization tool that provides a structured approach to brainstorming and categorizing potential causes of problems. These are also known as Ishikawa and cause-effect diagrams.

Frame of reference—A set of criteria from which measurements or judgments can be made.

Fulfillment—The opposite of an outage; when an order is received and all of the associated raw material is available in sufficient quantity.

Heijunka box—A visual scheduling tool used to smooth production flow.

Henry Ford—Founder of the Ford Motor Company who popularized the assembly line and pioneered many of the methods used in lean manufacturing.

Huddle boards—A tool for visualizing work and workflow. Huddle boards are often whiteboards that include cards or post-its to show status, progress, and issues related to a project or business initiative.

Ishikawa—Japanese management thinker who developed the cause-effect diagram.

Ishikawa diagram—A visualization tool that provides a structured approach to brainstorming and categorizing potential causes of problems. These are also known as fishbone and cause-effect diagrams.

Key performance indicator (KPI)—A measurable value that demonstrates how effectively a company is achieving key business objectives.

KPI—Key performance indicator.

KPI boards—Boards that display progress against KPIs to help track and reach objectives.

LAME—Acronym for *lean as mainly experienced.*

Lathe—A machine for shaping wood, metal, or other material by means of a rotating drive that turns the piece being worked on against changeable cutting tools.

Lead time—The time required for an order to be delivered. The time from order initiation to delivery.

Lean as mainly experienced (LAME)—A characterization of lean implementations that depart from ideal lean principles.

Level loading—Use of strategic inventory to smooth out differences when demands have similar average rates but divergent peak rates.

Maslow's Hierarchy of Needs—A motivational theory comprised of a five-tier model of human needs.

Min/max—Minimum and maximum stocking levels.

Muda—Activity that creates no value. Japanese word for waste.

Non-conversion—Activity that requires a man or machine's time and does not affect progress toward fulfilling a product's finished form. Typically, this is restricted to activities that are primarily moving, inspection, rework, and handling.

Offline—Activity that takes place away from production.

One-point lessons (OPL)—A tool used to educate operators to improve operations. The main point of learning for a particular process written in one or two sentences and accompanied by simple and explanatory diagrams.

Online—Activity that takes place during production.

Outage—Product being unavailable when an order is received. Takes place when an order is received and any or all of the associated raw material is insufficient in quantity for that order to be completed.

Outlier—An observation that lies outside the overall pattern of a distribution.

Pareto principle—Principle that states that 80% of effects come from 20% of the causes.

Potemkin lean—Lean implementations that emphasize style over substance.

Process capability—A statistical measurement of a process's ability to consistently produce parts within specified tolerances.

QLM—Quantum Lean maintenance.

Quantum Lean maintenance (QLM)—Total productive maintenance reconfigured to the Quantum Lean framework.

Raw inventory—Items that are purchased for incorporation into a company's finished product and have not yet been processed by the company. This can include manufactured parts that have been provided by a vendor.

Reorder point (ROP)—Stock level that triggers reorder. As an example, if a purchase order is initiated when the quantity of bolts falls below 1,000 pieces, the ROP for bolts is 1,000.

Reorder quantity (ROQ)—The quantity that is ordered when an ROP is reached. For instance, if the reorder quantity for bolts has been specified as 500 pieces, the ROQ for bolts is 500.

ROP—Reorder point.

ROQ—Reorder quantity.

Safety stock (SS)—A supply of material kept in case ROQs and ROPs prove inadequate.

Scope—The definition, extent, and content of an endeavor.

Setup—Preparation of equipment in order to switch it from processing a particular product so that it can produce another. Also known as changeover.

Shigeo Shingo—Japanese industrial engineer who developed the setup reduction method called *single minute exchange of dies* (SMED).

Single minute exchange of dies (SMED)—Method for reducing setup or changeover time.

SKU—Stock-keeping unit.

SMED—Single minute exchange of dies.

SS—Safety stock.

Statistical control—A process where the variation of the process is primarily due to factors that are inherent to that process.

Statistical process control (SPC)—The use of statistical techniques to control a process or production method.

Stock-keeping unit (SKU)—A distinct type of item, such as a product or service, and all the attributes associated with the item type that distinguish it from other item types.

Taiichi Ohno—Father of the Toyota Production System (TPS).

Takt time—For a production line, the average time between units leaving the line. To be takt time, this should match the average customer demand rate.

Tampering—Attempting to change a process that is in statistical control.

Time-in-system—The time that a product spends in the process of fulfillment including all delays, non-conversion activities, and conversion activities. Also known as cycle time.

Total productive maintenance (TPM)—Comprehensive system of improving uptime and resource durability.

Toyota Production System (TPS)—An integrated business management system developed by Toyota to efficiently organize sales, marketing, design, manufacturing, logistics, and procurement to minimize cost and waste.

TPM—Total productive maintenance.

TPS—Toyota Production System.

True north—In lean, this describes a state of perfection that a lean system should aspire to.

Type one muda—Activity that creates no value but is unavoidable with current technologies and production assets.

Type two muda—Activity that creates no value and can be eliminated immediately.

Value-added activity—As defined by the Lean Enterprise Institute, any activity that creates value for the customer.

Waste—Activity that creates no value.

WIP—Work-in-process inventory.

Work-in-process inventory (WIP)—Product that is partially processed but not ready for sale. In addition, WIP is typically stored on the production floor in the process of being manufactured.

APPENDIX C

SOURCES

4-1 The lean toolbox is similar to the house of lean model that is used by the National Institute of Standards and Technology's Manufacturing Extension Partnership (NIST-MEP).

5-1 Wagner, A., 2020. *The "LAME" Cargo Cult and Lean*—[online] Lean Blog. Available at: https://www.leanblog.org/2008/09/lame-cargo-cult -and-lean/. Note: I am very confident that I arrived at this observation independently. However, when searching online, I found sources that covered this subject prior to my making the observation. As a result, I attributed it in the bibliography just in case I happened to see it somewhere and subconsciously retained it.

5-2 Richter, L., 2011. [online] Frcatel.fri.uniza.sk. Available at: https://frcatel .fri.uniza.sk/hrme/files/2011/2011_2_07.pdf. Note: I am very confident that I arrived at this observation independently. However, when searching online, I found sources that covered this subject prior to my making the observation. As a result, I attributed it in the bibliography just in case I happened to see it somewhere and subconsciously retained it.

5-3 Outside of Quantum Lean maintenance (QLM), none of the lean tools presented are unique to QL. QL uses lean tools that have long been a part of lean implementations.

5-4 Davis, J., 1999. *Fast Track to Waste-Free Manufacturing*. Portland, OR: Productivity Press. Note: To the best of my knowledge, John Davis originated the idea that the goal for a lean operation should be that setup has no influence on a company's decision making, instead of the goal of outright eliminating it.

8-1 Weigel, A., 2000. [online] Web.mit.edu. Available at: https://web.mit .edu/esd.83/www/notebook/WomackJones.pdf.—Note: The section *LEI Lean* from Chapter 8 (QL versus other approaches) leaned heavily on this referenced article for facts about the Lean Enterprise Institute's version of lean systems.

301

8–2   Kutalik, C., 2009. *Will the Real Lean Production Please Stand Up?* [online] Labor Notes. Available at: https://labornotes.org/blogs/2009/10/will-real-lean-production-please-stand. Note: I was looking for a widespread term for typical lean implementations and found LAME. In this article, the acronym was short for: lean as mainly experienced. I liked and used this characterization.

8–3   Graban, M., 2007. Lean or L.A.M.E.? [online] Mark Graban's Lean Blog. Available at: https://www.leanblog.org/2007/03/lean-or-lame/. Note: I was looking for a widespread term for typical lean implementations and found LAME. In this article, the acronym was short for: lean as misguidedly executed. I liked the characterization from reference 8–2 better.

11–1   *Polishing Concrete Floors.* [online] Available at: https://www.concretenetwork.com/concrete/polishing/. Note: This website was used to research and fact check concrete polishing.

11–2   En.wikipedia.org. n.d. *Dry-Ice Blasting.* [online] Available at: https://en.wikipedia.org/wiki/Dry-ice_blasting. Note: This article was used to fact check the subsection about dry-ice blasting in Chapter 11 (5S).

13–1   Davis, J., 1999. *Fast Track to Waste-Free Manufacturing.* Portland, OR: Productivity Press. Note: To the best of my knowledge, John Davis originated the idea that the goal for a lean operation should be that setup has no influence on a company's decision making, instead of the goal of outright eliminating it.

13–2   Lynch, M., 1996. *Managing Computer Numerical Control Operations: How to get the most out of your CNC machine tools.* Society of Manufacturing Engineers. Note: In the example used for setup on a CNC lathe in Chapter 13 (Quick Changeover), this book was researched and fact-checked for CNC setups.

13–3   Castells, R., 2016. *Six Fascinating Facts about Fasteners.* [online] Element. Available at: https://www.element.com/nucleus/2016/06/29/six-fascinating-facts-about-fasteners.

13–4   Youtube.com. 2018. *Which Penetrating Oil is Best? Let's Find Out!* [online] Available at: https://www.youtube.com/watch?v=xUEob2oAKVs.

13–5   YouTube. 2019. *Is Seafoam Deep Creep the Best Penetrating Oil? Let's Find Out!* [online] Available at: https://www.youtube.com/watch?v=dObEK7V-TFU.

14–1   En.wikipedia.org. n.d. *Total Productive Maintenance.* [online] Available at: https://en.wikipedia.org/wiki/Total_productive_maintenance. Note: The article was used for fact checking the section about total productive maintenance (TPM) in Chapter 14 (QLM).

14–2 Overall equipment effectiveness (OEE) is a widespread metric utilized throughout industry and is in no way unique to QL.

14–3 En.wikipedia.org. n.d. *Overall Equipment Effectiveness*. [online] Available at: https://en.wikipedia.org/wiki/Overall_equipment_effectiveness. Note: This article was used for fact checking the section about OEE in Chapter 14 (QLM).

17–1 En.wikipedia.org. n.d. *Work Sampling*. [online] Available at: https://en.wikipedia.org/wiki/Work_sampling. Note: This article was used for fact checking the section about work sampling in Chapter 17 (Work Balancing).

17–2 En.wikipedia.org. n.d. *Maynard Operation Sequence Technique*. [online] Available at: https://en.wikipedia.org/wiki/Maynard_operation_sequence_technique. Note: This article was used to fact check the subsection about predetermined time systems in Chapter 17 (Work Balancing).

17–3 Unknown. *Assembly Systems and Line Balancing*. [online] Available at: https://bit.ly/2J7Moj5. Note: The section about line balancing in Chapter 17 (Work Balancing) was fact checked using this article.

20–1 En.wikipedia.org. n.d. *Ishikawa Diagram*. [online] Available at: https://en.wikipedia.org/wiki/Ishikawa_diagram.

20–2 Medium.com. n.d. *Pacing and Leading*. [online] Levers of Persuasion. Available at: https://medium.com/@leversofpersuasion/pacing-and-leading-133766efb463.

20–3 Adams, S., 2018. *Win Bigly: Persuasion in a World Where Facts Don't Matter*. Portfolio.

20–4 Krause, T., Hidley, J., and Hodson, S., 1990. *The Behavior-Based Safety Process: Managing Involvement in an Injury-Free Culture*. Van Nostrand Reinhold.

20–5 En.wikipedia.org. n.d. *Maslow's Hierarchy of Needs*. [online] Available at: https://en.wikipedia.org/wiki/Maslow%27s_hierarchy_of_needs. Note: The subsection "Maslow's Hierarchy of Needs" from Chapter 20 (Lean Implementations: Improving the Odds) was fact checked against the referenced article and reference 20–6.

20–6 McLeod, S., 2020. *Maslow's Hierarchy of Needs*. Available at: https://www.simplypsychology.org/maslow.html. Note: The subsection "Maslow's Hierarchy of Needs" from Chapter 20 (Lean Implementations: Improving the Odds) was fact checked against the referenced article and reference 20–5.

21–1 En.wikipedia.org. n.d. *Potemkin Village*. [online] Available at: https://en.wikipedia.org/wiki/Potemkin_village. Note: The historic background about Potemkin villages in the introductory paragraph in Chapter 21 (Potemkin lean) was fact checked against this article.

In the following list, I am crediting sources for ideas that aren't copywritten, but I want to give credit where it's due:

John Baker, Engineer—Prior to meeting John Baker, I used yellow post-it notes to document conversions, non-conversions, and delays during the development of product path diagrams. During a training session that Mr. Baker was attending, he suggested using red, yellow, and green post-its for the symbols. What an idea!

Kenneth Iverson (Founder of Nucor)—My first exposure to the idea that a well-trained genius gets it right 60% of the time came from Ken Iverson.

Victor Perrazoli, Consultant—He coined the 5S phrase, "Every tool has a home and no visitors are allowed." I liked it so much that I borrowed it.

Keith Terhune, Chemical Engineer—In the QL hierarchy, the first order of business is honoring commitments, regardless of how inefficient it may be. While I didn't swipe this idea from Keith (honest!), he arrived at this observation entirely independent of this book. When he said it to me, I considered it a total validation. The man is a sharp pencil!

This next list contains some great sources of information if you want to pursue lean in more depth:

Bhote, K., 1991. *World Class Quality*. New York, NY: AMACOM.—About Shainin Techniques.

Box, G., Hunter, J., and Hunter, W., 2005. *Statistics for Experimenters*. Wiley-Interscience.

Bozzone, V., 2002. *Speed to Market: Lean Manufacturing for Job Shops*. AMACOM.

Davis, J., 1999. *Fast Track to Waste-Free Manufacturing*. Portland, OR: Productivity Press.

Goldratt, E. and Cox, J., 1984. *The Goal: A Process of Ongoing Improvement*. North River Press.

Lareau, W., 1991. *American Samurai: A Warrior for the Coming Dark Ages of American Business*. New Win Publishing.

Lynch, M., 1996. *Managing Computer Numerical Control Operations: How to get the most out of your CNC machine tools*. Society of Manufacturing Engineers.

Montgomery, D. and Runger, G., 2013. *Applied Statistics and Probability for Engineers, 6th Edition.* Wiley.

Preston, R., 1992. *American Steel.* New York, NY: Avon Books.

Womack, J. and Jones, D., 1990. *The Machine That Changed the World.* Simon & Schuster.

Womack, J. and Jones, D., 1996. *Lean Thinking: Banish Waste and Create Wealth in Your Corporation.* Productivity Press.

INDEX

Note: Page numbers followed by "*f*" indicate figures.

ABC analysis, 88, 101, 102–103, 103 *f*, 289

accuracy, 101–107. *See also* inventory
  ABC analysis, 88, 101, 102–103, 103 *f*
  cycle counting, 88, 101–102, 103–104
  kanban, 88, 104–106, 105 *f*

agendas, motivation, 268–270

alignment, 80

analysis of variance (ANOVA), 212, 244, 246

andon, 36, 46–48, 47 *f*, 64, 175

anti-seize compound, 170

asking for help, 264

attitudes, 267

audits, 132

authenticity, 66

authority
  available to few, 263
  benefit *vs.*, 262, 263 *f*
  effort *vs.*, 262, 262 *f*
  limits, 262
  as self-defeating, 263

automated *vs.* human-based system, 67–68

behaviors, 267

belief, 66

Benn, Ernest, 239

bills of material (BOM), 144

break down steps, 221

Buddhist faith, 15

Burke, Edmund, 129

Burns, Robert, 259

buy-in, 80

Cadillac XLR, 279

Castaway, 2

cells/cellular flow, 48–50, 64, 237–238
  as sequential flow, 237–238
  U-shaped, 48–49, 49 *f*

cellular manufacturing, 48

change, resistance to, 6

Chevrolet Corvette, 279

Chimero, Frank, 193

Churchill, Winston, 261

cleaning method, 141–142

commitments, 22

competence, 66, 265

conceding an argument, 264

conversion, 17–18, 18 *f*, 57

Coolidge, Calvin, 260